Democracy
and Subjective Rights

Democracy and Subjective Rights

Democracy Without *Demos*

Catherine Colliot-Thélène

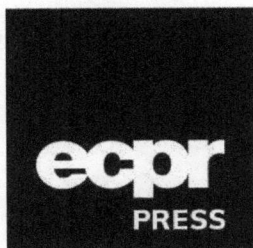

ecpr PRESS

Originally published in German as *Demokratie ohne Volk*
© 2011 by Hamburger Edition HIS Verlagsges. mbH, Hamburg, Germany
English edition © Catherine Colliot-Thélène and translated by Arianne Dorval

Published by the European Consortium for Political Research
Harbour House, 6-8 Hythe Quay
Colchester, CO2 8JF United Kingdom
www.ecpr.eu

British Library Cataloguing in Publication Data
A catalogue record for this book is available from the British Library

ISBN: HB 978-1-78552-262-8
ISBN: Ebook 978-1-78660-527-6
ISBN: PB 978-1-78661-306-6

Library of Congress Cataloging-in-Publication Data

Names: Colliot-Thélène, Catherine, author.
Title: Democracy and subjective rights : democracy without demos / Catherine Colliot-Thélène.
Description: London ; ECPR Press, [2017] | Includes bibliographical references and index.
Identifiers: LCCN 2017032345 (print) | LCCN 2017038980 (ebook) | ISBN 9781786605276 (Electronic) | ISBN 9781785522628 (hb : alk. paper) | ISBN 9781786605276 (ebook) | ISBN 9781786613066 (pb : alk. paper)
Subjects: LCSH: Democracy—Philosophy. | Civil rights. | Citizenship. | State, The. | Globalization—Political aspects.
Classification: LCC JC423 (ebook) | LCC JC423 .C653 2017 (print) | DDC 321.8—dc23
LC record available at https://lccn.loc.gov/2017032345

ecpr.eu/shop

Contents

Introduction

Since Hegel, we know that the figures of the subject change with the forms of the community, and that this is especially true of the political subject. The political philosophy of Hegel is to be found not only in *Elements of the Philosophy of Right*, but also, and perhaps most importantly, in *The Phenomenology of Spirit*. The latter was Hegel's first major political work (although it was also more than that), such that any interpretation of *Philosophy of Right* that does not rest on a proper reading of *The Phenomenology* is necessarily reductive. The central problem of Hegelian political thought is not the determination of the relationship between the individual and the state – as was assumed by liberal critics, who remained focused on the sacralisation of the state implied in their view, by Hegel's famous proposition that the state is the 'actuality of the ethical Idea'. For Hegel, the state is but the superior collective that represents, under the conditions of modern society, the last horizon of the individual's participation in the world of human relations. There had been other collectives before it, some of which (for instance, the Greek *polis* or the Roman Empire) are clearly identified in *The Phenomenology of Spirit*. And there were others next to it (families, corporations of civil society, churches, etc.), which, while occupying a subordinate position, contributed for Hegel to determining the identity, or rather, the identities of individuals. The central question of Hegel's philosophy is that of the becoming-subject in its various modalities, and the manner in which he addresses this question rests on the assumption that this becoming-subject is intimately linked to the forms of the collectives to which individuals belong – i.e., in which they are born, grow, live and die. The subject comes to himself through an experience shaped by a world which is a human world, not the world of an abstract humanity encompassing all humans, living and dead, but a historical world – a 'figure of the spirit' – that profoundly determines the subject's consciousness in both its cognitive and practical dimensions. This is the key point of Hegel's philosophy that the great Hegelian Jean Hyppolite had remarkably grasped. And it is to this truth of Hegelianism that Foucault was alluding, in a manner certainly skewed by the personal journey that had led him to rediscover it, when he concluded a lecture devoted to the 'hermeneutics of the subject' with a remark that must have seemed enigmatic to many of his listeners:

> How can what is given as the object of knowledge (*savoir*) connected to the mastery of *tekhne*, at the same time be the site where the truth of the subject we are appears, or is experienced and fulfilled with difficulty? How can the world, which is given as the object of knowledge (*connaissance*) on the basis of the mastery of *tekhne*, at the same time be the site where the "self" as ethical subject of truth appears and is experienced? If this really is the problem of Western philosophy—how can the world be the object of knowledge (*connaissance*) and at the same time the place of the subject's test; how can there be a subject of knowledge (*connaissance*) which takes the world as object through a *tekhne*, and a subject of self-experience which takes this same world, but in the radically different form of the place of its test?—if this really is the challenge of Western philosophy, you will see why *The Phenomenology of Mind* is the summit of this philosophy.[1]

My aim in the pages to come is not to interpret Hegelian philosophy; neither is it to deploy the two dimensions of experience – knowledge and ethics – which Foucault rightly considers as inextricably linked in Hegel's thought. The political subject alone will hold my interest. If it is not inappropriate to open this book by referring to Hegel, it is because, more than any other philosopher of the modern era, he reflected on the historicity of the figures of the subject while also relating each of them to successive incarnations of the *community*. Today, *democracy* is the name given to the ideal political community of which contemporary Western societies are generally agreed to constitute approximate forms. The central aim of this book is to identify the figure of the political subject that corresponds to democracy understood in its modern sense. In apparent continuity with Hegel, and even though he did not view himself as a democrat, I argue that the modern state is the collective that granted this subject his specific traits. Contemporary liberal democracies have more in common with the Hegelian state than liberal interpretations are willing to admit, and the democratic citizen may well recognise in the legal person, the subject of moral action, the economic man of civil society or the citizen of the state the various interdependent aspects of a multilayered

---

[1]   Foucault, 2005, p. 487.

identity that is still his today.[2] The Hegelian inspiration of this book, however, stops here. For if Hegel saw in the state another communitarian form of the collective, the thesis I defend is, on the contrary, that the modern political subject essentially escapes all communitarian assignation. This thesis runs counter not only to Hegel's thought, but also to all the theories that extol the virtues of the 'community of citizens' today. It also runs counter to those that, because they are dissatisfied with the social and political reality of contemporary liberal democracies, are concerned with the possibility or impossibility of a new form of community that might meet the latter's unfulfilled promises.

After having spent time, along with many of his contemporaries, dreaming of restoring something analogous to the 'beautiful ethical totality' of Greek antiquity, Hegel took note of the irreversible character of the ideological and socioeconomic transformations that shaped the modern world. The modern individual could not give to the collectives in which he belonged the full and immediate adhesion that Antigone had given to the family, or that Creon had demanded citizens to give to the *polis*. The complexity of modern societies manifested itself in the plurality of the collectives in which the individual was socialised, each of them contributing to determining a part of his identity. Yet what remains of the ideal of Hegel's youth in his work of maturity is an understanding of the different social inscriptions of the individual in terms of belonging. Both the legal sphere and the sphere of socio-economic relations based on work and exchange (what Hegel terms the 'system of needs') are insufficient precisely because they are ill-suited to the latter interpretation. Right in the strict sense (that of jurists) is qualified as 'abstract' because the identity it confers on the individual is purely exclusive (*PhR*, §34). As for socio-economic relations, they constitute the 'system of ethical life, lost in its extremes' (*PhR*, §184), by which Hegel means that the collective they produce appears merely as a means for individuals fully absorbed by their particular interests. Nevertheless, the ultimate subordination of these various spheres of action to the state allows for encountering, within modernity, a functional equivalent to the 'beautiful ethical totality' of old. In other words, it permits us to think of sociality as belonging, in spite of the difference introduced by the development of the different – legal, moral, economic – dimensions of the 'principle of subjective particularity': for Hegel, it is the 'highest duty' of individuals 'to be members of the state' (*PhR*, §258).

While one might hear echoes of the ideal of Hegel's youth in the conception of the state laid out in *Philosophy of Right*, this conception is by no means archaic; nor is it reactionary or authoritarian. If one is willing to admit that the Hegelian rational state grants most of the rights demanded by

---

2   See Hegel, 1991, *Elements of the Philosophy of Right*, §190. Hereafter I refer to *Philosophy of Right* in the text as PhR with mention of the paragraph.

liberalism to the legal person, the moral subject and the 'rational individual' of modern political economy,[3] then the affirmation of the primacy of the state merely translates in philosophy an ethics that was embraced by all the nation-states of the 19th and early 20th centuries. One commonplace interpretation, concerned mainly with highlighting the alleged characteristics of German political thought, has portrayed Hegel as the instigator of a state nationalism that, once relayed by the historians Ranke and Treitschke, could only end in the militarism of Wilhelm II's Empire and the charnel house of the Great War. In this perspective, the passage in *Philosophy of Right* that affirms the 'ethical moment' of war[4] has been widely denounced. Yet the type of nationalism defended by Hegel, which was remarkably devoid of any ethnic or cultural connotation, was not confined to Germany. It was nothing other than the nationalism in whose name 'dying for the fatherland' was considered in 1914, in Germany and elsewhere, as a sacrifice for which every good male citizen had to prepare himself. To this day, monuments to the dead in the cities and villages of Europe transmit the memory of this sacrifice, while the annual ceremony in homage to the Unknown Soldier in France attests to the ongoing import, in the symbolism of citizenship, of citizens' dutiful death on the battlefield.[5] Hegel, who was not and certainly did not wish to be a prophet, was likely thinking of the soldiers of year II when he evoked the sacrifice made to maintain the conditions of his freedom. Besides, the ethical significance of war is also praised by authors of our time who, without adhering to militarist ideology, associate democracy with the nation form. Thus, Dominique Schnapper, in a vigorous plea in favour of the democratic nation, regards the impossibility of requiring citizens to sacrifice their lives for the nation as a symptom of the erosion of the social bond and of democracy.[6]

The point here is not to criticise this specific form of nationalism, which, for better and for worse, constituted for a time civic virtue *par excellence*. For almost two centuries, the nation-state was one of the main collectives through which the individual could give meaning to his existence. Others vied against it – notably, the proletarian community. These collective identities were a

---

[3] See Kervégan, 2007, pp. 189–195.

[4] See *PhR*, §324 (Hegel, 1991, p. 361).

[5] The idea that dying for the fatherland could sanctify men in the same way as Christian martyrdom did first appeared in the 12th-13th century, when political power was beginning to undergo territorialisation. See Kantorowicz, 1951.

[6] Schnapper, 1998, p. 4 and *passim*. All things being equal, Dominique Schnapper is in agreement with Carl Schmitt when she quotes Benedict Anderson for whom it is absurd to expect anyone to die for the Comecon or the EEC (*ibid.*, p. 60). Indeed, in *The Concept of the Political*, Schmitt notes on several occasions (Schmitt, 1996, pp. 46 and 48) that 'to demand seriously of human beings that they kill others and be prepared to die themselves so that trade and industry may flourish for the survivors or that the purchasing power of grandchildren may grow is sinister and crazy'.

historically undeniable dimension of the political subject in the modern era. Aloïs Hahn speaks of 'participative identities' in this regard; he also sees in the nation a specifically modern form of segmentary social differentiation that not only coexisted with, but also operated as the necessary complement of functional differentiation – even though the latter had supposedly replaced the former.[7] Yet as novel as some of these participatory identities (nation and class) were, did they really constitute the specifically modern element of the modern *political* subject? The fact that national patriotism could invoke various precedents – for instance, the civic patriotism of Antiquity or that of the Italian republics of the Renaissance – gives us reason to doubt this assertion. A new reading of the Declaration of the Rights of Man and of the Citizen confronts us with an entirely different determination of the identity of the modern political subject, which ought to be viewed as the true innovation of modernity. This is the identity of the subject of rights, presupposed by the notion of 'subjective rights', which, far from referring to any given collective, is attached to the individual regardless of any affiliation. Though the notion of subjective rights has spawned a host of objections, it has played a non-negligible role in the political practices of the last two centuries. There are two reasons why placing this notion at the centre of our understanding of democracy seems necessary today. First, the lasting collective identities of nation and class that crystallised over two centuries in Western societies have lost much of their influence and power of attraction. Second, the fate of subjective rights no longer plays itself out merely on the national scale – a scale that, because the nation itself is a community, permitted to conflate the defence of subjective rights with that of the nation, but also with the defence of the alternative community of class that anticipated the communist society to come.

Regarding the first point, my aim is certainly not to dispute the fact that struggles for rights – for the respect and expansion of acquired rights and for the conquest of new rights – continue to require the formation of collectives that bring together and organise, more or less formally depending on each case, circles of individuals who mobilise *together* to obtain rights of which they feel deprived. Yet insofar as the 'minorities'[8] that intervene collectively in the public sphere to demand recognition of their rights are more numerous and more diversified today than they were during the nineteenth and much of the twentieth century, the collectives they form are also generally more evanescent than they used to be. These new collectives do not have

---

[7] 'Partizipative Identitäten', in Hahn, 2000, pp. 13–79.

[8] The term is obviously understood here in a political and not a quantitative sense. Among the 'minorities' that fought to obtain rights that had long been reserved for a fraction of the population of democratic nations are women, whose 'minority' was clearly of a legal and political nature.

the permanence of parties and trade unions; nor do they have the capacity to provide their members with living environments and interpretation grids that would enable them to form small and relatively autonomous societies within the national society, as parties and trade unions did when they believed they could offer a social project opposed to that of the political power in place. Women who mobilised in the 1970s to gain the right to abortion, or women in 'difficult neighbourhoods' who mobilise today against obscurantism and the violence of which they are victims, participate in a 'movement' in whose service some of them might invest a significant portion of their time and energy, but they do not base their entire lives on their identity as oppressed women. The same can be said of individuals who mobilise for the environment or become involved in various organisations for the defence of human rights. If I hesitate to include here the mobilisations of *sans papiers*, it is because state policies confine irregular migrants to a negative identity from which they can only hope to escape.

The second point is the most decisive argument in favour of thoroughly revising what we mean by democracy when we qualify modern liberal societies as democratic. It is, indeed, a reflection on the implications, for the definition of the political, of changes that have occurred in the place and role of the state within the general economy of places of power in the late twentieth and early twenty-first centuries that drove the investigation whose findings are presented in this book. The point of departure of this investigation was a study[9] I conducted on the historical significance of the notion of subjective rights, based on my analysis of the chapter Max Weber devoted to this theme in his 'Sociology of Law'. At the end of this analysis linked directly to the interpretation of the 'monopoly of legitimate violence', I suggested that the contemporary erosion of state sovereignty is significantly altering the conditions for the guarantee of subjective rights.[10] Contemporary legal pluralism, which results from the multiplication of supranational legal and judicial organs and the development of quasi-legal norms by private bodies (the *lex mercatoria* being the best-studied example[11]), entails the proliferation and increasing heterogeneity of the instances of power from which subjects can or must claim recognition of their rights. By the same token, the figure of the subject of right – itself produced, one must recall, by the destruction of the former legal pluralism that characterised medieval Europe's regime of special rights, under the centralising action of territorial sovereignty that is constitutive of the modern state – is being called into question.[12] I myself

---

[9]   Colliot-Thélène, 2005, pp. 23–46.
[10]   *Ibid.*, p. 46, note 70.
[11]   See especially the works of Gunther Teubner, 1996a and 1996b.
[12]   Colliot-Thélène, 2009a and 2009b.

interrogated this figure in two articles where I defended the thesis that the future of modern democracy (to be distinguished, of course, from ancient democracy, albeit according to criteria other than those of Benjamin Constant) remains tied to the future of the subject of right, despite the erosion of what was the condition for its formation, namely the state's legal monopoly. Yet I also argued that contemporary legal pluralism forces us to discard the classic notion of a *demos* conceived as a united community whose alleged will conditions the legitimacy of power. Indeed, while the plurality of powers does not preclude the defence of subjective rights, the diversity of rights addressees prevents groups of rights-claiming individuals from merging into a unified collective. The latter proposition was met with legitimate objections from some of my listeners and readers whom I could not suspect of being ill-disposed towards democracy, or of being hostile to the idea that democracy, understood in its modern sense, ought to recognise that the subject in and of himself – i.e., not as a member of a particular group – is entitled to claim rights. As I reflected on these objections, I became convinced that one of the main obstacles to understanding the reality of modern democracies lies in the notion of self-legislation. It is a truism that the participation of citizens in the elaboration of laws through the common, indirect method of electing their representatives weighs little in the determination of the content of these laws. Yet few democratic theorists are willing to concede that the control exercised by the 'people' over the actions of those who govern it – i.e., members of both the legislative and executive branches – is a fiction whose historical significance lies in a principle of legitimacy that developed in opposition to that of hereditary dynasties. In fact, this principle never implied that political power could lose its character of domination or that the citizen could cease to be subjected, and this not even in the eyes of the most unquestioned authority in modern democratic theory: Jean-Jacques Rousseau.

'The people, being subject to the laws, ought to be their author': this famous proposition from Rousseau's *Social Contract* is considered by many to be the fundamental axiom of democratic theory. It has since been deployed in various ways. Thus Seyla Benhabib rewrites this axiom in the terms of Habermasian discourse theory by claiming: '[A]ll those who are affected by the consequences of the adoption of a norm [must] have a say in its articulation'.[13] This, however, constitutes for her a meta-positive norm or abstract principle of legitimacy whose institutional consequences cannot be drawn without mediation. Hauke Brunkhorst translates this principle in a more directly institutional form when he writes that the constitutional norm of democracy is self-legislation, which is synonymous with the identity of

---

[13] Benhabib, 2004, p. 218.

the dominant and the dominated and therefore requires 'the exceptionless inclusion of all persons affected by the law in the process of legislation'.[14] Surely not all contemporary democratic theorists would be ready to claim that democracy tends towards the identity of the dominant and the dominated; as Brunkhorst himself points out, this would amount to the complete abolition of all domination in politics. Yet all consider that democratic power must at the very least be purged of any residue of '*violentia*'.[15] The alleged participation of the addressees of the law in the elaboration of the law, it is believed, entails a radical metamorphosis of power, the relative autonomy of which can then be explained only on functional grounds. Few, especially among philosophers, would now accept the brutal equations Max Weber established long ago between politics and power and between power and domination.[16] One speaks more readily today of an opposition between the rulers and the ruled than between the dominant and the dominated, and one stresses that public office is in principle open to all citizens. It is up to political scientists or sociologists to show, with supporting figures, the factual limits to this openness. Most will concede, of course, that the chances of holding a public office – especially the most important ones – are very unevenly distributed depending on the social background of individuals, that the professionalisation of politics leads to the formation of a 'political class' which tends to reproduce itself endogenously, that there exist political dynasties, etc. But so long as one remains within a national framework, one can argue that, even though social mobility is limited, ordinary citizens exercise control over those who govern them through voting. Thus, to the extent that this is possible in mass societies, the principle of self-legislation essentially finds its institutional translation in the process of leader selection via election. It is this process that gives political significance to the public sphere, namely the sites of communication – press, radio, television and (today) Internet – where public issues are discussed for the most part by experts or accredited representatives of power, but where ordinary citizens can also sometimes make their voices heard. This communication has political significance only because it is supposed to contribute to forming citizens' opinion, which determines their choices when they are called upon to elect their leaders. I shall leave aside here the questions that relate to the functioning and oft-emphasised ambivalence of this public sphere: whether it is a site for the elaboration of an informed public opinion emanating from civil society, or, on the contrary, a tool for shaping and even manipulating this opinion by those in power. My concern here is entirely different. Ultimately, the control exercised by citizens over their

---

[14] Brunkhorst, 2005, p. 73.
[15] See Habermas, 1998, p. 72.
[16] See Weber, 2009, p. 78.

leaders through periodic elections is the only thing that gives a semblance of reality to the principle of self-legislation. Yet this control is effective only over individuals who perform public functions within the framework of the national state. It is nevertheless well known that the rules to which the different spheres of collective activity are subjected are increasingly elaborated by instances made up of individuals who are not subjected to the control of voters. More than the internal dysfunctions of the public sphere on a national scale, it is this reconfiguration of places of power and rule elaboration that reveals the fictitious character of the principle of self-legislation, emptying it once and for all of any real signification. This principle is but a myth comparable to that of the divine origin of power, which in times past justified immutable social hierarchies and hereditary dynasties.

However, unlike divine will, the myth of self-legislation does not merely justify the autonomy of power by concealing its arbitrary character; it also obscures the very nature of power, namely its constitutive dissymmetrical structure. This obscuring is what leads some to imagine that the logic of democratic society tends towards the disappearance, if not of power, at least of domination. It is remarkable that the great figures of political philosophy of the last decades of the twentieth century abandoned the question of power (i.e., the question of the legitimacy of power in general, though not of the particular form of power embodied in liberal democracies).[17] As I will recall later, for Rousseau as much as for the founding fathers of the American Republic, the possibility that an oligarchy might reconstitute itself on the basis of elected representation was viewed as a key problem of modern republican institutions. Today, this question is largely repressed in favour of interrogations about the principles that ought to serve as a regulative idea for the action of leaders. The reality of the separation between the mass of individuals who are subjected to rules and those who elaborate, promulgate and enforce them, seems to become manifest again only when those rules are produced by instances other than legislative bodies and national governments. Democratic deficits are pointed out primarily when discussing the functioning of European institutions or the constraints and pressures that supranational instances of power such as the IMF or the World Bank exert on national authorities. In this regard, we can speak of the paradoxical invisibility of power in the contemporary moment. The more power is on display, the less it is perceived as power, and vice versa. The public staging of (essentially national) politics relativises the *difference of power*, insofar as it fuels the idea that leaders are only ever the representatives of the people and that their action is ultimately determined by the will of the people. Power becomes

---

[17]   I am thinking in particular of Jürgen Habermas and John Rawls. See Colliot-Thélène, 2009c.

manifest as a dissymmetrical structure only in the least visible instances of its exercise: in institutions whose name is well known, yet whose reasons and deliberations (conducted in small circles of experts) escape public knowledge and judgment.

The increasing influence wielded by various kinds of power which, because they are not selected by popular vote, are unaccountable to the populations that bear the effects of their decisions, is causing some to doubt that democracy has a future at all. The latter, they say, can only exist within a national framework.[18] Surely this is true so long as one persists in linking the concept of democracy to that of self-legislation, which, admittedly, tends towards purging power of its character of domination. However, very different perspectives open up when we recognise that the dissymmetrical structure of power is constitutive of what we call politics – the politics of times past, of the more or less absolute monarchies, of the city-states of the Italian Renaissance, or of the 'democratic' republics of the nineteenth and twentieth centuries. Modern democracy has only ever been a mode of organising power, that is to say, a mode of organising the relations between the dominant and the dominated. The nation-state was of course the specific territorial framework that set the conditions for this organisation. Must we conclude therefrom that democracy is doomed, in the short- or long-term, by the erosion of state sovereignty? Reading anew the history of the 'democratisation of democracies' (I will recall later that the political regimes born of the revolutions of the late eighteenth century were not designated by this term) reveals that the properly democratic component of such regimes owes not to this territorial framework, but to the transformations imposed on them by the claims of those who are excluded from power. By becoming the sole guarantor of rights, the nation-state created an unprecedented link between territory, political authority and rights – a link that has profoundly determined our conception of politics over the last two centuries. Yet as pointed out in particular by Saskia Sassen,[19] with whom I agree on several points, actors who, in this framework, were excluded from the formal organisation of politics nevertheless exerted considerable influence on its development. In particular, they contributed decisively to the formation of democratic citizenship in modern political regimes. This thesis can also be formulated in the terms of Jacques Rancière:[20] Disagreement – the claims of those who have no part (*les sans-part*) – is the living element of politics; it demands that we think the democratic 'people' not as a constituted community or a community to be constituted, but as the 'supplement' that frequently disrupts the always provisional order of all constitutions. I do not,

---

[18]   See Schnapper, 1998, p.165, and more recently, Crouch, 2004.
[19]   Sassen, 2006, pp. 279, 292–293.
[20]   See Rancière, 1998.

however, share Rancière's indifference towards institutions, which he places en bloc alongside the 'police' and the government, by which he means organisation in general, with all that it implies in terms of uneven distribution of places and functions. This indifference leads him to neglect the importance of rights recognition, which is nevertheless clearly the objective of those who have no part when they demand to participate. While a strictly legal conception of subjective rights, whose paradigmatic expression is found in Kelsen,[21] obscures the role of social dynamics in the history of those rights, Rancière makes the opposite mistake by forgetting that claims are meaningless when they have no addressee. Indeed, the conversion of claims into rights in the proper sense of the term depends precisely on the existence of addressees, as rights necessarily imply some form of guarantee.

From the perspective of the history of subjective rights, the novelty of our time is that state authorities are no longer the sole addressees of the claims made by those who are excluded from power: rights are now subject to negotiations that involve multiple partners. This makes it necessary to rethink the nature of citizenship.[22] Clearly, some of the rights guaranteed to individuals today are still linked to the status of citizen, which is itself tied to national affiliation. This is the case above all of political rights – the rights to vote and to stand for election – such that they are generally considered to form the very substance of citizenship in the proper sense of the term. Here we can gauge the influence of the principle of self-legislation, which ultimately leads to the double equivalence between citizenship and political rights and between citizenship and nationality. If we accept that democracy is a form of political organisation whose legitimacy rests on the participation of the people in the elaboration of the law, then the people-citizenry can only be composed of those who enjoy political rights. By the same token, the boundary between those who enjoy these rights and those who do not can never be entirely erased, even when calls are made to facilitate its crossing. Democratic citizenship necessarily excludes – 'passive' citizens yesterday, 'foreigners' today. Now as then, the excluded can only hope to be protected by the law, a protection that is conceded to them and thereby denies them recognition as autonomous political subjects. Neither the integration of universal norms of human rights into national laws, nor the recognition of foreign jurisprudences[23] or rules laid down in international conventions and treaties by national courts can change that fact. Between the citizen legislator and the foreigner (no matter how protected the latter may be) the difference is in kind. The difficulty of finding a satisfactory solution to the problems

---

[21] See *infra*, I. 2., p. 7–8.
[22] This is what Saskia Sassen attempts to do in chapter 6 of the cited book (Sassen, 2006).
[23] See Allard and Garapon, 2005.

posed by the status of foreigners owes not only to the demagogic and securitarian policies of governments in host countries – though this factor cannot be underestimated – but also to the impasses of a communitarian conception of democracy. The people that purport to instantiate the legitimation of power and to control its own fate through electing its leaders must be able to define itself, and it can do so only by setting its own boundaries.[24] Clearly, the territorial organisation of state power is that which permitted the individualisation of the subject of right and made him the fundamental form of the political subject; yet it is also that which nationalised citizenship. The whole question is to know whether these two products of state sovereignty are so intimately intertwined that they can only survive together, or whether, on the contrary, it is possible to invent a non-national citizenship without sacrificing the specific form of political subjectivity that has the subject of right as its core, and hence without relinquishing the emancipatory resources that have been attested by two centuries of history.

It is common today to attribute the contemporary impasses of democracy to globalisation. Yet, one of the great merits of the complex of phenomena designated by this term is to highlight anew the *difference of power*, that is to say, the essential and irreducible otherness of power in relation to those on whom it is exercised. Globalisation forces us to rethink the democratic reality of the political regimes born of the late eighteenth century revolutions. We ought to remember that, from Rousseau to Madison, the great thinkers whose reflection accompanied the mighty upheaval of social order that crystallised in these revolutions did not seek to abolish power, nor even to minimise it. This is why they rarely embraced democracy as such. It is well known that Madison, in particular, conceived the republic as different from democracy, which in his view could only mean the dictatorship of the majority.[25] But we often forget that Rousseau did not define himself as a democrat: between the three forms of government distinguished in the classic typology – monarchy, aristocracy and democracy – his preference went to the second.[26] The major concern of the theorists of the eighteenth century political revolutions as regards the organisation of institutions was not to eliminate the difference of power, but to prevent the 'abuse of government', namely the propensity of those in power to use power to their own benefit, and hence to lose sight of the public interest. For those who admitted the principle of electoral representation, the danger of abuse threatened both legislative bodies and the government understood in a narrow sense. All of them doubted that the possibility of such degeneration could be entirely ruled out; yet many also felt that the

---

[24] See Benhabib, 2004, pp. 45 and 219.
[25] See *The Federalist Papers*, 1961, p. 82*ff.*
[26] See *infra*, chapter 2.

periodic and sufficiently frequent election of political leaders by the people was the proper and perhaps the only conceivable means of preventing it.

Some may find that, as long as the rights to vote and to stand for election are no longer subject to restrictive conditions, except for the – 'natural' or allegedly inevitable – conditions of age and nationality, power is sufficiently transformed by regular electoral controls to no longer be assimilated to domination. This is the objection concerning self-legislation that I mentioned earlier, an objection whose recurrence requires that I specify what I mean by domination. It is true that the term was not in favour among the authors and theorists of the revolutions. 'To dominate', Mirabeau once said, 'is a tyrannical word that ought to be banished from our legislation'.[27] Yet what Mirabeau effectively banished was not the dissymmetry of the relationship between those who command and those who obey, that is to say, domination in the now ordinary sense of the term which is reproduced in Max Weber's 'sociological' definition: 'the probability that a command with a given specific content will be obeyed by a given group of persons'.[28] For Mirabeau, domination was a term from the Ancien Régime, the result of centuries of history during which the distinction established in Roman law between *dominium* and *imperium* was gradually erased, along with the clear perception of the difference between property and political power. By prohibiting the use of the term domination in the vocabulary of revolutionary legislations, Mirabeau did not dispute the need for power, and in particular for a power exercised through command (*imperium*). He simply called for the reconstruction, on new foundations, of the ancient distinction between *imperium* and *dominium*: political power cannot be the property of anyone; it is a public function performed by some in the name of the people and for the people.

As I mentioned earlier, the theorists of the revolutions anticipated the possibility that representation might give birth to a new oligarchy, which is something they wanted to avoid. Yet they also expected the electoral procedure to produce a government of the best, an aristocracy in the genuine sense of the term. According to Madison, the advantage of elections was that they 'refine and enlarge the public views by passing them through the medium of a chosen body of citizens, whose wisdom may best discern the true interest of their country'.[29] Rousseau came close to this view when he wrote that: 'The best and most natural arrangement is that the wisest should govern the many, when it is assured that they will govern for its profit, and not for their own'.[30] Unlike Madison and Hamilton, however, Rousseau hesitated to

---

[27] Quoted in *Geschichtliche Grundbegriffe*, vol. 3 (Brunner *et al.*, 1982), pp. 51–52.

[28] Weber, 1978, p. 53.

[29] *The Federalist Papers*, 1961, p. 82.

[30] *On the Social Contract, III, chapter 5* (Rousseau, 2003, p. 47).

attribute more wisdom to the affluent in general than to the multitude, even as he recognised that wealth does make it possible to devote all of one's time to the administration of public affairs. Yet despite these nuances, it seems obvious that the overwhelming majority of late eighteenth century theorists explicitly or implicitly agreed with what Bernard Manin calls the 'principle of distinction', whereby elected representatives of the people can only be 'distinguished citizens, socially different from those who elect them'.[31] Their aim was not to abolish power, nor even to purge power of domination understood in the modern sense.

How could it have been otherwise? The task to which these men devoted themselves was the conception and elaboration of a constitution, which is to say, of the fundamental rules that were to govern the administration of the social body. Yet, as Max Weber strongly emphasised, while it is true that every domination manifests itself concretely in an administration, it is also the case that every administration 'needs domination, because it is always necessary that some powers of command be in the hands of somebody'.[32] Administration without domination, which is what direct democracy aspires to be, was for Weber no more than a 'typological limiting case' whose conditions of existence were so restrictive (small communities, high levels of social homogeneity, low complexity of the issues to be addressed) that even the oft-cited examples of American townships and Swiss cantons could hardly satisfy them. The interest of this limiting case, which is of so little use for empirical analysis given the lack of fully corresponding examples, lies above all in its exposing domination where it is hidden: in those forms of power that are established according to constitutionalised procedures and exercised in the name of equal law. That the leaders or members of an administrative body present themselves as the 'servants' of those whom they command does not suffice to rid this body of its character of domination. However, there is no need to dwell here on Weber's caustic and disturbing analysis of democracy. For, to repeat, the theorists of the revolutions did not aspire to be democrats. They did not elaborate their constitutional projects based on the idea of a power *exercised by the people*; their sole aim was to ensure the governmentality of a society of free men, that is to say, a society independent of any personal subjection.

All this is well established and well known, and there would be no need to repeat the argument if the myths associated with the notion of self-legislation did not cloud our memory and our understanding. How, one might ask, does globalisation shed a new light on the issue of power? It is difficult to imagine that it will help us raise anew the question of governmentality *as it was*

---

[31]   Manin, 1997, p. 94.
[32]   Weber, 1978, p. 948.

asked at the end of the eighteenth century, insofar as one of the most manifest consequences of globalisation is the multiplication of the places and forms of power that influence the fate of all societies in the world, which renders illusory the idea that a state can independently determine the manner in which it organises and administers the 'social body'. We now know that the question of governance no longer arises merely in relation to the administration of states. Yet, what leads to the rediscovery that democracy is not a feature of the government of men is precisely the fragmentation of governance – the fact that we can speak of governance in large industrial companies, in universities and hospitals, in supranational and international institutions, and even of global governance. Democracy is not an attribute that distinguishes one type of governance from another; it can only be located in the relation of the ruled to the rulers. Government in general tends towards autonomy, and its action – what is now called governance – is exercised from the top down on individuals and populations that are naturally considered as objects to which laws, decrees and other administrative measures are meant to apply. It is in the logic of governance to suppose that wisdom – i.e., knowledge, but also a sense of the public interest along with the skills required to determine where it lies – belongs to an elite, to political leaders or experts recognised or appointed by them, all of whom always know what is in the interest of the people better than the people itself.

Most of these new powers are constituted via appointment or co-optation, and it is to these modes of constitution that we generally refer when we deplore their lack of democratic legitimacy. Does this mean that they are inaccessible to the action of the individuals or populations who bear the weight of their decisions and to whom their rules apply? The significant heterogeneity of these powers does not allow for a univocal answer, and an in-depth study should proceed with differentiated examples. Yet the answer cannot be entirely negative. Supranational legal instances can be formally called upon by individuals or associations, multinational consortia can be subjected to boycotts or campaigns of denunciation by consumer organisations or environmental protection associations, and social forums have been gaining the attention of political leaders. A whole literature has been documenting the emergence and considerable development, over the last decades, of forms of activist practice and organisation that are very different from those of what we might call the 'classic' period (from the late nineteenth to the third quarter of the twentieth century) in liberal democratic societies.[33] It is remarkable that this phenomenon occurred in the same years that the rise of voter abstention, the increasing fluidity of the electorate and the drastic

---

[33] See Soysal, 1994; Sassen, 2006.

reduction in party membership were prompting some to diagnose a depoliticisation of society – the latter being too quickly attributed to the rise of individualism and to the withdrawal of citizens into the private sphere. Political
scientists and journalists displayed surprising blindness at the time because of
their inability to rid themselves of a narrow and increasingly obsolete conception of politics and citizenship whose sole parameters are partisan membership and electoral participation. They failed to perceive, or perceived only
belatedly, the places and forms in which democracy was reinventing itself by
adapting to an institutional universe wherein the sovereign state had ceased
to be the only rights addressee.

One would be mistaken, however, in thinking that my aim in this book
is to deny any democratic significance to representative institutions and to
the specific rights that make them possible: the right to elect public officials,
freedom of expression, the existence of a public sphere free from censor-
ship, etc. I merely propose to reinterpret these by disconnecting them from
the myth of self-legislation. Representative institutions have only ever been
a means to compel certain categories of leaders to be *accountable* to the
populations over which their power is exercised. Thus, they are a means of
controlling power that ought to be included among the diverse set of democratic practices, without being made the exclusive model or even the core of
democracy. There are several other means to which the dominated can resort
– and indeed have always resorted – to act upon power. This is, in a way,
what Pierre Rosanvallon was observing, in the context of French political history of the last two centuries, when he identified and described the different
forms of 'counter-democratic surveillance', 'sovereignty of prevention' and
judicial control of power.[34] Yet, even as Rosanvallon recognised that these
phenomena constitute, along with electoral-representative government and
political reflection and deliberation, one of the 'three pillars of democratic
experience',[35] he made the mistake of construing them as forms of 'counter-
democracy'. In his view, these practices must be institutionalised lest they
become 'unpolitical', by which he means that they might lose the sense of
collectivity. No doubt Rosanvallon would like to see these modes of political participation that have developed outside the forms set by constitutions
become integral to democracy, but only as a supplement to the other modes,
and this to allow 'progress in self-government'.[36] The latter phrase echoes the
beautiful passage with which he concluded one of his previous books, and in
which he called for 'a renewed and demanding vision of the nation' while

---

[34]   Rosanvallon, 2008.
[35]   *Ibid.*, pp. 313–314.
[36]   *Ibid.*, p. 315.

also predicting a long future for the notion of popular sovereignty.[37] I argue, on the contrary, that this idea essentially belongs to the past. I defend the thesis that the development of forms of political intervention aimed at powers other than the nation-state retrospectively illuminates what the reality of popular sovereignty has always been, namely an institutional framework that organises the particular modalities of expressing rights claims when they are addressed to that equally particular form of power: the nation-state. So long as this framework remains in place – and nothing allows us to predict its near demise – the privileged means of controlling the national figures of power (including the public administration) will obviously have to be preserved. The defence of the representative principle wherever it may be applied, the fight for judicial institutions independent of political power, and the struggle for freedom of the press – not only vis-à-vis political power, but also vis-à-vis the large economic consortia on which press organs and radio and television channels increasingly depend – remain timely. Yet because the decisions that determine the fate of populations (the distribution of wealth, the nature and extension of effectively guaranteed rights, etc.) are being made less and less within the framework of the nation-state, the other means of controlling power that have accompanied the vote throughout the history of modern representative regimes, as well as those that are being invented today, will likely play an increasing role in democratic practice. These means of control should not be regarded as a mere supplement to what presumably remains, against all odds, the unshakable core of democratic institutions: representation. On the contrary, they reveal what representation has always been, while also forcing us to engage in a sober interpretation of its meaning and its reach. It may seem painful, in view of modern democracy's normative ideal, to renounce the idea of self-legislation and its related notion of constituent power; yet this is the price we have to pay if we are to perceive and understand the new conditions of democratic citizenship.

There is no shortage of works today that illustrate the ongoing transformation of citizenship and democracy: analyses of the new forms of civic engagement in contemporary megalopolises, investigations of the increasingly frequent cases of plural citizenship (including the addition of European citizenship to the national citizenship of European Union members), as well as a flourishing literature on participatory democracy. The only originality claimed by the present book lies in its invitation to think through the implications of these various phenomena from the perspective of the concepts of citizenship and democracy. At the risk of repeating myself: the more the figure of the subject of rights – i.e., the rights-claiming subject – acquires importance

---

[37] Rosanvallon, 2000, p. 42.

in terms of what we mean by democratic citizenship, the more the fiction of self-legislation loses credibility. Formulated in radical terms: the multiplication of powers to which the subjects of rights must address their claims *un-determines* the *demos* once and for all. The ambiguities of the concept of 'people' – which can mean humans considered collectively, the rabble, the body of citizens endowed with political rights, the nation, or groups of individuals who mobilise against an abusive power or a threatening foreign power – have been noted long ago.[38] It is only as a constituent power that the 'people' takes on an unambiguous political meaning. Thus understood, it does not derive its unity from any pre-political determination, ethnic or otherwise, but only from the unity of state power, which relies on the will of the people to establish its legitimacy. It is precisely this circle – whereby the political people is determined by the state and state power is legitimated by the postulated unity of the people – that is broken when the subjects of right discover that the state is no longer their sole interlocutor. The pluralisation of *kratos* makes the *demos* unidentifiable.

Reinterpreting modern democracy around the notion of subjective rights has required me to confront a long tradition of critique of this notion. In a recent article,[39] I tried to highlight the misunderstandings that underlie such critique (especially among jurists), while attempting to justify using subjective rights in a manner completely detached from the idea that the human individual has rights by nature. Chapter One of this book takes up the central argument of that article by inviting the reader to understand the emergence of the figure of the subject of rights in view of the great historical transformation that the abolition of the special rights (or rights-privileges) of the Ancien Régime represented for Western societies. The Weberian analysis of subjective rights is the foundation that underpins my interpretation. This chapter also includes a preliminary analysis of Kant's legal doctrine, to which I will continually return in the rest of the book while also discussing his political texts. Using Kant as a privileged interlocutor not only to think democracy, but also to propose a concept of democracy that justifies opposing institutionalised powers, will no doubt seem paradoxical – and I will explain later why I chose to do so.[40] Yet, it is clearly to Kant that we must return if we wish to free subjective rights from their interpretation as status, an interpretation that finds its exemplary legal expression in Kelsen and that, as I hope to show here, is entwined with the communitarian conception of democracy. After briefly recalling some elements of the modern history of the word

---

[38] *Translator's note*: The range of meanings covered by the term 'people' corresponds quite closely to that expressed by the French word 'peuple'.

[39] Colliot-Thélène, 2009b.

[40] See *infra*, IV.2: 'Liberal Individualism and Democracy'.

democracy, chapter Two devotes a fairly lengthy analysis to an author whose name is more expected in a discussion of democracy: Jean-Jacques Rousseau. Specifically, I show that the ambiguities of Rousseau's *Social Contract*, notably regarding the concept of 'people', anticipated the difficulties of modern democratic thought. Rousseau then takes us back to Kant, who, I argue, overcame without betraying Rousseau the ambiguities of his political theory by interpreting the original contract as an Idea of Reason, an interpretation that singularly limited the scope of the principle of self-legislation. These first and second chapters also include reflections on some aspects of the political thought of Hegel and the young Marx. The manner in which each revisited the legacy of the Enlightenment and the French Revolution (which Marx received through Hegel even as he opposed him) foretold the dilemmas of the second part of the nineteenth and much of the twentieth century concerning the place of laws and institutions in modern democracy.

After establishing the centrality of the individualisation of rights in the functioning of post-revolutionary forms of political domination, and after noting the difficulty of identifying the 'people' upon whose presumed consent the legitimacy of these forms rest, I interrogate the reasons that led to the designation of modern constitutional regimes as democracies. Chapter Three addresses this question by analysing the different stages of a process that culminated in the statutory conception of citizenship, a conception to which much of political theory and philosophy is still strongly attached. In the middle of the last century, Thomas H. Marshall defined the ideal type of citizenship, translating on the theoretical level the result of a history that had seen both an increase in the number of rights guaranteed by the state and an extension of the circle of rights beneficiaries. These phenomena, which were quite naturally interpreted as a democratisation of constitutional regimes, established a reciprocal link between citizenship and nationality that was not at all obvious for the revolutionaries of the late eighteenth century. From then on, individuals were presumed to enjoy rights based on their membership in a national community of which the state was both the interpreter and the instrument. The foreigner could only be granted minimal rights, human rights, which an anachronistic reading claimed were distinguished from the rights of citizens in the declarations of the revolutionary era. In such a configuration, it was inevitable that the status of foreigner, reduced to being the opposite of that of citizen, would become the focal point of the difficulties of a democracy necessarily attached to its own closure. Hannah Arendt raised this very problem in the aftermath of World War II. Today it is being raised again, with other referents (immigrants rather than stateless people) but in barely modified terms, prompting several contemporary theorists of democracy to try to elucidate the notion – as famous as it is enigmatic – put forward by Arendt: a 'right to have rights'.

In Arendt's view, the 'right to have rights' was at once necessary and structurally aporetic, because it depended on membership in a collective that was not institutionalised, and that she felt could never be institutionalised: humanity. Chapter Four of the present book aims to solve this aporia by resorting to the radical solution that consists in thinking democracy without *demos*, which is to say, by renouncing the idea or ideal of a democratic community, even one extended to the whole of humanity. A brief critical detour via Carl Schmitt will hopefully prevent any suspicion that I seek to break with the ideals of modern humanism in doing so. Here again, I invoke the authority of Kant, proposing an unusual reading of his cosmopolitanism and drawing on his concept of freedom – understood as 'innate right' – to reinterpret the 'right to have rights' in a resolutely individualistic fashion. As Kant himself points out, individualism does not mean egoism, and the importance I assign to the rights of the individual-subject does not imply that I deny the role of collective solidarities in the history of the democratisation of modern societies. Nevertheless, this history is also that of the repeated failure of attempts to establish lasting egalitarian communities, namely communities without domination. From Marx to Rancière through Arendt and Blanchot, I discuss various expressions of this demand along with its impasses, be these recognised or not by the different authors. It is these impasses that Weber addressed, in his own way, by positing the axiom of the impossible 'routinisation' of charisma, which was for him the figure of revolutionary exception.

'Democracy without *demos*' is first of all a reinterpretation of what modern democracy has been – of the history of democracy over the last two centuries. Any definition of democracy that fails to take into account the history that transformed republics and constitutional monarchies into liberal democracies is a dogmatic one, and it is easy to show how much the reality of the societies so designated contradicts the theoretical model that is said to reveal its foundations. The first interest of an interpretation of modern democracy centred on the subject of right is that it justifies using the sometimes disputed name 'liberal democracy' without uncritically accepting its naive or apologetic representations. As I indicated earlier, deconstructing the myth of self-legislation, and with it the communitarian conception of democracy, is made necessary by recent changes in the role of the nation-state within the space of the heterogeneous powers that shape the global world. The second interest of this interpretation is that it propels democracy into the future, instead of mourning its loss or contenting itself with a rump democracy bounded by the limited powers of the nation-state, which would entail abandoning to experts or to bureaucrats the most important decisions that determine the fate of us all. The analyses presented in chapter Five thus develop the points that initiated the reflection laid out in this book. These analyses, which are exploratory and ought to be further developed, draw on a few salient works on post-national citizenship to show that the denationalisation of citizenship (which is in part the work of nation-states themselves) is not incompatible with the affirmation of the autonomy of the subject of rights.[41] This autonomy, rather than the solidarity often invoked today to save what is left of the welfare state, should be viewed as the major political innovation of modernity, provided we agree that politics consists not merely of institutional arrangements but also of the dispositions and practices of the subject. The subject of right – i.e., the individual who claims equality rather than membership in a particular group to justify his rights claims – is not the entire reality of the modern political subject. Yet were he to disappear, either because of protective tutelage or under the pressure of anonymous constraints, democracy would become no more than an empty word.

---

[41] As will become clear further on (see chapter Four 4.2), autonomy is understood here as the refusal of tutelage.

Chapter 1

Subjective Rights

The National Assembly, wishing to establish the French Constitution on the principles that it has recognised and declared, irrevocably abolishes the institutions that have done injury to liberty and to the equality of rights. Nobility no longer exists, nor peerage, nor hereditary distinction of orders, nor feudal regime, nor patrimonial courts, nor titles, denominations or prerogatives deriving therefrom, nor any order of chivalry, nor any of the corporations or decorations for which proofs of nobility used to be required or which presupposed distinctions of birth, nor any other superiority than that of public officers in the exercise of their functions. [...] No privilege or exception to the common law for all Frenchmen any longer exists for any part of the nation or for any individual. (French Constitution of 3 September 1791)[1]

1.1 SUBJECTIVE RIGHTS: A DISPUTED CONCEPT

When did the term 'subjective rights' first come into use? While legal dictionaries and encyclopaedias do not precisely answer this question, we can at least say that the expression was coined fairly recently.[2] In the history of legal doctrines, it was the nineteenth century German Pandectists who made it famous by giving it a central place in legal theory. The idea, however, predates the term itself. For some it was Hobbes who fathered the notion, while

---

[1] The Declaration of 1789 is more succinct on this point. It simply affirms, in article 6, that all citizens are equal before the Law 'whether it protects or punishes', and that all 'shall be equally eligible to all high offices, public positions and employments, according to their ability, and without other distinction than that of their virtues or talents'.

[2] Olivier Jouanjan locates one of the very first occurrences of the term, under the phrase 'right in the subjective sense', in Christian Friedrich Glück's (1755–1831) *Ausfürhliche Erläuterungen der Pandekten nach Hellfeld* (Erlangen, Palm, 1790). See Jouanjan, 2009, p. 43.

1

for others it was Grotius; for others yet, the notion of subjective rights dates back even further in time. Thus, without claiming to have identified a specific origin, Niklas Luhmann[3] traced the genesis of this idea to the sixteenth century by drawing in particular on Richard Tuck's beautiful study of the sources and development of natural rights theories, a study that had itself explored the reception of Roman law in the twelfth century.[4]

The notion of subjective rights is not only recent; it is also highly controversial. Its obvious association with jusnaturalistic individualism has led some to believe that it could be dismissed by doing away with the very idea of natural law. Léon Duguit, for instance, rejected this idea in the name of the fundamentally social nature of the rule of law, which he explicitly opposed to the conception of natural and individual rights. In this conception, 'man, by the very fact of his birth and his life, is invested with effective powers that we term rights, and that legal doctrine qualifies as subjective rights', these being presumably fixed, 'by virtue of a superior and transcendent force, on the head of each individual, not because he lives in society, nor because he shows solidarity towards his fellow men, but by virtue of his humanity'.[5] Hans Kelsen also rejected natural law, but on the grounds that the notion of right derives from that of duty: 'The traditional view that the right and the obligation are two different objects of legal cognition, that, in fact, the former has a priority in relation to the latter, is probably rooted in the natural-law doctrine. This doctrine assumes the existence of natural rights, inborn in man, that are valid before any positive legal order is established'. Kelsen further noted that one merely needed to dismiss the notion of natural rights and to recognise that the only existing rights are those established by a positive legal order to see the notion of subjective rights – provided that we would want to keep it – change meaning entirely. '[I]t becomes evident', he wrote, 'that a subjective right (as a reflex right) presupposes a corresponding legal obligation – that indeed, it *is* this legal obligation'.[6] While this critique was forgotten in later years, both because of the rehabilitation of the idea of natural law in the post-war period and because of the widespread (though purely technical and non-ideological) use of the notion of subjective right among legal practitioners, Michel Villey revived it in a highly controversial manner in the 1970s and 1980s. Villey traced the philosophical roots of the notion of natural rights to the nominalism of William of Occam, and denounced its belated effects in the political philosophy of his time.[7] In his view, the essential feature of

---

[3] Luhmann, 1982.
[4] Tuck, 1979.
[5] Duguit, 2003, p.140.
[6] Kelsen, 2005, pp. 129–130.
[7] See Villey, 1983, 2003.

this philosophy that made human rights the criterion by which to judge the legitimacy of political regimes could be summed up in a formula whose simplicity bordered on oversimplification: 'From what "man" is, deduce his "right."'[8] To this conception, he himself opposed what he claimed was the truth of the Roman doctrine of law, consistent with the Aristotelian position. For Aristotle as for Roman jurists and the first glossators, law was *jus*, synonymous with *justum*, by which they meant the unity of rights and obligations that constituted an individual's part in the objective order of the world, and that it was the judge's responsibility to determine in the event of disputes (according to the principle of *suum cuique tribuere*). This doctrine ignored the 'subject of right', which Villey consequently invited his readers to discard: law would know no subjects, only beneficiaries.[9] More recently still, Vincent Descombes took up Villey's critique, while displacing it onto a different argumentative terrain. As part of a comprehensive critical study of the various philosophies of the subject, he developed a Wittgenstein-inspired grammatical analysis that challenged the semantic consistency of the notion of subject of right, and with it that of subjective rights.[10]

The jurists of the first half of the twentieth century, however, were not the first to criticise the notion of natural law; nor was Villey the first to deride human rights.[11] As regards natural law, Hegel had already stressed the confusion that underlay the expression. He noted in the *Philosophy of Mind* that '[t]he phrase "Law of nature," or Natural Right, in use for the philosophy of law involves the ambiguity that it may mean either right as something existing ready-formed in nature, or right as governed by the nature of things, i.e. by the notion'.[12] And yet, Hegel did not renounce using the phrase. The *Philosophy of Right* does bear the subtitle: 'Natural Law and Political Science in Outline'. It would be wrong to see this as a concession to the traditional denomination of a theoretical genre to which *Philosophy of Right* still belonged, despite the revision that this genre underwent in the book.[13] Unlike critics of the twentieth century, Hegel was well aware that what lay behind this naturalisation of rights was something quite different from simple naivety. Relating rights to the nature of man was a way of expressing the individualisation of the legal subject, namely the fact that the Moderns consider the individual as a subject

---

8 Villey, 1983, p.153.
9 *Ibid.*, p. 96.
10 Descombes, 2004, part IV.
11 See Binoche, 1989. This text was republished in the second part of *Bentham contre les droits de l'homme* (Binoche and Cléro, 2007).
12 *Philosophy of Mind*, §502 (Hegel, 1894, p. 112). Concerning Hegel's re-elaboration of the notion, see Kervégan, 2007, pp. 85–110.
13 Hegel would have preferred another designation to avoid this ambiguity. See Kervégan, 2007, p. 92.

of freedom and, by virtue of this, as a holder of rights. Hegel knew perfectly well that the notion of subject of right, thus understood, was alien to Roman law. In the latter, he noted, legal personality was a status, which made sense only in opposition to other statuses, and above all that of the slave. 'The right of persons in Roman law is therefore not the right of the person as such, but no more than the right of the *particular* person'.[14] By contrast, the fundamental principle of modern law, which Hegel enunciated in the form of an injunction, was addressed to every individual regardless of status distinction: *'Be a person and respect others as persons'*.[15] The naturalisation of rights merely reflected the individualisation of the legal subject. It was the product of history – of a history that dated back several centuries and that had seen status differences gradually lose their self-evident legitimacy, until the French Revolution declared them abolished.

1.2 KANT: PRIVATE LAW AS A DOCTRINE OF SUBJECTIVE RIGHTS

Hegel's account of what constituted for him the first level of law – which was nevertheless a fundamental level that developed all dimensions of the individual's legal personality – came with a recurring critique of Kantian positions. And yet it is Kant who presented with the greatest consistency the implications of the individualisation of the subject of right. Of the entire Kantian corpus, the *Doctrine of Right* was not the best served by exegetical commentary.[16] Specialists in moral philosophy have tended to view it as a mere appendix to Kant's body of work, while political scientists have more readily focused on his opuscules, in particular the *Idea for a Universal History with a Cosmopolitan Purpose* (1784), the essay on *Perpetual Peace* (1795), or the third part of *The Conflict of the Faculties* (1798). I will later comment on some of the arguments presented in those texts. Nevertheless, the key to Kant's legal *and political* philosophy does lie in the *Doctrine of Right* and, above all, in the mystery of its construction. For in this text, Kant preceded a description of public right – in other words, of right established and guaranteed by the state, which is what we normally refer to as positive

---

[14] *PhR*, §40 (Hegel, 1991, p. 71). 'But as for what is called the *right of persons* in Roman law, it regards a human being as a person only if he enjoys a certain *status* [...]; hence in Roman law even personality itself, as opposed to slavery, is merely an *estate* [*Stand*] or condition [*Zustand*]. [...] The right of persons in Roman law is therefore not the right of the person as such, but no more than the right of the particular person'.

[15] *Ibid.*, §36, p. 69.

[16] At least in French exegetic commentary. In German, one now has access to the remarkable studies of Wolfgang Kersting (Kersting, 2004).

right – with an account of private right construed as determinable prior to any political institution. This is all the more mysterious since Kant himself acknowledged that the private condition, which is another name for the state of nature, is 'one that is not rightful'.[17] There can be no right in the strict sense of the term – i.e., no 'conclusive' right, to use Kantian terminology – without a state. What interest did Kant have, then, in speaking of right, and especially of *legal* right, with regards to relationships that escape the constraints of the state or of any other instance of public power, when he himself claimed that 'right and authorization to use coercion […] mean one and the same thing'?[18] What interest is there in thinking something like a 'provisional' right that would be distinct from a 'conclusive' right?

If we are entitled to speak of mystery concerning the link that Kant established between private right and public right, it is because this link has often aroused perplexity among commentators. The book by Simone Goyard-Fabre, one of the few works in French to be entirely devoted to the *Doctrine of Right*,[19] exemplifies this perplexity, which she sought to overcome by putting forward a highly questionable interpretation. Private right, she wrote, is certainly not a-legal, but pre-legal – that is to say, it is legal in anticipation of the civil condition. This distinction allowed her to argue that, for Kant, 'the truth of private right resides in its subsumption under public right, namely in the guarantee which only civil law is authorised to give to the structures of society. Political right confers on natural right its truth and its legal validity'.[20] Alain Renaut, who recently published a beautiful translation of the *Doctrine of Right*, comes close to this interpretation. In a note where he comments the Kantian formula whereby 'only in a civil condition can something external be mine or yours' (the determination of 'something external' as 'mine or yours' being the entire content of the 'right of men', i.e., the right of jurists), he claims that this formula expresses 'the most famous thesis of the *Doctrine of Right*', namely that 'it is public law which founds private law'[21] This sort of interpretation does not help us understand why Kant, always so scrupulous in his choice of terminology, insisted in qualifying as legal the provisional rights of the private condition. The most explicit passage in this respect is found in the remark to paragraph 44 of the *Doctrine of Right*: 'If no acquisition were cognized as rightful even in a provisional way prior to entering the civil condition, the civil condition itself would be impossible'.[22]

---

[17] *Doctrine of Right*, §44 (Kant, 1996, p. 89). Hereafter I refer to the *Doctrine of Right* as *DR*.
[18] *Ibid.*, Introduction, §E, p. 26.
[19] Goyard-Fabre, 1975.
[20] *Ibid.*, p. 125.
[21] See Kant, 1994, p. 381, note 29.
[22] *DR*, §44 (Kant, 1996, p. 90).

The mystery is solved, however, as soon as we take into consideration the (generally implicit) critique that Kant levelled in all of his legal and political writings against the temptation of legal positivism, whose extreme (because logically rigorous) expression he found in Hobbes's positions. To be sure, 'only in a civil condition can something external be mine or yours'[23] and this 'something external' which is 'mine or yours' – the matter of private right – is found, with nothing added or subtracted, in the civil condition.[24] But it is not up to the state to determine the content of private rights. These must, on the contrary, be thinkable (which is what Kant meant by 'possibility') not only in their form, but also specifically in their content, regardless of the guarantee that the existence of an instance of coercion, that is of a political power, might offer them. Concerning the justification for property, which constituted for Kant the core of private right, Hobbes defended a completely opposite thesis: in his view, the foundation of property could only be institutional.[25] The anti-positivist signification of the logical anteriority of private right to public right appears clearly in one of the few passages where Kant explicitly mentions Hobbes, namely the second part of *Theory and Practice*, which bears the subtitle 'Against Hobbes', and more specifically the conclusion. In general, readers mainly remember from this text Kant's reaffirmation of his unreserved condemnation of the right to resist. No violation of right, no abuse of power on the part of rulers or legislators could justify for him a people's rebellion. In the last pages of the text, Kant claimed he was confident that despite everything, he would not be reproached for being overly flattering to monarchs – something about which he was certainly deluded. But it is to another potential critique that he unexpectedly devoted most of his attention: that according to which he excessively favoured the people by positing that it possessed imprescriptible rights in the face of power, even though these rights could not be binding. It is only in this short passage that Hobbes's name is mentioned,[26] and this in a text that was supposed to be entirely devoted to criticising him. The context clarifies the meaning of this critical reference. By declaring rebellion illegitimate, regardless of the reasons for it, Kant seemed to veer dangerously close to Hobbes's absolutist conception of sovereignty, which implied that it is power ('the head of state') which is responsible for

---

[23]   *Ibid.*, §8, p. 45.

[24]   *Ibid.*, §41, p. 85.

[25]   See *Leviathan*, chapter 24, 'Of *the* NUTRITION *and* PROCREATION *of a Common-wealth*', in Hobbes, 1982, pp. 295–296: 'The Distribution of the Materials of this Nourishment, is the constitution of *Mine*, and *Thine*, and *His*; that is to say, in one word *Propriety*; and belongeth in all kinds of Common-wealth to the Soveraign Power'. See also *ibid.*, p. 297: 'From whence we may collect, that the Propriety which a subject hath in his lands, consisteth in a right to exclude all other subjects from the use of them; and not to exclude their Soveraign, be it an Assembly, or a Monarch'.

[26]   Kant, 1991a, pp. 84–85.

defining the just and the unjust – to determine what right is. It is precisely this thesis, which Kant deemed 'terrifying',[27] that the construction of the *Doctrine of Right* permitted to rule out. The anteriority of private right to public right means that, contrary to what Simone Goyard-Fabre argues, the truth and validity of private right *do not depend* on its subsumption under public right.

Clearly, Kant is not Kelsen. In the book that the latter devoted to refuting one by one – from Durkheim and Tönnies to Jellinek and Weber (among others!) [28] – all the theorists of the state that introduced in its concept determinations other than that of the legal order, the passage dedicated to Kant is surprisingly short.[29] Kelsen saw in the Kantian theory of law and state merely 'the typical expression of the doctrine of natural law'. Kant remained a contractualist and therefore presupposed – contradictorily, according to Kelsen – that the idea of rights preceded the state in one way or another. In his view, Kant came very close to perceiving the law and the state as identical when he defined the latter as the 'union of a multitude of human beings under laws of right'.[30] Provided that we correct the image suggested by the term 'under', this formula means, again according to Kelsen, that the state is the behaviour of a multitude of human beings bound by norms of right. Yet because Kant failed to take this definition to its logical conclusion, he, like other theorists of natural law, juxtaposed to his legal concept of the state another concept which he unduly presented as equivalent: the state is a fact of power that produces right.[31] The casualness with which Kelsen rushed through the Kantian case is indicated by his silence regarding the nonetheless crucial distinction Kant established between private right and public right. This is because the meaning of this distinction was imperceptible to him.

Indeed, in order to exorcise once and for all the notion of 'natural law', Kelsen reversed the priority of rights and obligations by placing obligations at the legal forefront. In his view, the major defect of what he vaguely referred to as traditional legal theory – in its German and French variants at least – was to take subjective rights as a starting point, such that obligations would, so to speak, disappear behind them.[32] Unlike Duguit, Kelsen did not completely reject the use of the expression 'subjective rights', but he broke the term down between reflex rights, political rights, subjective rights 'in the technical sense' and positive permissions.[33] Yet despite their differences, these four types of

---

[27] *Ibid.*, p. 84.
[28] Kelsen, 1928.
[29] *Ibid.*, pp. 140–143.
[30] *DR*, §45 (Kant, 1996, p. 90).
[31] On the status of power in Kelsen's thought, see Norberto Bobbio's 'Kelsen and Legal Power' (Bobbio, 1999, pp. 435–450).
[32] Kelsen, 2005, p. 125.
[33] See Kelsen, *Pure Theory of Law*, chapter 29 (Kelsen, 2005, p. 125–145). See also the aforementioned article by Norberto Bobbio.

subjective rights can be regarded as species of a same genus, in the sense that each of them is established by state-created norms, the state being the one and only source of right. As the term suggests, reflex rights are merely the correlate of prohibitions, accompanied by sanctions in the case of violation, which influence behaviours. Moreover, even the powers (in the sense of *capacitas*) of legal subjectivity, such as that of participating, directly or indirectly, in the elaboration of the political will or that of initiating a legal procedure through filing a complaint (i.e., subjective right 'in the technical sense', to use Kelsen's terminology) always proceed from an *Ermächtigung* – a term which the English 'authorisation' imperfectly renders. The individual has power only in so far as it is conceded to him. Behind the authorisations and powers granted by the state, there is nothing. The legal subject, and with him the political subject, has no consistency of his own; he is merely the point of convergence of norms determined by the state. These norms target the human individual through behaviours, which they prohibit or render possible depending on the situation. But they do not presuppose the individual as subject; on the contrary, they treat him as an object, as the object to which these norms apply.

In short, this position implies that rights and obligations are the constitutive elements of a status, that which the state confers on the citizen. Kant, who was the heir of Rousseau and a fervent admirer of the constitutional work of the French Revolution, could not share this conception. The fact that he associated right with constraint should not mislead us. This constraint can only be the guarantee of rights that are determinable independently of it. The fundamental argument of Kant's legal theory is formulated in paragraph 9 of the *Doctrine of Right*: 'Any guarantee [...] already presupposes what belongs to someone (to whom it secures it). Prior to a civil constitution (or in *abstraction* from it) external objects that are mine or yours must therefore be assumed to be possible [...]'[34] Clearly, only one right can be qualified as 'innate': the equal freedom of all. But it is from this innate right that one can infer the 'right of men', namely the concrete rights which legitimate powers ought to respect.[35] If these rights could not be determined in *abstraction* from the existence of the state, the need for the latter would be based merely on psychological motivations such as the fear of death (as in Hobbes). These motivations, however, do not suffice to found a duty, which is why the normative necessity of the state remains unintelligible. This is what is meant by the formula cited earlier whereby 'the civil condition itself would be impossible'[36] if right were not given consistency independently of this condition. If

---

[34] *DR*, §9 (Kant, 1996, p. 45).
[35] On the meaning of this 'innate right', see *infra* chapter 4.2: 'Liberal Individualism and Democracy'.
[36] *DR*, §44 (Kant, 1996, p. 90).

we are to give a normative meaning to Hobbes's famous injunction that 'we should leave the state of nature', then *we must admit* that the notion of right has meaning even before we take into consideration the conditions for the guarantee of rights.

The difference between the position of Kant and that of Kelsen is reflected in the fact that the latter substitutes the terminology of *being* for that of *having* to qualify the relation between the subject and his rights. To understand the significance of this substitution, we must first clarify the meaning of the Kantian notion of 'what is externally mine or yours'. It would be reductive to conflate this notion with what is commonly referred to as 'property', by which is meant the guaranteed possession of wealth, whether in the form of movable or immovable goods. It is true that this sort of property – and especially property of the land – plays an important role in a large part of Kant's argument. But the Kantian 'what is externally mine or yours' generally includes any object that an individual can claim to have 'under his control': sensible objects, clearly, but also the 'will' of another and the 'status' of another in relation to me. The will of another is the performance I consider myself entitled to demand from someone who made a promise to me (the domain of contract law). The status of another in relation to me refers to my husband or my wife, my child, my servant. Of all these 'objects', I can say that they are mine so long as I can claim rights to them, even as I do not effectively have them 'under my control'. This 'something external' is not a thing, because exteriority is not conceived here as a spatio-temporal determination, but as a difference from the subject.[37] It is this purely intelligible relation of appropriation of an object that I do not presently have under my control (or may not have under my control) that Kant designates as mine. The Kantian doctrine of property is a reflection on the concept of 'mine' in general, regardless of the object to which it applies. More directly, it is *a theory of subjective rights in general*. This is why Kant noted that it is inappropriate to say that one possesses a right to an object, because 'a right is already an intellectual possession of an object and it would make no sense to speak of possessing a possession'.[38]

For Kant, rights are something that the subject *has* – that he can claim as his – which implies a distinction between this subject and his rights. For Kelsen, on the contrary, obligations and rights, which are both created by state norms, constitute the *being* of the person understood as a legal subjectivity. It is in the name of this conception of obligations and rights that he

---

[37] *Ibid.*, §7, p. 42: 'So too the expression *external* does not mean existing in a *place other* than where I am, or that my decision and acceptance are occurring at a different time from the making of the offer; it means only an object *distinct* from me'.

[38] *Ibid.*, §5, p. 39.

refutes, in particular, the relevance of the distinction between real persons and fictitious persons:

> The person as a holder of obligations and rights is not something that is different from the obligations and rights, as whose holder the person is presented – just as a tree which is said to have a trunk, branches, and blossoms, is not a substance different from trunk, branches, and blossoms, but merely the totality of these elements. The physical or juristic person who 'has' obligations and rights as their holder, *is* these obligations and rights – a complex of legal obligations and rights whose totality is expressed figuratively in the concept of 'person'. 'Person' is merely the personification of this totality.[39]

This difference between being and having encapsulates the opposition between a statutory and a universal conception of the subject of right. Kelsen's conception, as we saw earlier, is statutory in that for him the subject of right is constituted as such by the norms that determine what is forbidden and what is permitted to him. Insofar as legal norms are necessarily determined by a state (the legal order and the state being one and the same thing), it is by virtue of his membership in a specific state that an individual is a subject of right. By contrast, Kant's conception is universal in that for him the subject of right is thinkable independently of the rights he 'possesses'. Of course, the subject only truly possesses those rights, as conclusive rights, when they are guaranteed by a state power. But the key point here is that the content of those rights is independent of the power that guarantees them. If, as is generally recognised, Kant is the philosopher who gave the subjectivisation of right 'its most accomplished expression',[40] it is because he separated the figure of the subject of right from any presupposed membership in a collective, including the state. However, the implications of this separation are difficult to admit not only by proponents of all types of legal positivism, but also by theorists of the republican tradition, especially in its French variant, because it is so difficult for them to think citizenship – whether civil or political – independent of nationality. I will return to this point later.

1.3 THE INDIVIDUALISATION OF RIGHTS

It is a commonplace observation that the individualisation of rights constitutes the great legal innovation of modern times. I will further argue here that this individualisation actually forms the core of the modern *political* revolution. To put it in unambiguous terms, this process was central to the radical

---

[39] Kelsen, 2005, pp. 172–173.
[40] Pierre Rosanvallon, 1992, p. 140.

transformation of political power that began well before the revolutions of the late 18th century and that was merely continued by them, culminating in the liberal democratic states of today. The thesis whereby the history of right and that of the modern state are closely linked is also commonplace – so much so, in fact, that it borders on platitude. This link is generally understood as the subjection of a political power that was once largely arbitrary, and whose only limit (more or less respected depending on the circumstances) was the natural right which Christianity founded in divine authority (the 'laws of God and of nature', to use the words of Bodin[41]). From this perspective, the modern legal innovation consisted in secularising the laws that limited power, which necessarily resulted in their codification. Ultimately, the constitutionalisation of power – the mode of its formation and that of its exercise – was the high point of centuries of mingled legal and political histories. Along with it came a well-known paradox – the ever-recurring difficulty faced by all sovereignty and reason of state theories since the late sixteenth century: insofar as this right which is supposed to limit power is cut off from any transcendence, it can have no other source than power itself. This is the paradox of 'the limit of an ultimate, unlimited authority'.[42]

The paradox nevertheless disappears when we understand this subjection of power to the law, not as a limitation of power by a heterogeneous instance, but as a specific form of rationalisation of power from which power itself consequently derives some advantage. The symbolic impact of the declarations of the rights of man of the revolutionary period, as well as the dramatic aspect of the revolutionary episode itself, prompted many theorists of the next two centuries – liberals and democrats alike – to overestimate the importance of the break that the eighteenth century political revolutions represented in the Western history of the forms of power. The political recognition of the natural equality of men, which founds and justifies their equality before the law, is generally traced back to these declarations. Thus, it is argued that the French and American revolutions translated for the first time in political terms an equality that had been professed by Christianity for nearly two millennia, yet had until then concerned merely man's relation to God. In this view, the Pauline idea – rewritten here in the terms of Hegel – that 'a *human being counts as such because he is a human being*, not because he is a Jew, Catholic, Protestant, German, Italian, etc'.[43] acquired legal and hence political significance with the declarations of the rights of man. Yet, while it is undeniable that the revolutions abolished a whole range of privileges and status differences that subsisted in the Ancien

---

[41] *On Sovereignty: Six Books of the Commonwealth*, I, 8 (Bodin, 2009, p. 68).

[42] Luhmann, 1989a, p. 79.

[43] *Elements of the Philosophy of Right*, §209 (Hegel, 1991, p. 240). This is an implicit allusion to Paul, Epistle to the Colossians, III, 11 (*The Bible*, 1997, 251): 'Where there is neither Greek nor Jew, circumcision nor uncircumcision, Barbarian, Scythian, bond *nor* free; but Christ is all, and in all'. See also the Epistle to the Galatians, III, 28.

Régime societies of the second half of the eighteenth century, the figure of the individual who holds rights by virtue of a nature that knows no inequality does not date from this period. This figure lay at the foundation of the social contract theories of the seventeenth century – from Hobbes's to Locke's – all of which had individualism as their starting point, regardless of the political institutions (possibly even absolutist ones) that they ultimately sought to justify. How could this figure be thinkable at a time when the life of most individuals was still entirely determined by their membership in particular groups – 'closed' groups, to use the language of Weber[44] – that protected the 'opportunities' reserved for their members by jealously guarding this closure, and that were themselves integrated into a network of relationships where dissymmetry, that is hierarchy, was the rule? This is because the process of eradication of legal pluralism in which social, legal and political dimensions were inextricably linked had been underway for several centuries.

It is symptomatic that the archaeology of the notion of subjective rights (which, as I recalled earlier, was explicitly codified in legal texts only starting in the nineteenth century) detects the first signs of its appearance as far back as the twelfth century.[45] Indeed, the genesis of subjective rights coincides with the period in which territorial states were being formed in Europe, namely from the twelfth to the nineteenth century.[46] I will not attribute this coincidence to the 'reception of Roman law', which, as Villey and others have rightly pointed out, did not even know the notion. What began in the twelfth century was a process of centralisation of power whose driving force was the monarchy. This slow process, which spanned seven centuries, was punctuated by a few important theoretical works that pondered its meaning – from Bodin's to Hobbes's – and that are interpreted today as different stages in the elaboration of the concept of state sovereignty.[47] While the reception, adaptation and 'nationalisation' of Roman law did play a role in this history,[48]

---

44 I am alluding here to the distinction Weber made between 'open and closed' social relationships. In an open relationship, participation in the reciprocal social action that constitutes said relationship is not denied to anyone who is in a position to join (i.e., who is qualified) and has the desire to do so. By contrast, in a closed relationship, the very content or the rules of the relationship exclude and limit such participation or else subject it to restrictive conditions. See Weber, 1976, pp. 23–24 (in English: Weber, 1978, p. 43).

45 See Tuck, 1979.

46 For more details on the centuries-long history of the formation of the modern state, see Wolfgang Reinhard, *Geschichte der Staatsgewalt* (Reinhard, 1999).

47 For a discussion of this history, and especially of Bodin, see Quaritsch, 1986,

48 See Reinhard, 1999, pp. 285–290. Reinhard, who recalls how the School of Bologna rediscovered and developed the Justinian compilation in the 12th century, nevertheless observes that this work long remained an object of pure academic interest. In his view, the new legal culture that developed in the 12th century owed more to Canon law, itself impregnated with the Roman legal tradition, than to the work of Bologna jurists. The 'reception of Roman law', he writes, is not easy to date or to define. It is, rather, an extremely diffuse process (*ibid.*, p. 287). Concerning the 'nationalisation' of Roman law, Reinhard mentions (*ibid.*, p 301) the existence of Roman-German, Roman-Swedish, and Roman-Dutch laws as early as the 17th century.

the main factor behind it lay in the weakening, elimination or subjection by territorial powers of the various authorities – Church, nobility, *Stände*, free urban communes, etc. – with which they competed for the control of law and justice. Hobbes occupies an exceptional place in the philosophical reflection on this long transformation, which saw the gradual co-emergence of a new form of political power and a novel conception of right. He is indeed the most prominent theorist of modern sovereignty (which Bodin's *Sovereignty,* still burdened with medieval conceptions, had merely heralded) and the first to have extricated the notion of subjective right from the confused accounts of his predecessors. To be sure, he did not yet use this expression. But the difference he established between right, which is synonymous with freedom, and law, which is constraining, clearly anticipated the opposition between subjective right and objective law. Against what had been until then a common conflation between *jux* and *lex* – i.e., right and law – he affirmed, on the contrary, the necessity of distinguishing between the two, 'because RIGHT consisteth in liberty to do, or to forbeare; Whereas LAW, determineth, and bindeth to one of them: so that Law, and Right, differ as much, as Obligation, and Liberty; which in one and the same matter are inconsistent'.[49] With Hobbes, Luhmann writes, right became 'a capacity to have and make claims', and henceforth 'the subjective rights recognised in civil society, as well as the legal codification performed by the state, appeared as variants of a right itself founded on a claim'.[50] The individualisation of the rights-holder was not only, as I indicated earlier, the signification of the link established between rights and the nature of man; it also constituted a 'subjectivisation of natural law' whose initiator was precisely Hobbes.[51] The connection between this 'subjectivisation' and the presuppositions of state sovereignty appears clearly in the chapter in *Leviathan* devoted to 'Of Systemes Subject, Politicall, and Private'.[52] Here, Hobbes states that all temporary or permanent collectives other than the state can legitimately exist only with the explicit (written) or implicit authorisation of the 'Soveraign Power of the Common-wealth'. As a result, the individual always maintains the ability to dissociate himself from such collectives. This is the case, for instance, when a debt is incurred by a collective – where it is 'not onely lawfull but expedient' for a member to 'make open protestation' against the decisions taken by it – or, more generally, when a dispute pits a particular member against an entire 'Body Politique', which it is up to the sovereign (the state), and never the particular

---

[49] *Leviathan*, ch. XIV (Hobbes, 1982, p. 189).
[50] Luhmann, 1982, p. 59.
[51] *Ibid.*, p. 60.
[52] *Leviathan*, ch. XXII (Hobbes, 1982, pp. 274–288). I am grateful to Etienne Balibar for bringing my attention to this chapter, as well as to the work of David Runciman, *Pluralism and the personality of the State* (1997), which examines how the heirs of Hobbes have dealt with the personality of the groups that are subordinated to the state.

body itself, to judge.[53] Hobbes clearly indicates here that the obligations of an individual towards a particular collective are always mediated by the state, for which the only subject of right is the individual as such – that is to say, the individual in abstraction from his various community affiliations (family, profession, corporations of all kinds, religious community, etc.).

To be sure, it is only with the revolutions of the late eighteenth century that the natural and legal equality of all men was established as a principle of right and political organisation. But the revolutions merely completed the transformation of how European societies operated – a process that had been initiated centuries earlier and that, by disrupting the relationship between the individual and the powers to which he was subjected, turned the subjected into the modern subject. The ambivalence of the term 'subject' is likely the product of that history. While Kant expressed the originality of the modern subject in the language of autonomy, Niklas Luhmann did so in the language of 'self-reference'. Some view these philosophical concepts as mere speculative window-dressing for the reference to human nature, which they claim was simply converted into rational nature. But rather than attempting to defend this ultimate rational foundation of right in philosophical terms, one can more easily explicate it through the lens of history. Indeed, for historians as for sociologists, the originality of the self-reference of the subject of right acquires concrete meaning as soon as it is contrasted to the legal and political conditions with which it broke.

Max Weber, who combined the skills of the historian with those of the sociologist, gave us the key to this historical understanding of self-reference by characterising the modern state as the monopoly of legitimate violence – a characterisation as famous as it is generally misunderstood. The best-known version of this 'definition' of the modern state, which is found in the speech on 'Politics as a Vocation', puts excessive stress on the dimension of violence, and especially physical violence. It is this dimension that later commentators emphasised, often to reproach Weber for having transposed to sociology an authoritarian conception of power, and of politics in general, by completely ignoring the links between politics and freedom.[54] Yet various passages from *Economy and Society* – namely those in the chapter 'Basic Sociological Terms',[55] which includes the definition of the state later presented in 'Politics as a Vocation', as well as in the 'Sociology of Law', especially the section on subjective rights entitled 'Forms of Creation of Rights'[56] – allow for an entirely different interpretation of the 'monopoly of legitimate violence'.

---

[53] *Leviathan*, ch. XXII (Hobbes, 1982, pp. 278 and 281).
[54] See for instance Arendt, 1970, p. 36*ff.*
[55] Weber, 1976, pp. 29–30 (in English: Weber, 1978, p. 54). See paragraph 17 of the chapter 'Basic Sociological Terms'.
[56] Weber, 1978, pp. 666–752.

First, it is notable that Weber speaks in *Economy and Society* of the monopoly of 'coercion' as much as he does of the monopoly of 'legitimate physical violence'. This variant allows us to recognise, in the Weberian definition of the state, a thesis that was widespread among German jurists and historians of his time. Weber merely took up and reworked this thesis as part of his own project: the establishment of a sort of fundamental dictionary of sociology. Before him, Rudolph von Ihering and Rudolph Sohm[57] had already evoked the state's monopoly of coercion. So had Georg Jellinek, a jurist and close friend of Weber,[58] who, in his *Allgemeine Staatslehre*, had summed up the process of state formation in these terms: 'The development of the state is everywhere accompanied by the absorption of the autonomous creation of law, such that, ultimately, only the state has control over the means of legal coercion. Today, any systematic new creation [...] of law is the work of the state itself, or else is transferred or conceded by it'.[59] Like these jurists and legal historians, Weber interpreted the sovereignty of the modern state in view of the intertwined histories of political organisation and law in the West. In this interpretation, the modern sovereign state appears as the outcome of a process that saw a certain type of political community (consecrated thereby as the political community *par excellence*) monopolise the exercise of legitimate coercion at the expense of various 'law communities' (*Rechtsgemeinschaften*) – feudal powers, orders, Churches, cities, etc. – that previously guaranteed special rights to their members.

Second, reading the section on subjective rights in the 'Sociology of Law' allows us to perceive the close connection between state sovereignty thus understood and a profound upheaval in the conception of right. The nature of this upheaval (to which the title of the section, 'Forms of Creation of Rights', directly refers)[60] is somewhat obscured, both by the extremely dense nature of the chapter in question – in which Weber tried, as he often did, to accomplish several things at once – and by the liberty he took in speaking

---

[57] Rudolf Von Jhering (1818–1892) was a professor of law in Göttingen. His most famous work is *Der Zweck im Recht* (two volumes, 1877–1883). Rudolph Sohm (1841–1917) was a professor of legal history in Leipzig and a specialist of Canon law. Weber claims to have found the concept of charismatic power in his work. For more details on the texts that these two authors devoted to the monopoly of coercion, see Anter, 2001, p. 125, notes 7, 8 and 9.

[58] Georg Jellinek (1815–1911) was named professor (with tenure) of constitutional and international law and of political science at the University of Heidelberg in 1891. It is in Heidelberg that an intellectual and personal relationship developed between him and Weber, himself appointed professor at the chair of national economy and finance in the same university in 1896. On the intellectual dimension of the relationship between Weber and Jellinek, see Anter, 2000 and Breuer, 1999. For a discussion of Jellinek's theory of public subjective rights, see Jouanjan 2005a and 2005b.

[59] Jellinek, 1976, p. 124. I discussed the pre-Weberian history of the concept of monopoly of legal coercion in an article entirely devoted to this topic (Colliot-Thélène, 2005). Anter (2014 and 2001) analysed this history in even greater detail.

[60] In German: 'Die Formen der Begründung subjektiver Rechte'. It seems to me when reading this chapter that the term 'Begründung' should be understood not only in the sense of foundation ('creation' in the English translation), but also of justification.

of 'subjective rights' regarding societies that did not know the concept. To understand the nature of this upheaval, we ought to consider another element in the Weberian characterisation of the state. As can be read in the chapter 'Basic Sociological Terms', the modern state is a 'compulsory political organization with continuous operations (*politischer Anstaltsbetrieb*)', which successfully claims 'the monopoly of the legitimate use of physical force'.[61] The notion of *Anstalt* (rendered in English by the not very telling expression 'compulsory organisation') covers two related characteristics: the codification of legal and administrative regulations and territoriality. Likewise, the speech on 'Politics as a Vocation' emphasises that territory is a key element of the modern state.[62] The state's monopoly of legal coercion is indeed effective only within the limits of a territory. But these limits, which primarily evoke the borders separating nation-states, also imply that the state, as the only instance legitimised to guarantee right, has no rivals within its borders. In other words: the fact that the limits of this particular form of political power known as the state are territorial means that there can be no statutory rights. The state monopolises legitimate legal coercion in the same gesture by which it territorialises power. It is the effects of this double-sided process on the understanding of the foundation of right that are described in the second part of the section devoted to subjective rights in the 'Sociology of Law' – namely, the transition from a regime of rights attached to persons by virtue of their membership in a determined community to the law of a territorial power that applies to all without distinction. 'In the past', wrote Weber, the rights attached to individuals depended on their membership in 'law communities' that were based on very diverse criteria: birth, political, religious and ethnic affiliations, mode of life, or voluntary association. These rights were constitutive of the status of the individual, who carried them with him and claimed them as privileges: 'The individual carried his *professio juris* with him wherever he went. Right was not a "lex terrae" [...] but rather the privilege of the person as a member of a particular group'.[63] The modern state put an end to this heterogeneity of 'special rights' by imposing itself as the only legitimate source of law, and by subordinating the validity of subsisting 'special rights' to its authorisation: 'The state insisted almost everywhere, and usually with success, that the validity of these special rights as well as the extent of their application, should be subject to its consent'.[64] Given this subordination,

---

[61] Weber, 1978, p. 54.
[62] The complete characterisation of the modern state in 'Politics as a Vocation' is as follows: 'Today [...] we have to say that a state is a human community that (successfully) claims the monopoly of the legitimate use of physical force within a given territory. Note that "territory" is one of the characteristics of the state' (Weber, 2009, p. 78).
[63] Weber, 1978, p. 696 (modified translation).
[64] *Ibid.*, p. 695 (modified translation).

which Weber designated in German with the legal term '*Mediatisierung der Rechte*' (mediation of special rights), these rights were now, under the conditions of the political and legal order of the state, attached to individuals on 'a basis which differ[ed] in many important respects from that of the privileges of the older corporate status groups'.[65] What this entirely new basis consisted of is expressed in a note where Weber remarked that in the bygone era of legal pluralism, in which all rights 'appeared as the privilege of particular individuals or objects [...] the idea of generally applicable norms was not, it is true, completely lacking, but it inevitably remained in an undeveloped state'.[66] The victory of the sovereign state over the legal-political pluralism of medieval society, at the end of a centuries-long process which the late eighteenth century revolutions completed, is precisely what made possible the development and generalisation of this 'idea'.

Before political thought focused, in the second half of the nineteenth and much of the twentieth century, on the opposition between the formal character of legal equality and the reality of socio-economic inequalities, many authors still had in mind the magnitude of the transformation that the eradication of status differences – and its corollary, the individualisation of the subject of right – had introduced in the symbolic understanding of right. In the second half of the twentieth century, this theme no longer really held the attention of political theorists. It is sociologists who preserved the memory of this upheaval, reflecting it in the various dichotomies with which they sought to characterise the specificity of modern Western societies: status and contract, community and society, mechanical and organic division of labour, etc.[67] Far more than political theory or political philosophy, it is sociology that has transmitted to us – to some representatives of the discipline at least – a broad historical perspective on the question of the individualisation of the subject. In this respect, Luhmann was a worthy heir to Durkheim and Weber (though he did not dwell much on the second) when he noted that the notion of subjective rights was at the heart of a new, individualising semantics, and when he interpreted the development of the language of subjective rights as the sign that the stratified differentiation of past societies had been replaced by a new form of differentiation which he termed 'functional'. What constituted the identity of a human being was no longer the particular place he occupied in an objective cosmo-social order, but self-reference, which had the paradoxical property of allowing for the social inclusion of an individual unbound from membership in any determined collective.

---

[65] *Ibid.*, p. 698.
[66] *Ibid* (modified translation).
[67] These distinctions are, in order, those made by Henry Sumner Maine, Ferdinand Tönnies and Emile Durkheim.

The semantics of subjective rights refers to subjects as individuals. [...] It is only starting in the mid-17th century that the (still prevailing) medieval conceptuality, whereby the *subjectum* signified no more than what lies at the foundation, could begin to change. With the Cartesian turn in philosophy, the term 'subject' took on a new meaning: the individual himself now founded the justification for his rights. Independently of this change in Subject/Object terminology, there was in the second half of the 17th century a growing interest in self-referential figures and modes of argumentation. In the case of subjective rights [...], the question was no longer that of reflex rights in an objective order, but that of the transfer of the substance of right in the self-reference of the subject. The criteria that separated right from non-right were no longer the natural demands of the social order; nor were they the *prima regula boni et mali* that could be found in the nature of man. On the contrary, they now had to refer to the subject's relation to himself and to discriminate in function of this relation. In this sense, one could also attribute an absolute character to the self-referential subjective foundation of right: from then on, this foundation depended only on itself.[68]

1.4 MARX, LEGAL EQUALITY AND DEMOCRACY

Marx was one of the authors who, in the first half of the nineteenth century, continued to reflect on the significance of this transformation. In fact, all of his works, whether the texts published during his lifetime or those left unfinished and published long after his death, illustrate the shift in the framing of political and social issues that occurred around the mid-nineteenth century. Marx substituted the socio-economic question of exploitation for that of domination and generally viewed the law, which he essentially reduced to the contract, as the device that rendered possible, at the same time that it camouflaged it, the extortion of surplus-labour in its specifically capitalist form. There is no doubt that, in so doing, Marx helped to push into oblivion the extraordinary emancipatory scope of equal law, as reflected by the prominence given to the opposition between formal legal equality and real social inequalities in the critical argumentation of his heirs. Only in Marx's texts from before 1850 can one still hear echoes of the great transformation effected by the break with the logic of status-based societies. Thus, in *Critique of Hegel's 'Philosophy of Right'*, Marx writes:

> In general, the significance of the estate [*Stand*] is that *difference*, or *separation*, constitutes the *substance* of the individual [translation corrected]. His manner of life, activity, etc., is his privilege, and instead of making him a functional

---

[68]   Luhmann, 1982, pp. 80–81.

member of society, it makes him an *exception* from society. The fact that this *difference* is not only *individual* but also established as community [*Gemeinwesen*], estate, corporation, not only fails to abolish the exclusiveness of its nature, but is rather its expression. Instead of the particular function being a function of society, the particular function is made into a society for itself.

Not only is the *estate* [*Stand*] based on the *separation* of society as the governing principle, but it separates man from his universal nature; it makes him an animal whose being coincides immediately with its determinate character. The Middle Ages constitutes the *animal history* of mankind, its zoology.[69]

Marx, then, could recognise that the particularity of bourgeois society lay in the 'accomplished principle of individualism'.[70] Yet this characterisation was extremely ambiguous coming from him, for it combined both positive and negative elements. On the one hand, insofar as individualisation meant that man no longer coincided with his status 'determinacy', it brought the animal history of mankind to an end. On the other hand, Marx's interpretation of modern individualism was already then burdened by the critique of the atomisation of civil society,[71] which was central to his reading of Hegel's *Philosophy of Right* and of the Declaration of the Rights of Man and of the Citizen – a reading that appeared the same year in both the *Critique* and *The Jewish Question*. This interpretation bias led him to identify the overthrow of the political yoke of domination relations that prevailed in the Ancien Régime with the eradication of the 'bonds which restrained the egoistic spirit of civil society'.[72] Marx was well aware that the individualisation of the subject was a product of the modern state, insofar as state formation was accompanied by the disentanglement of politics and society. 'The abstraction of the political state', he further noted in the *Critique*, 'is a modern product. In the Middle Ages there was serf, feudal property, trade corporation, corporation of scholars, etc., that is, in the Middle Ages property, trade, society, man was political; the material content of the state was fixed by reason of its form; every private sphere had a political character or was a political sphere, or again, politics was also the character of the private spheres'.[73] But because Marx reduced the meaning of individualisation to the privatisation of existence, it was impossible for him to consider the revolutionary significance of legal equality – and this long before he elaborated the theory of exploitation. Thus he was able to see a form of democracy in the lack of differentiation between

---

[69] Marx, 1983, p. 285 (in English: Marx, 1977, p. 82, emphasis in the original German).
[70] *Ibid.*, p. 285 (in English: Marx, 1977, p. 81).
[71] Hegel himself had already formulated this critique.
[72] Marx, 1983, p. 369 (in English : Marx, 1977, p. 27).
[73] *Ibid.* p. 233 (in English: Marx, 1977, p. 32).

the political and the social that characterised medieval societies, even though this was a 'democracy of unfreedom'.[74]

As paradoxical – and no doubt deliberately provocative – as this expression may be, we should dwell on it for a moment. One could indeed quote several passages from Marx to show that he saw many virtues in individualism. The fact remains, however, that his concept of democracy was not only inchoate but also profoundly a-legal. This, in my view, deserves to be pondered by contemporary theorists of radical democracy who rehash the famous formula, drawn from the same text, according to which democracy is the 'resolved mystery of all constitutions'[75]; for if one does not specify what Marx meant by democracy, the repetition of this formula remains purely incantatory. The manner in which Marx described medieval society gives a few clues to his concept of democracy. If the Middle Ages were the 'zoology' of mankind, it is because the reality of the individual was entirely determined by his status (in the language Hegel used to speak of the animal, it coincided with its determinacy). But if they were 'democratic', it is because the political and social domains were not yet distinguished. Both these characteristics were of course closely linked: it is indeed in the logic of societies based on status differentiation that the being of the individual is determined by the place he occupies in a cosmo-social order that does not know the functional differentiations of modernity. Nevertheless, the dream that Marx expressed in this text – and that likely constituted, until the end of his life, the utopian dimension of what he conceived as the communism to come – was to separate these two inseparable aspects of medieval society. It was to build a society that would abolish functional differentiations without restoring hierarchies, and in which the individual would not be imperatively assigned to a particular place in the general economy of social life. Of course, one cannot accuse Marx of having completely ignored the meaning of legal equality. He indirectly celebrated it by interpreting as a form of progress the transformation of the political estates of the Middle Ages into mere social estates – that is to say, the autonomisation of the political that had made it possible to conceive the 'universal nature' of man.[76] The political abstraction of the universal appeared to him as a necessary moment in the affirmation of the universal, i.e., of the representation of something resembling the general interest. But insofar as Marx also condemned, via the critique of Hegelian 'mediations', the separation between civil society and the state, he left open the question of whether the representation of the universal – of the very idea of public interest – could survive the elimination of political abstraction. Put differently, he did not ask

---

[74] *Ibid.*
[75] *Ibid.*, p. 231 (in English: Marx, 1977, p. 30). See, for instance, Negri, 2009.
[76] *Ibid.*, pp. 283–285 (in English: Marx, 1977, pp. 81–82).

whether legal equality might not be fundamentally linked to the functional differentiation characteristic of modern societies.

It was the experience of totalitarian societies in the last century that prompted political thought to rediscover – belatedly – the democratic poten-tialities of legal equality. If I write 'belatedly', it is because this rediscovery did not take place on the side of traditional liberal thought – which, ever since the nineteenth century, played liberalism against democracy and felt obliged to defend a strict legalism against the threats of social subversion – but rather among leftist critics of Soviet society, such as Claude Lefort in France.[77] In the early 1980s, Lefort proposed an extremely insightful reading of the texts just mentioned, in which he reproached Marx for ignoring the dimen-sion of law and, more generally, of institutions. According to Lefort, this ignorance was tantamount to a rejection of the political that was motivated by the ideal, formulated by Marx in the Feuerbachian vocabulary of generic being, of a society that would know neither power nor law. What seems to me particularly interesting in Lefort's text is that he explains the erasure of the dimension of law in Marx's early writings by the narrowness of his historical perspective, despite his allusive references to the Middle Ages. Marx, writes Lefort, failed to analyse the bond of filiation between the bourgeois state and the monarchical state – the latter having 'established itself by destroying', long before the revolution, 'both the organization and the spirit of feudalism'. As a result, Marx ignored the fact that 'far from the state arising out of the emancipation of bourgeois society, shaking itself free of the feudal world, it was much more the case that the establishment of territorial kingdoms, unified by the common allegiance of subjects to the monarch and gradually levelled down by state power, created the conditions for the expansion of the bourgeoisie'. The institution of human rights in the declarations of the revolu-tions may have marked a transformation of the political, but one that occurred 'on the boundaries of a unique history, the history of the emergence of that state which embodies right, the *état de droit* [state of law]'.[78]

The monarchical state was already a state of law, not in the current under-standing of the term but in the sense that, by ending the plurality of powers that characterised feudal society, territorial monarchy created the conditions for a unification of law that allowed for its autonomisation. Surely, the link between the centralisation of power and the autonomisation of law calls for more precise analyses than those Lefort outlines in his text (or those I myself outline here). Lefort nevertheless touches upon a key point when he states that the real innovation of the 'political revolution', by which he means the revo-lutions of the late 18th century, was not the dissociation between the instance

---

[77] See Lefort, 'Politics and Human Rights', in Lefort, 1986, pp. 239–272.
[78] All citations in this paragraph, *Ibid.*, pp. 254–255

of power and the instance of right (a dissociation already initiated under the monarchical state), but 'a phenomenon of disincorporation of power and disincorporation of right'.[79] Of course, I would add, this disincorporation of power and right did not mean the abolition of power, nor even a weakening of it. It constituted rather a new stage in the process of rationalisation of power initiated by monarchical centralisation. The fact is that the French Revolution sought to destroy *both* the absolutism of royal power and the privileges – 'special rights', to use the language of Weber – that subsisted in the last years of the Ancien Régime.[80] Yet, far from challenging the centralisation of legal and political power, the French Revolution actually reinforced it, in particular through mythologising the unity of the nation. The joint affirmation of human rights and of the unity of the body of the nation, in which some see a tension and even a fundamental ambiguity of the French Revolution, shows rather that the figure of the individual subject of rights, which must have appeared at the time as a break from the last privileges, was the ultimate outcome (though not the goal) of the territorialisation of political power.

The 'disincorporation of power' implies that the constitutions of the revolutionary period had as one of their main objectives to prevent the appropriation of power by individuals or groups of particular individuals. This included past appropriations by the noble aristocracy or dynasties of hereditary monarchs, but also any new form of appropriation that might constitute itself on the basis of the difference between the dominant and the dominated – a difference deemed irreducible even when it was rewritten in the terms of representation. Already for Rousseau, the government's propensity to monopolise sovereignty contained the germ of a degeneration that was as inevitable as old age and death were for the human body.[81] While the possibility of degeneration could never be entirely eliminated, he thought it important to try to prevent it by turning the depositaries of the executive power into simple officers of the people, which the latter would appoint and could depose at any time.[82] As is well known, the danger that the political elite might transform itself into a new aristocracy was also central to reflections on the nature of representative government in both France and the United States. The electoral procedure, and hence the right to vote, were first and foremost conceived as a means to prevent the appropriation of power, and not as a form of participation in the elaboration of the law, that is to say, in the formulation of the general will.[83]

---

[79] *Ibid.*, p. 255.
[80] See Balibar, 2014, p. 47.
[81] See Rousseau, *On the Social Contract*, III, 10.
[82] *Ibid.*, III, 18.
[83] See Rosanvallon, 1998, pp. 56–57. I will return – in order to criticise it – to the conflation that later occurred between the right to vote and the expression of popular sovereignty understood as self-legislation.

To return to Marx, it is remarkable that, upon commenting on the paragraphs Hegel had devoted to the *idealism* of sovereignty, he missed precisely this determining aspect of the political revolution of the eighteenth century, and thereby failed to perceive that this revolution had, from this perspective, merely completed the transformation of the mode of exercise of political power that the centralised monarchy had initiated. Obsessed as he was with the opposition between the sovereignty of the people and that of the monarch, Marx allowed himself to deride, with all the verve that made the charm of his prose, Hegel's justification of hereditary monarchy. In paragraph 280 of the *Philosophy of Right*, Hegel had inferred the rationality of hereditary monarchy from the fact that the political decision is always made in the last resort by individuals, and the ultimate decision by a single individual (since modern republics are also incapable of functioning without a head of state or government). Commenting on this paragraph, Marx quipped: 'Hegel thinks he has proven that the subjectivity of the state, sovereignty, the monarch, is "essentially" characterised as *this* individual, in abstraction from all his other characteristics, and this individual is *raised* to the dignity of monarch in an immediate, natural fashion. [...] Birth would determine the quality of the monarch as it determines the quality of cattle. Hegel has demonstrated that the monarch must be born, which no one questions, but not that birth makes one a monarch'.[84] Even if we grant to Marx that Hegel's argument was weak on this point, it is more difficult to follow him in his commentary to paragraphs 277 and 278 of the *Philosophy of Right*. For it is precisely in these paragraphs that Hegel identified the specificity of modern political power, namely that 'the functions and powers of the state cannot be *private property*' (*PhR*, §277, emphasis in the original German). This forbidden appropriation, along with the interdependence of the various authorities – legislative, executive, judicial, administrative – through which state power is exercised without division, constitutes what Hegel calls the idealism of the state (*PhR*, §278). Marx, who was haunted by the ideal of an immediate coincidence of the social and the political in the individual, misinterpreted the meaning of 'private' in this passage. Where Hegel said that the various expressions of public power could not be *appropriated*, Marx understood that those who exercise power do so not by virtue of their private qualities – individual and natural (even physical, according to Marx) – but by virtue of their social ones. This was an argument that Marx could easily denounce as tautological.[85]

---

[84] Marx, 1983, pp. 234–235 (in English: Marx, 1977, p. 33). My emphasis.

[85] *Ibid.*, p. 222 (in English: Marx, 1977, p. 21): 'The activities and agencies of the state are attached to individuals (the state is only active through individuals), but not to the individual as *physical* but *political*; they are attached to the *political quality* of the individual. Hence it is ridiculous to say, as Hegel does, that '*it is in an external and contingent way* that these offices are linked with particular persons'. On the contrary, they are linked with them by a *vinculum substantiate*, by reason of an essential quality of particular persons. These offices are the natural action of this essential quality' (my emphasis). The rest of the passage specifies that this essential quality is the social quality of man.

The *Critique of Hegel's 'Philosophy of Right'*, which was left unfinished at Marx's death and was later published in 1927, often inspired leftist critics of orthodox Marxism as it prevailed in social democracy and in communist parties and states. This seductive and enigmatic text does give a few clues to some of Marx's fundamental positions, which were not affected by his shift in theoretical interest towards the economic foundation of socio-political structures in modern societies. The most important is, of course, Marx's distrust of 'mediations', which he thought could only fail to reconcile what had first been separated (namely the political and the social). Yet this interpretation of Hegel's *Philosophy of Right* cannot be of much use because it is based on a giant misunderstanding. One can certainly identify anachronistic residues in Hegel's text – for instance, the notion of a corporate organisation of society and of its political representation, or, as we have just seen, the supposedly logical-speculative justification of hereditary monarchy. But what Hegel presented in the *Philosophy of Right* was precisely the modern state as it resulted from a double rationalisation (i.e., monarchical and then revolutionary), in all its distinct yet united moments: abstract right (based on the equality of persons), civil society (already upset by the emergence of class divisions) and the organisation of public power into impersonal functions. The notion of 'idealism of sovereignty', in the name of which Hegel denounced the confused character of what is designated by the term 'popular sovereignty', may seem mysterious to a reader of today. It is further obscured by the fact that he purported to justify hereditary monarchy by resorting to it. Hegel's main objective was nevertheless clear: it was to defend the unity of the state against all particular powers, whether that of the monarch, of the people (understood as the rabble) or of any other portion of the social body. Such unity relied on the universality of the foundation of right – namely personality, a capacity that is granted equally to all independently of difference in status.

This conception of the state and of its relations with particular groups in society, which Hegel derived from a reflection on the examples of England, revolutionary France and Napoleonic France, was ahead compared to the reality of the conditions that prevailed in Prussia in the 1820s. What Hegel could not anticipate was that legal equality, once expressed in the language of the rights of man and of the citizen, would open a breach for the movement of democratisation of constitutional regimes. He was well aware that modern socioeconomic structures produce poverty and wealth simultaneously, and that they are responsible for the development of the rabble. But all he saw in this rabble was its distress and the deficiencies (in the domains of culture, civic-mindedness, etc.) that result from it. The political and trade union organisation of propertyless workers had yet to come. That the poor might constitute themselves as political subjects through this organisation, and that they might win new rights by appealing to the principle of legal equality, was not yet imaginable. For Hegel, the right of the person was reduced to the right of property – i.e., the property of 'things', which nevertheless also included talents and abilities, or what Hegel called 'internal property'. Marx was right on this point.[86] The list of more specific rights that were deduced from this right of property (the rights of usufruct, disposal and contract, but also the right to file a complaint in court in case of violation of rights) was closed. To my knowledge, Hegel did not explicitly address the undetermined character of human rights, which is a common *topos* in the conservative critique of the French Revolution. In his view, the question of human rights was settled with the opposition between right understood in 'an immediate, natural fashion' and right as governed by the notion.[87] It was the task of the rational thought of the world – i.e., of philosophy – to deduce such rights from the concept of freedom. This implies that rights could not be indeterminate. And yet, the dynamic potential of rights resided precisely in their indeterminacy. Unlike statutory rights in societies of old, the rights of the individual-subject are not immutable. Though they presented themselves as 'natural – and we saw that this naturalness means nothing more than their individualisation – they are in reality an empty form whose content has been clarified and enriched in the movement of history. Put in the words of Lefort, insofar as right is reduced to a basis 'without shape', the rights of man 'go beyond any particular formulation which has been given of them; and this means that their formulation contains the demand for their reformulation, or that acquired rights are necessarily called upon to support new rights'.[88] Hegel and Marx both failed to perceive, though for different reasons, that the representation of the individual as a subject of rights could be the anchor point for the democratisation of constitutional regimes – a process that was to profoundly transform the traditional notion of democracy.

---

[86] See Marx, 1983, p. 303*ff*. (in English: Marx, 1977, p.98*ff*.).
[87] Marx, 1983, p. 234 (in English: Marx, 1977, p. 33).
[88] Lefort, 1986, p. 258 (modified translation).

Chapter 2

Democracy

The conditions of administration of mass structures are radically different from those obtaining in small associations resting upon neighbourly or personal relationships. As soon as mass administration is involved, the meaning of democracy changes so radically that it no longer makes sense for the sociologist to ascribe to the term the same meaning as in the case discussed so far. (Max Weber, 1978, p. 951)

2.1 SOME ELEMENTS OF THE MODERN HISTORY OF THE TERM 'DEMOCRACY'

Before questioning the current meaning of the term 'democracy,' a brief reminder of its fortunes and misfortunes in the eighteenth century may be in order. As Robert Roswell Palmer observed in an article published in 1953, 'democracy' has become a 'general symbol of widely held political and personal values'.[1] To put it more simply, the word today is the name of the good political regime, one that Western societies pride themselves on and that they strive to spread to all the peoples of the world, by the force of example, if not by military intervention. These political regimes trace their origins to the revolutions of the late eighteenth century, and favour either the French or the American variant. It is curious, though well known to historians of political thought, that in the decisive years of the two revolutions those who were sympathetic to the revolutionary movement rarely used and even explicitly rejected the term democracy in favour of the word republic. By contrast, opponents of the revolution did speak of democracy, but only to expose it to

---

[1]   Palmer, 1953, p. 203.

the contempt of their readers. The most famous example is that of Edmund Burke, who noted in 1790: 'A perfect democracy is the most shameless thing in the world'.[2] In the Germanic sphere, Christoph Martin Wieland echoed Burke's position when he denounced the 'democratic folly' of French revolutionaries who were spreading a 'political gospel of democracy' that could only result in a 'kakistocracy' of the 'plebeian nobility'.[3]

In this section, I draw on the aforementioned text by Palmer (which is limited to the decade 1789–1799), Hans Maier's more comprehensive study published in 1971, and the article 'Demokratie' in Brunner *et al's Geschichtliche Grundbegriffe*.[4] Until the eve of the late eighteenth century political revolutions, which largely contributed to forging both the institutions and the political semantics of the next two centuries, the term democracy was found essentially in the scholarly literature – namely, the political philosophies and theories that renewed Aristotle's division of governments according to the number of people exercising power: one, many and all. Scepticism about the possibility of achieving 'pure' democracy was commonplace in this literature. However, a more concrete use of the term began to appear in the 1730s to designate both past regimes (Athens, Sparta, the Roman Republic) and contemporary ones (primarily the small republics of Switzerland and Holland, but also some free cities of Germany), a usage that became widespread in the Enlightenment. One of its first occurrences can be found in Luther's *Table Talk*, which cites Switzerland and the land of Dithmarschen as examples of democracies.[5] Considering the importance that the French Revolution acquired in the democratic imagination of the nineteenth and twentieth centuries, the rarity of the term in the texts that record the constitutional debates of the years 1789–1793 in France is quite surprising. Palmer remarks, in particular, that the term was absent from the debates on universal suffrage in 1790.[6] Some notable exceptions should nevertheless be mentioned, for they indicate

---

[2] Burke, 1955, pp. 106–107.

[3] Wieland, *Über Constitutionen* (1792), quoted in *Geschichtliche Grundbegriffe*, vol. 1 (Brunner et al., 1972, p. 849).

[4] Maier, 1971. Maier is also one of the authors of the article 'Demokratie' in Brunner *et al's Geschichtliche Grundbegriffe*. Palmer reproduced the best part of his 1953 article in the first chapter of *The Age of the Democratic Revolution* (Palmer, 1959, pp. 13–20). Here I trace only the uses of 'democracy', and not those of 'democrat', a term whose history does not rigorously parallel that of 'democracy'. 'Democrat' could indeed be used as the opposite of aristocrat to designate a member of the lower classes. It appears that this usage had currency especially in Belgium and Holland (Palmer, 1953, pp. 206–07).

[5] *Geschichtliche Grundbegriffe*, vol. 1 (Brunner et al., 1972, p. 845, note 160). Dithmarschen is the name of a region located in Schleswig-Holstein (in Germany) that had developed its own autonomous government and was considered a free republic of peasants.

[6] See also the concurring remarks of Rosanvallon, 2000, pp. 22–25. Rosanvallon notes concerning 1789 that: 'Though popular sovereignty became the key organising principle, the term democracy was hardly used to characterise the political regime. The term was not part of the language of 1789'.

a shift in meaning that heralded the new usage of the term that was to prevail in the next century. The first exception predates the revolution: it is Marquis d'Argenson's *Considerations on the Government of France*, which was published in 1764, though it had been circulating in manuscript form since the 1730s. D'Argenson observed the progress of democracy in France and attributed it to the fight waged by the kings against the privileges of the noble aristocracy. In his view, the enemy was the aristocracy and not the monarchy, the latter being, on the contrary, compatible with democracy. Hardly thinkable within the traditional division of governments,[7] this affirmation signalled a shift in the range of meanings associated with the term: democracy no longer served to designate specific political institutions, but to characterise a social logic. When he employed the word 'democracy,' d'Argenson was not thinking of self-government, but of 'equality'. Both Palmer and Maier underscore that this usage – later adopted by Tocqueville – remained an isolated case in the language and representations of the eighteenth century. The possibility of a 'royal democracy' was nonetheless raised in the early months of the French Revolution, and in particular by Baron de Wimpffen, who advocated using this expression during the constitutional debates of 1789. Though his proposal was not adopted, it caught the attention of Mirabeau, who on this occasion stressed that the Prince and the people had converging interests since both could only hope to see the aristocracy stripped of its privileges.[8]

The second exception is the frequently quoted speech that Robespierre delivered to the Convention on February 5, 1794. According to Palmer's careful count, the term 'democracy' appeared eleven times in a sequence of 700 words, that is, in five minutes of speech. Robespierre appropriated the term only to make it synonymous with republic, which no doubt excluded the possibility of a democratic monarchy or aristocracy, but also implied a critique of the ideal of direct democracy. Democracy is not, he stressed, a state in which the people meets continually to regulate for itself all public affairs, but one in which the people as sovereign is guided by laws of its own making, accomplishes for itself what it can, and leaves the rest to delegates. The key word of this speech was not self-government either, but equality and full civil rights. The 'soul' of democracy was 'public virtue' and 'love of equality,' and

---

[7]   Except if we take into consideration the theme of 'mixed governments'.

[8]   See Hans Maier, 1971, p. 135, but also *Geschichtliche Grundbegriffe*, vol. 1 (Brunner *et al.*, 1972, p. 847, note 176). In the *Courrier de Provence* 34 (7), Mirabeau commented Baron de Wimpffen's proposal in these terms: 'By uniting two words that had heretofore been kept apart, Baron de Wimpffen expressed an important truth: Democracy is the natural ally of monarchy. There exists no opposition between their interests insofar as the wish of the King is sufficiently strong to oppose the introduction of an aristocracy, which always tends towards independence, and the power of which is necessarily exercised at the expense of the Prince and the People'. As for Marquis d'Argenson, he did not mince his words: the 'measures' he proposed in his *Considerations* to 'spread Democracy in France' included the 'destruction of the Nobility'.

revolutionary terror was justified by the need to break the tyranny that stood in their way.

Among the texts that helped to fix the terminology of the legal and political doctrines of the nineteenth and twentieth centuries, those of Kant occupy a central place. Was it his meditation on the French revolutionary experience that led him to reject the equivalence between republicanism and democracy[9] – an equivalence that could be found here and there in those years and not just in Robespierre's famous speech? The fact remains that the essay on *Perpetual Peace* took up the traditional division into three regimes – i.e., autocracy (in lieu of monarchy), aristocracy and democracy, or, the power of the prince, the power of the nobility and the power of the people – while introducing an innovation that was to set a precedent for later constitutional doctrines. For Kant, these three regimes constituted forms of domination (*forma imperii*) that needed to be distinguished from forms of government (*forma regiminis*), that is to say, from the mode of exercising power. From a normative perspective, the decisive difference lay in whether the form of government was republican or despotic: in a republican regime executive and legislative powers were separate, whereas in a despotic one there was no such distinction. This separation, which was for Kant the defining criterion of 'representative' government, guaranteed that laws were not the instrument of a private will. In the wake of Kant's text, Friedrich Schlegel proposed to push the Kantian idea of perpetual peace one step further by interpreting it as the focal point of morality and politics, which would 'make an end of all rule and dependency'.[10] For Schlegel, this meant accepting the fiction that allowed the will of the majority to function as a surrogate for the *a priori* of an absolutely universal will. Under this condition, it would be possible to reunite what Kant had separated, namely democracy and republicanism: 'Republicanism is [...] necessarily democratic, and the unproven paradox that democracy is necessarily despotic cannot be correct'.[11] While this utopia somehow anticipated the future of the terms 'democracy' and 'republic,' it seems to have found no echo in the political and constitutional literature of the time.

This brief overview of the history of the term 'democracy' in the eighteenth century and the revolutionary years would be incomplete without also mentioning the uses made of it by some priests and bishops. Laicism, and most importantly the anti-clericalism that marked the dominant interpretations of the French Revolution (especially in France) in the two centuries that followed, repressed the memory of Christian democratism, in particular

---

[9] See *Perpetual Peace and Other Essays*, First Definitive Article (Kant, 1983, pp.113–14).
[10] F. Schlegel, *Versuch über den Begriff des Republikanismus* (1796), quoted in *Geschichtliche Grundbegriffe*, vol. 1 (Brunner et al., 1972, p. 852).
[11] *Ibid.*

because of the continuity that was established between this revolution and those conducted later under the banner of communism. It seems that the specific expression 'Christian democracy' appeared for the first time in a speech delivered to the Legislative Assembly by the (constitutional) bishop of Lyon, Antoine-Adrien Lamourette, on November 21, 1791.[12] Maier also cites the sermon 'On the Accord of Religion and Liberty,' pronounced on February 4, 1792 by Claude Fauchet, who argued that the laws of democracy were the very laws of God and that Christ had died 'for the democracy of the universe'. For his part, the Abbé Grégoire spoke of 'the natural alliance of Christianity and democracy'. The most astonishing document is surely the homily issued by the Bishop of Imola (the future Pope Pius VII) on Christmas Eve, 1797, who not only affirmed the compatibility of democratic government with the Bible, but also urged his followers to defend equality before the law and to establish 'the greatest possible union of sentiments, of hearts, of physical and moral forces, whence a gracious fraternity may enter into society'. 'Be good Christians,' he concluded, 'and be the best of democrats'.[13] Maier is right to observe that this Christian notion of democracy was an 'emphatic' concept, one 'that, in the first years of the Revolution, had no immediate political significance'.[14] Yet by putting emphasis on fraternity, the notion anticipated the social inflection of the term that would come to prevail, in the late nineteenth and early twentieth centuries, in the interpretation of social rights as a form of solidarity.[15]

2.2 DEMOCRACY AS THE GOVERNMENT OF THE PEOPLE, OR, 'WAS ROUSSEAU A DEMOCRAT?'

From the nineteenth century to the present, the fundamental reference of democratic theorists has been a text published nearly thirty years before the start of the French Revolution: *On the Social Contract* by Rousseau (1762 [2003]). Given the history that I have just recalled, it seems legitimate to ask: was Rousseau a democrat? Lest readers think that I cultivate a dubious taste for gratuitous paradoxes, let me formulate the question differently: was Rousseau a democrat in the sense intended by those who currently invoke his name when reflecting on the democratic character of contemporary liberal

---

[12] All citations are taken from Maier, 1971, p. 141.
[13] Quoted in Palmer, 1953, p. 221. Palmer himself quotes the Bishop of Imola's homily from A. Dufourcq, *Le régime Jacobin en Italie: Étude sur la république romaine, 1798–1799* (Paris, 1900). According to Palmer, it is in Italy that the term 'democracy', understood in a positive sense, was most commonly used between 1796 and 1799.
[14] Maier, *Geschichtliche Grundbegriffe*, vol. 1 (Brunner *et al.*, 1972, p. 859).
[15] See Brunkhorst, *Solidarity*, 2005, and *infra*, p...

democracies? Or better yet: was it only natural that the doctrine of the general will should result in the defence of democratic government and, furthermore, in those forms of government that are qualified as democratic today? We know that Rousseau's thought has been interpreted in contradictory ways. We also know that these interpretations were fraught with the shadow of the Bolshevik regime, which purported to have realised genuine democracy – one that was anticipated by the French Revolution, the Paris Commune and some other rare moments of revolutionary rupture, and that was essentially different from the 'formal' democracy of bourgeois political regimes. Insofar as the champions of 'real' democracy claimed the legacy of Rousseau, it was only fair that the defenders of liberal regimes should discern in his work the matrix of totalitarianism. Had Rousseau not conceived the social contract as a 'total alienation' of each individual together with all his rights to the community? Had he not determined the relations between the sovereign power – i.e., the state – and its subjects in a decidedly asymmetrical fashion, by positing that it 'need give no guarantee to it subjects' and that these, insofar as their particular will does not necessarily coincide with the general will, could, on the contrary, be occasionally constrained, that is to say, forced to be free? Had he not condemned representative government (because the general will cannot be represented)? And had he not proscribed 'partial associations,' a move which, when combined with all of the above, could easily be interpreted as a justification in advance of the ban on political pluralism? Liberal theorists had no difficulty building the case against Rousseau. And neither the scholarly exegeses of historians of philosophy, who underscored the fundamental individualism of all contractualist conceptions of the state, nor the central role played by the notion of liberty in Rousseau's thought carried much weight in a debate whose stake was less the concept of democracy than the justification of liberalism. This is precisely how it was understood by Schmitt, who further reinforced the case against Rousseau by overstating the opposition between democracy and liberalism, and by attributing to him the theoretical paternity of a homogeneous conception of the people – one that, in the case of Schmitt at least, could be interpreted in racial terms.[16]

A brief excursus via Schmitt will help to end all ambiguity in this regard. Schmitt built his *Constitutional Theory* (Carl Schmitt, 1928 [2008]) on a clear opposition between the liberal and political components of modern constitutions. Freedom, which is presumed to be unlimited, entails a limitation of state power, and fundamental rights belong to this liberal component. As for institutional arrangements, their necessary correlate is the separation of powers, interpreted by Schmitt as a division that allows for the mutual

---

[16]   See Carl Schmitt, 2008, pp. 235–49.

control of distinct (legislative, executive, judicial) bodies, and hence as a system destined to hamper the power of the state – though such an arrangement does not constitute in itself what Schmitt called a 'political form,' by which he meant the unified organisation of a people. This organisation can, in turn, rest on two antagonistic concepts: representation and identity. In both cases, it is the political unity of the people that is in play. But while representation (*Repräsentation*, which Schmitt emphatically distinguished from *Vertretung*, a term he reserved for the representation of orders in the Ancien Régime or that of interests in modern political regimes) establishes this unity by conferring a radically new type of being – precisely that of a political unity – on what is at first merely 'some human group living together,'[17] identity presupposes, on the contrary, the immediate coincidence of the political people with its material reality. As a principle of democracy, identity resists all mediation. If Schmitt could consider the *Social Contract* to be the purest theoretical expression of this identitarian understanding of democracy, it is because Rousseau had explicitly rejected the representation of the general will. For Schmitt, of course, the opposition between representation and identity could only be understood in an ideal-typical sense. It goes without saying that there has never been a state without representation and, conversely, that no state has ever been completely devoid of structural elements in which the principle of identity manifests itself. Strictly interpreted, identity implies the complete lack of differentiation between the dominant and the dominated, the rulers and the ruled, those who command and those who obey. In other words, it entails that all citizens exercise direct decision-making power over public affairs.[18] In the conditions of modern states, only referendums on a concrete question come close to realising this ideal; yet nowhere do referendums constitute the normal modality of political decision-making, and this no doubt because they can never do so. Schmitt suggested that Rousseau himself had recognised the inevitable contamination of the principle of identity by the principle of representation when he noted that, as a member of the sovereign, 'the individual state citizen' is 'present not in his "natural" condition as individual person. [...] He is present as state citizen, as "citoyen."'[19] I shall return later to the challenges posed by this splitting of the individual in the *Social Contract*. But whatever Schmitt may have thought, the fact that Rousseau did not view this splitting as a concession to the principle of representation suggests he was fully aware that the real people is never homogeneous. The *Social Contract*

---

[17] *Ibid.*, p. 243.
[18] For that matter, Schmitt recognises that the 'substantial similarity of the people' is an 'ideal mental construct', and that as such it is dangerous. Its full realisation would imply a minimum degree of government, which in turn would deprive the people concerned of political autonomy. See Schmitt, 2008, p. 248.
[19] *Ibid.*, p. 240.

does not presuppose the homogeneity of the people. On the contrary, it confronts the problem that its lack of homogeneity presents to anyone who wants to think the conditions of a political constitution based on individual liberty, and hence to prevent 'usurpations of government,' that is to say, to contain the power of the state. Whereas Schmitt considered state power to be antithetical to freedom, Rousseau's whole ambition was, instead to found the first on the second. Ultimately, Schmitt's highly truncated reading of Rousseau merely replicates that of a certain liberalism, which considers that democracy and the state of law – i.e., the rule of law – are fundamentally irreconcilable.

Leaving Schmitt aside for a moment, we can return to the question with which this section began. Expressing doubts about the democratic character of Rousseau's political philosophy might simply mean that one has joined the camp of his liberal critics. Indeed, it might reveal that one takes as self-evident the thesis that pluralism of opinions and political parties, along with the guarantee of individual freedoms, are essential elements of democracy as understood by the moderns, and that neither can be reconciled with the radicalism of Rousseau's concept of democracy, which revisited the ideals of Antiquity (be they Greek or Roman) instead of preparing the future. Such a reading can certainly be supported by numerous quotes from Rousseau, as can, for that matter, the interpretations that have been produced by Schmitt or Rousseau's democratic disciples. However, it is not from a liberal perspective that I wish to examine the relationship between the logic of the *Social Contract* and the institutions of modern democracies. My aim is not to judge Rousseau's positions based on a predetermined conception of democracy, whatever that may be. It is, on the one hand, to question the manner in which Rousseau understood his own work, and, on the other, to specify the institutional translation of the principles he laid at the foundation of legitimate power, as can be reconstructed on the basis of his texts. Did Rousseau conceive the social contract as a contribution to a political theory that would establish the normative superiority of democratic *government*? Did he reject in advance the institutional forms (the distinction between the rulers and the ruled, the separation between legislative and executive powers, the election of deputies, the majority principle) that pertain to regimes qualified as democracies today?

Regarding the first point, the answer is obviously negative. Anyone who has read the *Social Contract* in its entirety knows that Rousseau used the term democracy only in the conventional sense of his day, namely as part of the classical division of governments according to the number of those exercising power (democracy, aristocracy, and monarchy) – the very division that Hegel would declare obsolete one century later.[20] There is no denying that Rousseau

---

[20]   *PhR*, §273 (Hegel, 1991, p. 310).

felt sympathy towards the forms of government in which the people met at frequent intervals to openly express its adherence to the laws. This sympathy, however, did not prevent him from recognising that the concrete conditions that made this sort of government possible (limited size of the state's territory, small population, relatively homogeneous material conditions of existence, etc.) were so stringent that it was doubtful whether genuine democracy had ever existed, and, indeed, whether it could ever exist.[21] The chapters in the third book of the *Social Contract* that are devoted to comparing the three forms of government – the selection of either of which is conditioned by the specific features of the people for whom government is intended – suggest that elective aristocracy was for Rousseau the most recommendable. The sixth of the *Letters Written from the Mountain*, in which Rousseau sums up the general argument of the *Social Contract*, makes the same point: after comparing the three main forms of government – monarchy, aristocracy and democracy – in terms of their advantages and their inconveniences, he gives the preference to 'the one that is intermediate between the two extremes and that bears the name of Aristocracy'.[22] And this, not because he sees it as a second-best solution, as a sort of substitute for a democracy that is impossible in large states, but because he feels that only aristocracy has the potential to provide enlightened government. The election of magistrates (government members) is the means to ensure that these will distinguish themselves by 'uprightness, understanding, experience and all other claims to pre-eminence and public esteem,' thus offering 'further guarantees of wise government'. This is why 'it is the best and most natural arrangement that the wisest should govern the many [multitude], when it is assured that they will govern for its profit and not for their own' (*SC*, III, 5).

The mention of the multitude underscores a problem that haunts the *Social Contract* from beginning to end, and that leaves its argument locked in an aporia which Rousseau is unable to resolve: the irreducible gap between the people as a body politic and the real people. Tracing the deployment of this aporia will help to answer my second question: what would Rousseau have thought of the way modern liberal democracies operate? Rousseau details in three chapters of Book II all that distinguishes real peoples from one another: the size and configuration (climate, soil fertility, etc.) of their territories and the importance of their populations, but also their histories, which are encapsulated in customs that render them more or less amenable to discipline and that make it possible to speak of young and old peoples.

---

[21] *On the Social Contract*, III, 4. In the rest of this section, references to the *Social Contract (SC)* are included in the text with mention of the book and chapter number. When the page is indicated, the reference is to: Rousseau, 2003.

[22] Rousseau, 2013, p. 233.

Notwithstanding these differences, mentioned by Rousseau only to identify the most favourable conditions for establishing a political regime in line with the requirements of the social compact, there is one characteristic that is shared by all real peoples: that of being multitudes. The multitude, however, lacks both unity and enlightenment. Regarding the second, Rousseau notes that the multitude is 'blind' and 'often does not know what it wills, because it rarely knows what is good for it' (*SC*, II, 6). This is why he cannot imagine assigning it the task of determining the fundamental laws that will establish it as a people – what today we would call its constitution – but feels obliged to appeal to the mythical figure of the legislator (*SC*, II, 7). Yet the greatest difficulty does not lie in the multitude's lack of enlightenment, but in its lack of unity, that is to say, in the divisions among the real people. For while the intervention of the legislator can supplement the ignorance of the people without compromising its legislative authority, divisions among the people prevent all the particular wills from ever coinciding with the general will, making it impossible to abolish domination.

The ambiguity of Rousseau's concept of the people is already manifest in the chapter on the social compact (*SC*, I, 6). What this compact produces is a 'moral and collective body, composed of as many members as the assembly contains votes,' that is, a 'common identity,' a 'public person'. Rousseau refers to the latter not as people but as state or sovereign, and reserves the name people for associates taken collectively. From the outset, then, we have two collectives: the sovereign and the people. Rousseau never succeeds in making them coincide, and this, even though he presents the social compact as the act by which a people becomes a people (*SC*, I, 5, p. 8), he identifies on several occasions the will of the sovereign with that of the people (*SC*, III, 2, p. 42), and he sometimes says of the people that it is only sovereign or subject (*SC*, III, 17, p. 68). The sovereign people is not the real people, but the 'body politic' (*SC*, II, 6) created by the social compact.[23] Yet the latter must precede itself, in the sense that there is admittedly a common good on which all particular wills can agree in spite of everything that separates them (*SC*, II, 1): 'Were there no point of agreement between them all, no society could exist'.

This point of convergence can only be the will to agree itself, provided there is equality between the contracting parties, and hence between the commitments they make. To be sure, this condition prohibits the acceptance of any sort of contract of submission. This is why, against Hobbes in particular, Rousseau refuses to view the institution of government as a contract (*SC*, III, 16). The clear distinction between legislative and executive powers is generally recognised as an essential aspect of Rousseau's politics. However, by

---

[23] On the notion of 'body politic', see Bernardi, 2006.

insisting on this distinction, one also often obscures the fact that, in the logic of legislative power itself, the dimension of subjection is not abolished. The citizen in Rousseau does not replace the subject, but merely duplicates him. Indeed, to the difference between the 'moral and collective body' and the associates taken collectively there corresponds another within the individual between his quality as citizen – as a member of the sovereign – and his quality as subject – as one subjected to the laws of the state. The tension between citizen and subject directly proceeds from the problem to which the social compact must respond, and which Rousseau famously stated as follows: 'To find a form of association which will defend and protect with the whole common force the person and goods of each associate, and in which each, while uniting himself with all, may still obey himself alone, and remain as free as before' (*SC*, I, 6). To obey and to be free, to be subjected and at the same time not to be: such is the 'difficulty' that the total alienation of each associate, but also of all without reserve, must solve. Obedience is exclusive of domination, so long as it is obedience to oneself. Yet the loop that is supposed to help one think subjection without domination implies a transmutation of the individual that, because it cannot be truly accomplished, induces a split within this individual which is registered as a distinction between citizen and subject. Citizens are 'on the one hand sovereign and on the other subject' (*SC*, III, 1). Rousseau took this transmutation as an inevitable consequence of the contract. By ensuring the passage of man from the state of nature to the civil state, the contract produces in him 'a very remarkable change [...] by substituting justice for instinct in his conduct, and giving his actions the morality they had formerly lacked' (*SC*, I, 8). Yet the persistence of the subject beneath the citizen, which reveals the lack of coincidence between the particular will and the general will, continues to make itself felt throughout the four books of the *Social Contract*. It compels Rousseau to produce convoluted arguments that sometimes border on sophistry, the first of these being the paradox – now an axiom of contemporary republican and democratic thought – that one can force an individual to be free (*SC*, I, 7).

As I have just mentioned, the clear distinction between legislative and executive powers makes it possible to recognise the need for the autonomy of government without justifying this autonomy by a contract of submission. The people retains the 'right of legislation' (*SC*, II, 7, p. 27). 'The legislative power belongs to the people, and can belong to it alone' (*SC*, III, 1). But what people is doing the legislating? Is it the 'body politic' constituted by the compact or else the real people? What are the meaning and practical implications of the notion of self-legislation, which in the eyes of our contemporaries sums up Rousseau's contribution to the determination of modern democracy? Of course, one must take into consideration the fact that Rousseau understood the term 'law' in a very narrow sense, one that did not cover all that is designated by this name in the political practices of modern states. The law, in the strict sense Rousseau gave to the term, is universal both by virtue of its origin – namely, the general will – and by virtue of the object it applies to – which can only be the people as a whole (*SC*, II, 6). This second dimension of law's universality implies that a norm that is enacted by the sovereign but concerns merely a part of the people is not a law but a decree (according to the terminological convention proposed by Rousseau). Only the rules that determine the 'conditions of civil association' – that is to say, constitutional laws – can be construed as laws. And it is for these fundamental legislative provisions alone that the principle of self-legislation is relevant. 'The people, being subject to the laws, ought to be their author: the conditions of the society ought to be regulated solely by those who come together to form it' (*SC*, II, 6). Yet it is also at this point that the loop of subjection without domination reveals its fragility, not because the people which authors the law is not identical to the people which is subjected to the law, but, paradoxically, because it is exactly the same: the multitude always lurks behind the abstraction of the sovereign, just as the subject is forever present beneath the citizen. If Rousseau must resort to the problematic mediation of the legislator, it is because, as I recalled earlier, the people is never but the people – the 'multitude, which often does not know what it wills, because it rarely knows what is good for it,' and which, for this reason, cannot draw up the laws. Not only *should* the people *not* govern, but it *cannot* legislate, not even when it comes to the fundamental laws that determine its own organisation. What, then, is left of 'self-legislation'? The answer is the 'right of legislation,' which is not the power to legislate, but the authority that confers an obligatory character on laws elaborated by an instance that is always distinct from the people.[24]

One might ask whether it was necessary to make such a detour to reach the trivial truth that the sovereign people of the *Social Contract* is nothing other than constituent power – that abstract instance, that body without corporeality which has been construed, for the last two centuries, as the source of all legitimate political authority in the constitution of almost every Western state. While the detour did lead to a truism, it was nevertheless worthwhile for it frees us from the illusion that Rousseau's notion of self-legislation helps to conceive a political regime that can realise, or can tend to realise, the identity of the dominant and the dominated – a regime, in other words, that can abolish domination. The sovereign does not succeed in erasing the difference of the people any more than the citizen succeeds in erasing the difference of the subject. The real people cannot be so easily forgotten. And the principle whereby 'the people, being subject to the laws, ought to be their

---

[24]   *SC*, II, 7, p. 27: 'He, therefore, who draws up the laws has, or should have, no right of legislation, and the people cannot, even if it wishes, deprive itself of this incommunicable right [...]'.

author' compellingly suggests that the 'people in person'[25] needs to be physically present in assemblies that occupy, at regular and frequent intervals, the entire field of power by temporarily suspending both the elected magistracy (deputies) and the executive one (the government).[26] Thus, even as Rousseau says and repeats that truly democratic government is impossible, and even as he limits himself to determining forms of organisation of civil association that are adapted to a variety of peoples, he cannot escape the fascination that the conditions of small states exert on him: 'All things considered, I do not see that it is possible henceforth for the Sovereign to preserve among us the exercise of its rights, unless the city is very small' (*SC*, III, 15, p. 66).

Far from it being the case that Rousseau postulated the homogeneity of the people, it is on the contrary the people's heterogeneity that haunted him and that he tried, without success, to exorcise. For this heterogeneity is the main obstacle to the universality of the law. The main effect of the recurring mention of the presence of the people in person is to underscore the irreducibility of the gap between the real people and the body politic. In some passages, Rousseau does seem to believe that this presence, wherever it can be secured (that is, in small cities), might solve the difficulty. Yet regardless of its size, the real people is never equal to the spontaneous merging of particular wills into the unity of the general will. This is why, even as Rousseau grants the assembled people the right 'of stating views, making proposals, dividing and discussing' (*SC*, IV, 1, p. 72), he immediately negates that which might give meaning to such deliberation: in a well-constituted state, deliberation has no object, insofar as it involves the confrontation of different opinions. It is important that the right to deliberate be granted to ordinary citizens against those who would want to reserve its monopoly for government officials. But there is really no reason to deliberate, because the goal is not the pursuit of a reasonable compromise between divergent interests and opinions, but the formulation of what each and all – *omnes et singulatim* – necessarily want in as much as they want to build a body politic together. Such is the condition for the validity of the self-legislation theorem: the projection onto the real people of a unanimity that can only be the doing of the sovereign's 'moral and collective body'. In order to prevent the risk of autonomisation of the legislative and executive magistracies, Rousseau needs the sovereign to incarnate itself in the real people. But the latter can fulfil the function of the sovereign only on condition that it is transformed, that is to say, on condition that it

---

25 See *SC*, III, 15, p. 65: 'Every law the people has not ratified in person is null and void – is, in fact, not a law'. It is in light of this maxim that Rousseau rejects the idea of 'representation'.

26 See *SC*, III, 12, p. 61: 'The Sovereign, having no force other than the legislative power, acts only by means of the laws; and the laws being solely the authentic acts of the general will, the Sovereign cannot act save when the people is assembled'. The people assembled as a sovereign body does not govern, but suspends executive power, see *SC* III, 14.

is *derealised*. The 'moral and collective body' precedes itself in a people purged of particularity, one that can institute only on condition of being itself somehow already instituted: one ought to ban 'factions' and 'partial associations' and atomise the people so as to prevent differences from crystallising and making themselves heard.[27] The impossible coincidence between the real people and the sovereign is concealed in the transmutation of the real people, the correlate of which is the transmutation of the natural individual into a moral being. Is it the social compact that accomplishes this transmutation (*SC*, I, 8)? Or is it the legislator, whose grandiose task it is, so to speak, to change human nature, to transform 'each individual, who is by himself a complete and solitary whole, into part of a greater whole from which he in a manner receives his life and being' (*SC*, II, 7)? The question is pointless: the inception of the sovereign is atemporal; the conversion of the sum of particular persons into the 'moral and collective body' occurs instantly (*SC*, I, 6); and the institution of government is 'accomplished by a sudden conversion of Sovereignty into democracy' (*SC*, III, 17). Rousseau cannot plot the different moments of institutional elaboration in temporal sequences because the differences and divisions among the real people can only vanish with the suspension of time. Unanimity is possible only in suspended time – for the primitive contract and it alone. 'Apart from this primitive contract,' the ordinary exercise of legislative power by popular assemblies must follow the prosaic rule of the majority: because the real people is divided, one must accept that 'the vote of the majority always binds all the rest' (*SC*, IV, 2).

Would Rousseau have accommodated himself to the institutions of contemporary liberal democracies? Is 'representative democracy' a *contradictio in adjecto* in the proper Rousseauian orthodoxy? The text of the *Social Contract* seems perfectly clear on this point. 'Sovereignty, for the same reason as makes it inalienable, cannot be represented; it lies essentially in the general will, and will does not admit of representation: It is either the same, or other; there is no intermediate possibility' (*SC*, III, 15). Nevertheless, this proposition is aimed at a 'feudal' concept of representation, whereby the representative is not the spokesperson of those he represents, but one who speaks and acts for them, as does the tutor for his pupil.[28] Consequently, this concept refers not to the principle of deputation, but to how the function of the deputy must be interpreted. The deputies of the people must be construed not as its representatives (in the 'feudal' sense of the term), but as its 'stewards'. Rous-

---

[27] See *SC*, II, 3, in which Rousseau formulates the famous difference between the general will and the will of all.

[28] Echoes of this conception may be found in Hobbes's *Leviathan*, chapter 18 (Hobbes, 1982, p. 228*ff*): The representative shall be given the 'Right to present the Person' of those whom he represents.

seau did admit that there had to be deputies, and that their mode of selection had to be election.[29] One might object that he limited the scope of application of deputation to the constitution of government, and that, as regards the legislature, he continued to dream of a presence of 'the people in person'.[30] But this would not necessarily have led him to challenge the legitimacy of modern parliamentary representation, insofar as the work of the legislature, as he understood it, was limited to determining constitutional laws. The ordinary legislative work of our parliaments belongs, on the contrary, to what Rousseau construed as the realm of government. His *Considerations on the Government of Poland,* in particular, make clear that this legislative work naturally falls to assemblies of elected deputies, in which the normal and legitimate mode of agreement is the rule of the majority, unlike how the terms of the constitutional compact are themselves determined. Unanimity is required only 'for the formation of the body politic and for the fundamental laws that pertain to its existence,' whereas 'for those multitudes of points that have ridiculously been put into the number of fundamental laws, and which merely make up the body of legislation, as for the ones arranged under the title of matters of State, by the vicissitude of things they are subject to unavoidable variations that do not allow one to require unanimity in them'.[31]

There is in the *Social Contract* a 'pragmatic' dimension that has led some readers to consider that the work joins two books into one, the first dealing with the primitive contract, and the second with the constitution of government. Some have suggested that the break occurs between the first two books, which address the 'idea' and the last two, which focus on its 'feasibility'.[32] This pragmatic dimension is apparent in Rousseau's stated intention to determine a 'sure and legitimate rule of administration, men being taken as they are' (*SC*, I, p. 1), and, more concretely, in his effort to adapt laws to the diverse conditions of peoples. To be sure, Rousseau's pragmatism is continually undermined by the undeniable sympathy he feels towards that democratic form of government he deems impossible, yet whose approximate forms he perceives in small cities. But do the problem and source of the contradictions one encounters in the *Social Contract* lie in this sympathy to which the archaic features of the book are linked? What I have tried to show, on the contrary, is that the core of the difficulty, the source of the contradictions, is more fundamental: it stems from the impossible coincidence between the real

---

29 Rousseau also mentions election by lot, which he claims would certainly be preferable 'in a real democracy'. Yet, he also notes that there is no such thing as 'real democracy' (*SC*, IV, 3, p. 76). On the history of election by lot, see Manin, 1997 and Sintomer, 2007.

30 This is why Rousseau ultimately confesses that he does not think it possible for the sovereign to preserve the exercise of its rights other than in small cities (*SC*, III, 15).

31 Rousseau, 2005, pp. 203–204.

32 See Sternberger, 1990, p. 161 and note 6.

people and the body politic of the sovereign. In this sense, while it is true that one can distinguish, in the *Social Contract*, between a *metapolitical* level of reflection, which deals with the foundation of legitimate power, and a pragmatic one, which is closer to what one would normally expect of a political theory, these two levels cannot be distributed between two successive parts of the book. They are necessarily intertwined, because the identities that result from the social compact (the identity of the sovereign and the people, and that of citizens and subjects) must demonstrate their capacity to determine the legitimate forms of civil association against the determination of political institutions (the 'political [laws], which determine the forms of the government,' *SC*, II, 12). The remaining difference haunts the *Social Contract* from beginning to end: it is the deployment of the aporia inherent to those postulated yet unrealisable identities. The *Social Contract* demonstrates the impossibility of democracy to anyone who views the notion of self-legislation as the decisive element in the concept of democracy.

But surely it is a mistake to understand self-legislation in a literal sense. The meaning of the term must be sought rather in the aforementioned concept of the law, which combines the generality of its source with that of the object to which it applies. That 'the people, being subject to the laws, ought to be their author' simply means that the law must be equal for all.[33] If subjection is not servitude, and if the necessary autonomy of power can be recognised without domination being thereby posited as inevitable, it is because this power rests on laws whose double generality guarantees citizens 'that they all bind themselves to observe the same conditions and should therefore all enjoy the same rights' (*SC*, II, 4, p. 20). The laws in which sovereignty manifests itself are legitimate and just conventions because they are common to all: 'So long as the subjects have to submit only to conventions of this sort, they obey no-one but their own will' (*ibid.*). As regards large modern states, the fiction of the people assembled 'in person,' which underlies Rousseau's recurring references to the conditions of ancient democracies or of the small republics of yesterday and today, has no other signification than this requirement: the law must be such that each individual, so long as he aspires to the unity of civil society, must necessarily accept it. Yet this necessity can impose itself on each individual only if the law recognises neither individuals, nor groups of individuals – if, in other words, it is *impersonal*. While it is true that this term does not belong to Rousseau's vocabulary, it does convey what he meant by equality.[34] Indeed, equality as understood by Rousseau is not equal-

---

[33] This simple requirement was highly revolutionary at the time.

[34] In a similar vein, see Rosanvallon, 1992, pp. 215–16: 'The general will retains [in Rousseau] a strong liberal dimension, as it does in Montesquieu: It expresses the impersonal and uniform character of the law, which guarantees equity'.

ity of conditions, though differences in wealth should not be such that one individual can buy another, or, conversely, that another individual may be forced to sell himself (*SC*, II, 11). Nor is it the absence of privileges: the law can establish privileges, provided that it does not 'confer them on anybody by name' (*SC*, II, 6). What is more, Rousseau's equality is not incompatible with monarchical – even hereditary – government, so long as the law does not designate the individual who will be king or 'nominate' a royal family (*ibid.*). Equal law does not imply the absence of differences of wealth or rank, differences which the social criticism of the nineteenth and twentieth centuries accustomed us to regard as the foundation of the opposition between the dominant and the dominated. It does not entail the abolition of domination, thus understood, but the opening up of access to it. Privileges, whatever they may be, must not be attached to individuals, and positions of domination must not be statutorily reserved for some while being forbidden to others.

The two 'objects,' liberty and equality (*SC*, II, 11), which Rousseau construes as the end of well-constituted states, are, in reality, indistinguishable. To put it differently, equality does not merely render liberty possible; it completely determines its content. Equality of individuals means that 'power [...] shall always be exercised by virtue of rank and law' (*ibid.*), and that power thus exercised presupposes the eradication of all relations of personal dependency. It is here that the enigma of the citizen/subject – of he who is a member of the sovereign, yet who, when 'taken singly, exercises no function of Sovereignty' (*SC*, III, 2, p. 42) – is resolved. Because the citizen is a being of flesh and blood whose particular will rarely coincides with the general will he must obey. But this obedience is liberty because it is obedience to an impersonal power exercised in the name of the law: 'The essence of the body politic lies in the reconciliation of obedience and liberty, and the words subject and Sovereign are identical correlatives the idea of which meets in the single word "citizen"' (*SC*, III, 13). From this perspective, one can agree with the theorists who today defend the idea that democracy and the state of law are one and the same thing. The geneses of the two notions are of course different. But while democracy means nothing other than the rule of law, it is indeed inseparable from the state of law.[35] However, it is a fallacy to conclude that the state of law is a state without domination. Like Rousseau's 'well-constituted' state, it does not abolish domination, but merely transforms the mode in which domination is formed and exercised.

No doubt there are archaic aspects to Rousseau's text. Among these should be mentioned not only his fascination with the conditions of face-to-face democracy – with those peoples in which 'every member may be known by

---

[35] For instance, in Habermas, 'Du lien interne entre État de droit et démocratie' (On the internal connection between the state of law and democracy) (1998, pp. 275–86).

every other' (*SC*, II, 10, p. 33) – but also his distrust of both the monetary economy and the privatisation of existence that reduces citizens' interest in public affairs.[36] By reserving the term democracy for one of the three forms from the traditional division of government, Rousseau merely conformed to the language of his day. Neither his choice of examples – whether the ancient republics or the Switzerland and Holland of his time – nor his doubts concerning the possibility of pure democracy (reserved for 'a people of gods,' *SC*, III, 4) were in the least original.[37] Leaving these aspects aside, however, we can admit that Rousseau might have agreed overall with the forms currently taken by democracy in the regimes to which we refer as liberal democracies. But shall we say that he was a democrat in the sense intended by those who invoke his name today? The answer, it seems to me, must be negative, if we make the identity of the dominant and the dominated – i.e., the absence of domination – the criterion of democracy.

It is true, as Hauke Brunkhorst remarks,[38] that the opposition established by liberals between the constitutional state (*Rechtsstaat,* or the state of law) and democracy rests on the idea that the function of rights is to protect individuals against the liberticidal potentialities of democracy, understood as the domination of the majority. It is also true that we find in Rousseau an entirely different concept of the state of law. But when, in order to reject this opposition, Brunkhorst characterises democracy as 'self-legislation by the people' and as 'autonomy of the *demos*,' when he associates this characterisation with the thesis that democracy realises the paradox of a 'rule by the ruled' in which domination is abolished, and when, finally, he infers from the strict identity of the ruling and the ruled the requisite of 'exceptionless inclusion of all persons affected by the law in the process of legislation,'[39] he draws from Rousseau's work consequences that only the 'archaic' part of the *Social Contract,* at the very most, might warrant. The citizen of the *Social Contract* does belong to the sovereign, but he does not legislate if by legislating we mean 'making the law'. As I mentioned earlier, the citizen has only the 'right of legislation' (*SC*, II, 7, p. 27), meaning that his consent – which is presumed so long as the law decrees merely on the general – confers authority on the law. This is not insignificant, but it is something other than 'inclusion in the process of legislation'.

The confusion that surrounds contemporary references to the notion of self-legislation obscures the fact that modern social contract theories, including the radical version proposed by Rousseau, have as their object the justification of power, or, what amounts to the same thing, the justification of subjects'

---

[36] See *SC*, III, 15, p. 64: 'Make gifts of money, and you will not be long without chains. The word finance is a slavish word, unknown in the city-state. In a country that is truly free, the citizens do everything with their own arms and nothing by means of money'.

[37] See Maier, 1971, pp. 127–61.

[38] Brunkhorst, 2005, p. 68.

[39] *Ibid.,* p. 68 and p. 73.

obedience to authority. No matter how deeply Rousseau transformed the notion of sovereignty inherited from Hobbes and, beyond him, from Bodin, sovereignty essentially remained a domination over subjects. As Judith Shklar remarks about Hobbes: 'Sovereignty is a matter of making and enforcing laws, and citizenship is at its height when subjects understand why they should obey them and do so invariably unless their lives are threatened, at which point they cease to be subjects. Until that extreme moment, subject-citizens are in one respect alike and equal: all are subjects to a sovereign'.[40] The abolition of status differences, already a given in Hobbes, in no way altered this fundamental determination of sovereignty. This is why Shklar can rightly consider that Bodin is 'the real inventor of the modern state and its limited but essentially equal and inclusive notion of citizenship'.[41] The same applies to 'self-legislation'. Much as he excoriated Bodin and Hobbes, Shklar adds, 'Rousseau, the most coherent theorist of democratic citizenship, owed a lot to Hobbes and Bodin. His republican citizen is certainly not one who rules. The magistrates govern him, but he does take part in legislation, and thus he is both a member of the sovereign and a subject'.[42]

If citizenship fails to reduce subjection, it is because from the outset it was conceived only as a modality of the latter. Citizens do vote in Rousseau; yet insofar as this vote is an election, and hence concerns singular persons, it is not the expression of the sovereign's 'right of legislation', but an act of government (*SC*, III, 17; IV, 3). By contrast, theorists of contemporary representative democracies see in elections, and especially in the election of the members of legislative bodies, the essential act by which the people exercises its sovereignty. It is this presupposition that leads them to conflate self-legislation with participation in the power to legislate. Obeying the law whose *elaboration* one has contributed to, even if indirectly, is by no means a subjection; hence, the citizen seems at last to have eliminated the subject within himself, and, correlatively, power seems to have freed itself of domination. If we remain within Rousseauian orthodoxy, however, we must maintain that the freedom of the citizen does not abolish obedience, and that the first of these two terms, which Rousseau tried hard to link together ('the essence of the body politic lies in the reconciliation of obedience and liberty'), enjoys a sort of priority. Obedience to the law is not servitude; because it is not linked to status inequalities other than those established by a general law, that is, by an impersonal law. Yet this is still obedience, a term which implies that the law is a command. Thus, against Carl Schmitt, I argue that the rationalisation

---

[40] Judith Shklar, 1991, p. 32.
[41] *Ibid.*, p. 33.
[42] *Ibid.*, p. 34. By stressing that the citizen never ceases to be a subject, Shklar appears to reject the idea of self-government, not that of self-legislation. Yet she is under no illusion regarding the reality of citizens' 'participation' in the elaboration of the law, as is made clear at the beginning of her chapter on voting. Her entire argument consists in highlighting the mostly symbolic character of the right to vote. Whether it is exercised or not, this right is the mark of equality.

of the law via its universalisation does not eliminate its character of command. The political order is still conceived as the product of the will of a legislator, a conception wherein the import of the Judeo-Christian core of the Western tradition manifests itself. While it is customary to emphasise, in the passage from medieval Europe to modernity, the positivisation of the foundation of power involved in the substitution of human will for divine will, one cannot fail to recognise the persistence, through this transformation, of a determined conception of the form of power. The figure of the God of Moses can still be distinguished in the sovereign people.

The rule of law signifies the impersonalisation of power: not that power ceases to be exercised by individuals, but that these individuals are merely magistrates holding offices from which they may, in principle, be removed at any time. As is well known, the correlate of the positivisation of the foundation of the legal-political order is its mutability. Power cannot be appropriated. That the notion of freedom is entirely configured by that of equality means that it has no other signification than the rejection of *perennial* status differences. So long as this condition is met, all forms of government are possible and compatible with the self-determination of the sovereign, including, as I mentioned earlier, hereditary monarchy. The important thing is that the sovereign decides on the form of government, and not on the individuals who hold the positions of power thus instituted. The sovereign only needs to exercise its inalienable right to alter this form for the positions of power to immediately lose their legitimacy. If Rousseau was a 'democrat' at a time when the term did not exist,[43] it is because he reflected on the extreme consequences of the mutability of powers, whose only legitimacy rests on the presumed consent of the men over whom they are exercised. Here we are far, very far from the axiom of contemporary political theories whereby the respect for intangible principles and values is the criterion by which democratic governments are recognised. For all that, 'democracy' as Rousseau understood it is not the government of the people; it does not even entail the people's participation, whether direct or indirect, in the elaboration of the law.

2.3 FROM ROUSSEAU TO KANT

Historians of political philosophy have difficulty agreeing on the nature of Kant's relation to Rousseau. What the moral and political philosophies of Kant owe to Rousseau – namely the concept of liberty as self-determination – is hardly contestable. Yet, for the most part, Rousseau is regarded by posterity as the father of a conception of democracy that entails the illimitation

---

[43] At least as it is understood today, see supra, pp: 27–31.

of the people's power, whereas Kant, thanks to his justification of individual subjective rights (and despite his rejection of the right to resist), is viewed, on the contrary, as having laid the foundations of the state of law, which implies a limitation of power. While we may concede the relevance of such analyses, we should nevertheless conclude that Kant read Rousseau properly, and that he took from the *Social Contract* that which was preparing the future, despite the book's ambiguities and archaisms. By interpreting the original contract as 'merely an *idea* of reason,'[44] Kant clearly distinguished between the metapolitical level and that of political theory. The main issue for Kant was not to dismiss the question of whether such a contract had a historical reality – something to which most social contract theorists never gave any credence or importance anyway – but to refine the concept of this contract by removing all references to the 'people in person.' Not only was there no need for the real people to assemble in order to give its assent to the law, but this had to be rigorously proscribed: a people that claims to judge by itself the legitimacy of power is already seditious.[45] The possibility that the real people might reappear in the place of the sovereign people is eliminated so long as the people's assent to the law is merely presumed, and so long as citizens' participation in the elaboration of the law is allowed on the mode of the 'as if.' The original contract does have a 'practical reality,' in that it 'can oblige every legislator to frame his laws in such a way that they could have been produced by the united will of a whole nation, and to regard each subject, in so far as he can claim citizenship, as if he had consented with the general will. This is the test of the rightfulness of every public law.'[46] It is significant that, in order to illustrate the implications of this idea of reason, the first example that came to Kant's mind is that of a law that would establish hereditary privilege for 'a certain class of subjects': it is impossible, he observed, that an entire people could give its consent to such a law (*ibid.*). Also significant, from another perspective, is the fact that Kant affirmed immediately after that a law should be considered just so long as it is *only possible* that a people could consent to it, and this even if the real people would probably refuse its consent. Ultimately, the idea of the original contract is nothing other than the idea of the equal freedom of men, that one and only 'innate right' which Kant, in the introduction to the *Doctrine of Right*, lays out in its two dimensions – freedom, defined as 'independence from being constrained by another's choice,' and equality, namely an individual's quality of being his

---

[44] Kant, 1991a, p. 79.
[45] See *DR* §49 (Kant, 1996, p. 95): 'A people should not *inquire* with any practical aim in view into the origin of supreme authority to which it is subject, that is, a subject *ought not to reason subtly* for the sake of action about the origin of this authority, as a right that can still be called into question (*ius controversum*) with regard to the obedience he owes it'.
[46] Kant, 1991a, p. 79.

own master *sui juris* – while concluding that they are in the end one and the same thing.[47] The condition of equal freedom, which is the very meaning of the original contract and hence the true criterion of the legitimacy of public laws, constitutes the juridical state by proscribing not inequalities of wealth, nor even inequalities of rank, but inequalities of birth alone – that is to say, the principle upon which the hierarchical organisation of the estates (*Stände*) of the Ancien Régime rested. For 'birth is not an act on the part of the one who is born, it cannot create any equality in his legal position and cannot make him submit to any coercive laws' that would be added to the coercion of public law, which is indifferent to inequalities of birth.[48]

The explicitly fictional character of the original contract allows Kant to completely separate the metapolitical level from that of political theory. The difference between the real people and the sovereign people no longer undermines the interpretation of the rule of law, because one of the two terms of this difference has been eliminated. At the historical level (the 'pragmatic' level of the *Social Contract*), the existence of the state, in whatever form it takes, can only be accepted as fact. It is the authority of the state that turns the people into a politically significant entity, which is to say (and this amounts to the same thing for Kant), into a legally constituted entity. Between Rousseau and Kant there was the French Revolution, and among the supporters of the Enlightenment who observed it from the outside, the revolution first aroused enthusiasm, and then perplexed horror as they watched it unfold. It is likely that this experience played a role in the virulence with which Kant attacked the right to resist. Yet should we see in this merely an expression of hostility towards revolutionary violence – one against which Kant argued the merits of gradual institutional reform initiated by the leaders themselves under the guidance of an enlightened public opinion? Rather than seeking the cause of Kant's condemnation of sedition in his personal psychological dispositions, we ought to understand the meaning of the revolutionary rupture from the standpoint of a legal conception of power. That Kant rejected the right to resist established powers, but also attempts at restoring the destroyed political order once a new one is established,[49] appears to some as a paradox. In reality, this paradox is merely the admission that the irruption of the real people on the political scene – which is what a revolution is about – is unthinkable within the framework of a coherent legal philosophy of political power. So long as one identifies, as Kant did, the political people with the people constituted by the legal order of the state, resistance to power – no matter its abuses

---

[47] *DR* Introduction, B (Kant, 1996, pp. 30–31). See infra...
[48] Kant, 1991a, p. 76.
[49] See *DR* §49, General remark on the effects with regard to rights that follow from the nature of the civil union, A (Kant, 1996, pp. 93–98).

and no matter how far it has strayed from the requirements of the idea of the original contract – is necessarily illegitimate. The illegality of resistance is what makes it illegitimate: the people 'as subject' cannot be made 'sovereign over him to whom it is subject.'[50] Between the destruction of the old political order and the establishment of a new one, there is a vacuum during which the concepts of legal-political theory fail to apply.[51]

For some contemporary authors, it is axiomatic that the rule of law cannot be a domination. But we must agree on what this term signifies. Of course, if the term is dogmatically reserved to designate relationships of command and obedience based on hereditary status differences, then the rule of equal law abolishes domination. This argument, however, rests on a tautology. It seems more consistent with ordinary usage to speak of domination whenever certain individuals are in a position to command others, who are in turn obligated to obey them. This definition of domination is that proposed by Weber: 'the probability that a command with a given specific content will be obeyed by a given group of persons.'[52] And yet this obligation is found even where social and political hierarchies are based on – real or supposed – merit, and no longer on birth. The persistence of the subject in the citizen is already explicit in Rousseau. Kant merely glosses him when he justifies the establishment of '*civic dignities*' that 'comprise the relation of a *superior* over all (which, from the point of view of laws of freedom, can be none other than the united people itself) to the multitude of that people severally as *subjects*, that is, the relation of a *commander* (*imperans*) to *those who obey* (*subditus*).'[53] For those who might not have heard him properly, Kant is even more specific in his 'General remark on the effects with regard to rights that follow from the nature of the civil union.' In addition to the right to levy taxes, the rights of the 'supreme commander of a state' include 'the distribution of offices' and 'dignities'. 'Dignities' (which, unlike offices, are not salaried) establish a 'division of rank into the higher (destined to command) and the lower,' wherein the latter 'though free and bound only by public law, is still destined to obey the former.'[54]

Kant read Rousseau properly, which is to say: the Republic of Kant is the truth of Rousseau's democracy. It is the truth, not of what Rousseau

---

[50]   *Ibid.*, §49 (p. 97).

[51]   It is the concepts of legal-political theory that fail to apply, and them alone. This does not mean that interim periods (between two 'juridical states' to use Kant's terminology), which are often accompanied by outbreaks of violence, irreducibly escape all theories of law in general. On this point, see Derrida's commentary on the theme of 'founding violence' in Walter Benjamin; this violence is not 'alien to law', even though it is 'in law, what suspends law' (Derrida, 2002, p. 269).

[52]   Weber, 1978, p. 53.

[53]   *DR* §48 (Kant, 1996, p. 92).

[54]   *Ibid.*, General remark on the effects with regard to rights that follow from the nature of the civil union, D (p. 102).

designated with this name, but of what he meant by popular sovereignty. Rousseau, for that matter, already employed the term republic in this sense. 'I therefore give the name "Republic,"' he wrote, 'to every State that is governed by laws, no matter what the form of its administration may be: for only in such a case does the public interest govern, and the res publica rank as a reality. Every legitimate government is republican' (*SC*, II, 6, p. 24). Popular sovereignty did not imply that the people should govern itself, nor even that it should be invested with the power to make the law; it was merely one form of rationalisation of the exercise of power. Power was henceforth exercised through equal law, which did not abolish the opposition between the 'higher,' 'destined to command,' and the 'lower,' 'destined to obey,' but transformed it by opening the possibility for everyone to access the functions of command. This, of course, was a possibility in principle. Merit, but also the vagaries of birth, which conditioned differences of wealth and culture if no longer differences of legal status, mediated the distribution of individuals between positions of command and ones of obedience. Hegel would later clearly recognise the element of contingency that intervened in the social – and thereby also political – destinies of individuals.[55] Kant himself was aware of the formal character of this opening up of access to social hierarchies under the effect of equal law. This is evidenced by the distinction he made between active and passive citizens – a distinction too quickly glossed over when it is simply attributed to the yet inchoate character of the conditions of modern societies in the Germany of his time. The right to vote was extended to the entire adult population belatedly, in the nineteenth century, and this initially to men alone (women would have to wait until the twentieth century). For those who view this extension as the main criterion of democracy's progress, the Kantian distinction indicates that his conception of the rule of equal law was incomplete. And yet this distinction does not cover that of censitary regimes, the principle of which Kant explicitly criticised. It is at once more innocent (it does not stem from the desire to reserve power for the rich) and more profound. According to Kant, political qualification – i.e., the authority that grants the right to decide on public affairs – requires that the individual be his own master.[56] However, only property opens this possibility, and property is and will always be unevenly distributed. *Beati possidentes*![57] The civil condition guarantees that something external can be yours or mine, and therefore validates differences in property, from the greatest wealth to the complete

---

[55]   *PhR*, §200 (Hegel, 1991, pp. 233–34).
[56]   This same idea was apparently shared by Blackstone (cited in Shklar, 1971, p. 37), who felt that property qualifications for voting were reasonable 'to exclude such persons as are of so mean a situation as to be esteemed to have no will of their own'.
[57]   See *DR* §9 (Kant, 1996, p. 46).

lack of possession that condemns individuals to dependency. For the freedom and equality of all to be respected, it suffices that no one be prevented from trying to rise from the passive to the active state.[58]

2.4 CRITIQUES OF DEMOCRACY: THE PEOPLE AND THE RABBLE

There was a sudden surge in the tumult outside – the revolution had reached the windows of the assembly hall. The excited exchange of opinions inside stopped short. Hands folded over their stomachs and, mute with shock, they stared at one another or toward the windows, where they could see raised fists and hear boisterous hoots, inane and deafening yowls that filled the air. But then, quite unexpectedly, as if the rebels were suddenly appalled at their own behaviour, it was as quiet outside as it was in the hall; and the deep hush that fell over everything was broken only by the sound of one word, spoken slowly and with cold intensity, emanating from somewhere in the bottom rows, where Lebrecht Kroger had taken his seat: 'Rabble [*la canaille*]!' [59]

Kant, I wrote, read Rousseau properly. By clearly distinguishing between the metapolitical level and that of political theory, by identifying the republic with the rule of equal law, Kant purged the notion of popular sovereignty of the archaisms that had led Rousseau himself to doubt whether democracy could be realised under the conditions of large modern states. But did Rousseau's theory really have to stand the test of revolutionary experience for such an interpretation to become possible? In fact, it was not this 'liberal' reading of Rousseau that had the most decisive influence in France between 1789 and 1793. Rather, it was the identification of the nation with the people – a people that fully mobilises to determine what the public interest is, and therefore has to participate, one way or another, in *the exercise of sovereign power*. The original ambiguity of the Rousseauian concept of the people largely contributed to the difficulties that the actors of the French Revolution encountered in defining the forms of the political regime that was to be instituted after the overthrow of absolute monarchy. These difficulties were reflected in the

---

[58] I shall return later to the compatibility of the distinction between passive and active citizens with the Kantian concept of citizenship, see *infra*, pp. 64–65.

[59] Thomas Mann, *Buddenbrooks: The Decline of a Family* (1994, pp. 184–85). The scene takes place in Lübeck in 1848. The meeting is that of the local council, which brings together the notables of the city. Lebrecht Kroger, father-in-law of Consul Johann Buddenbrooks, is a noble. He embodies a world of values that predate the bourgeois culture represented by Buddenbrooks and his son Thomas. Kroger's generation still often expresses itself in French: 'Rabble' is in French ('*la canaille*') in the original German text. Kroger dies of a heart attack upon leaving the meeting.

divergent interpretations that were proposed of how the sovereign people should be represented – a representation which all deemed essential, but which some feared would allow for the constitution of a new aristocracy of power, thereby reducing popular sovereignty to a mere fiction.

In revolutionary France as in America,[60] the most determined supporters of representative government conceived the latter as something radically different from democracy, and even as an antidote to it. The opposition between democracy and representative government could be defended in any number of ways, but in the final analysis it was always inspired by a fundamental distrust of the *real people*. What the term 'people' evoked was not even the multitude of Rousseau (or that of Hobbes or Spinoza before him) – that is, the entire population of a state understood as the juxtaposition of individuals driven by particular interests – but a part of this population, namely those who lack not only property, but also and especially culture and interest in public affairs. The people was, quite simply, the rabble, the mob of paupers whose gatherings easily turn to rioting, to destructive actions which no constructive action can quell.[61] That this uncultured fraction of the population might wish to participate in the exercise of power, or even merely to influence it, was a revolting idea for the major actors of the French and American Revolutions – those children of the Enlightenment who were elaborating the constitutions aimed at determining the form of the new political regime. And yet there were others who, without disputing the need for representation, justified it with the sole technical argument that direct rule was impossible under the conditions of large states. This line of argument made it possible to reconcile the power of the people with representation, and hence to think something like 'representative democracy.' This people whose participation in power they wished for could not be the 'people principle' invoked to found the legitimacy of power in opposition to dynastic or theological legitimacies. But neither was it the people-rabble. It was something closer to Rousseau's 'people in person,' the real people actually assembled in all its components to make their voices heard. Indeed, such was one of the effects of the revolution that long obscured the ambiguity of Rousseau's notion of popular sovereignty: 'The people in person' – which belonged to the archaic part of the *Social Contract* where Rousseau provided examples, banal at the time, from the ancient democracies or the small republics of Switzerland and Holland – had acquired a new reality in mobilisation, that is to say, in the politicisation of the masses via the revolutionary process. This mobilisation, the 'people as event' to borrow an expression from Rosanvallon, seemed to resolve, 'for a time, the constitutive

---

[60] See in particular Madison, *The Federalists Papers*, letters 10 and 14 (1961, p. 81*ff* and pp. 100–101).

[61] See Rosanvallon, 1992, pp. 75–78.

aporia of representation.' The people had become visible, 'in the tumult of the street or in the good behavior of patriotic festivals.'[62]

For reasons that I recalled earlier, Rousseau wished the 'people in person' to hold periodic assemblies. But he also considered, as did the actors of the French and American Revolutions who played representation against democracy, that the people was insufficiently enlightened to draw up the laws. On the other hand, Rousseau granted good will to this multitude. To the rhetorical question as to whether the 'blind multitude' had the ability to legislate, he replied negatively of course, but he also justified this response in these terms: 'Of itself the people wills always the good, but of itself it by no means always sees it. The general will is always in the right, but the judgment which guides it is not always enlightened.'[63] An entirely different perspective can be found in Hegel, who not only remarked that the people lacked enlightenment but also questioned the integrity of its will.

Hegel has never been regarded as a democrat. It is therefore not surprising that he penned one of the most articulate critiques of an interpretation of popular sovereignty that sought to draw immediate institutional consequences from it. In a famous passage from his *Philosophy of Right*, after having rapidly discussed the signification of the term 'popular sovereignty' from the standpoint of external relations between states (a people is sovereign if it has constituted a state of its own), he pondered the meaning of this same expression from the standpoint of internal politics. He admitted that it could have meaning, but on condition that it signified the same as state sovereignty: 'We may also say that *internal sovereignty* lies with the *people*, but only if we are speaking of the *whole* [state] in general, in keeping with the above demonstration (see §§ 277 and 278) that sovereignty belongs to the *state*.'[64] However, as Hegel remarked, popular sovereignty was not then evoked in this sense, but made rather to stand in opposition to the sovereignty of the monarch. This interpretation was for him one of the confused thoughts that resulted from the empty notion of the people, and it provided him with the opportunity to clarify what he meant by people:

> *Without* its monarch and that *articulation* of the whole which is necessarily and immediately associated with monarchy, *the* people is a formless mass. The latter is no longer a state, and *none* of those determinations which are encountered only in an *internally organized* whole (such as sovereignty, government, courts

---

63 *SC*, II, 6, p. 25. See also *SC*, II, 3, p. 17: '[...] the general will is always right and tends to the public advantage; but it does not follow that the deliberations of the people are always equally correct. Our will is always for our own good, but we do not always see what that is; the people is never corrupted, but it is often deceived, and on such occasions only does it seem to will what is bad'.
64 *PhR*, §279 (Hegel, 1991, p. 318).

of law, public authorities [*Obrigkeit*], estates, etc.) is applicable to it. It is only when moments such as these which refer to an organization, to political life, emerge in a people that it ceases to be that indeterminate abstraction which the purely general idea [*Vorstellung*] of the *people* denotes.[65]

The people, provided that the term is given a comprehensible meaning from the standpoint of the rational state, was not the formless mass, devoid of constitution. Neither was it the rabble. Indeed, when a few paragraphs later Hegel discussed the legislature, in which he wished to see the monarch, the executive power and the estates (*Stände*) represented all at once, he had the opportunity to return to the many 'warped and erroneous'[66] ideas that had passed into current opinion concerning the people, the constitution and the estates. He specifically tackled two fundamental ideas, which inspired in his view those who wished the deputies of the estates to prevail in the legislature, if not constitute all of it.[67] The first was that these deputies, and even the people itself, knew best what was in their interest; the second was that these same deputies were also those most willing to bring that interest into existence. Hegel contested both of these presuppositions. To the first, he violently objected that, 'if the term "the people" denotes a particular category of members of the state, it refers to that category of citizens *who do not know their own will.*' This diagnosis was literally identical to Rousseau's, but with the difference that Rousseau was speaking of the multitude in general, whereas Hegel was specifically referring to one category of members of the state. The meaning of this difference becomes clear in Hegel's objection to the second preconceived idea, which he suspected lay behind the argument that the deputies of the estates should prevail in the legislature: the presumption of their good will. Here, Hegel resolutely opposed Rousseau's thesis and concurred with the anti-democratic supporters of representative government of the revolutionary period. To argue that the deputies of the estates were more willing to bring the universal interest into existence was an expression of the 'negative viewpoint,' namely the distrust towards government that was characteristic of the rabble [*Pöbel*][68]

As soon as there was question of the people, the anti-democratic thinkers never failed to evoke the spectre of the rabble. It may be true, as Rosanvallon suggests, that this *topos* of eighteennth century anti-democratic thinking had a cultural and even anthropological signification rather than a political or

---

[65] *Ibid.*, §279 (p. 319).
[66] *Ibid.*, §301 (p. 340).
[67] All things being equal, the representation of the estates (*Stände*) constitutes the popular element of the legislature, which, in the Hegelian rational state, must also include representatives of the government along with the monarch himself.
[68] *Ibid.*, §301 (p. 341).

social one, in the sense that for many philosophers of the period, the 'rabble' designated a sort of 'pre-humanity,' a population believed to have 'remained in a state of nature, governed by instincts and needs.'[69] And yet, it should be noted that Hegel had the means to understand this otherwise. Hegel was not the Lebrecht Kroger of *Buddenbrooks*; his rabble was not just the *'canaille'* whose critical dispositions and revolutionary inclinations could be simply attributed to innate wickedness. To be sure, the rabble did not know what the good was, be it that of the state or its own; consequently, it could not recognise the good in the action of the rulers it distrusted. But the rabble was the way it was because of the logic of civil society as a whole. This logic indeed produced misery, just as it produced, at the other end of the social spectrum, the accumulation of wealth. Among those who lacked personal property and hence had to work to provide for themselves, and this in activities that were generally both too demanding and too dreary to allow them to enjoy the freedoms and spiritual benefits of civil society, the most destitute did not even have the means of living deemed the minimum necessary for civil life in the society of their time. The latter, who by the same token lost the 'feeling of right, integrity, and honour which comes from supporting oneself by one's own activity and work', formed the rabble.[70] Though Hegel did not say this, they had every reason to believe that the monarch and the members of government cared little about what was good for it.

For Hegel, the expression 'popular sovereignty' could have meaning from the standpoint of internal politics only on condition that by people was meant something other than the formless masses imagined as devoid of constitution – something other than the rabble, other even than all the individuals who composed the population of a state. Even admitting that the estates somehow represented the people in the legislature, as compared to the monarch and the members of government, this was so in the sense that they were quantitatively the most important element: 'the many,' as the Greek said (*oi polloi*), and not 'all.'[71] For as Hegel remarked, echoing the prejudices of his time, it went without saying that this 'all' did not include children or women, to mention only these. No matter how one approached the issue, the political people – the sovereign people – coincided with none of the confused notions invoked by the proponents of democracy to contest the legitimacy of the institutions of constitutional monarchies. It was because Hegel defended this legitimacy that he attacked the confused notions of democrats. But leaving aside the question of monarchism, as I earlier suggested we do, the core of Hegel's argumentation consists in saying that the constituent people is constituted as such by the

---

69   Rosanvallon, 1992, p. 77.
70   *PhR*, §244 (Hegel, 1991, p. 266).
71   *Ibid.*, §301 (p. 339).

state. Or, to use a more Hegelian formulation: popular sovereignty is nothing other than the principle of legitimation of modern rational power, which is itself a product of the double – economic and political – revolution that rendered necessary the elimination of status differences and that made codified law the preferred means of exercising power. By significantly broadening the notion of law, Hegel came close to identifying the state with the legal order, as Kelsen later would. It is not surprising, then, to find under Kelsen's pen the thesis that the political people could have no consistency other than that conferred on it by the unity of the state. As the latter wrote in 1928 in his book on *Democracy*: 'at bottom, only a juristic fact is capable of circumscribing the unity of the People with some accuracy, namely: the unity of the state's legal order whose norms govern the behaviour of its subjects.'[72]

---

[72] Kelsen, 2013, p. 36.

Chapter 3

The Democratisation of Democracies

Since the Rights of Man were proclaimed to be 'inalienable,' irreducible to and undeducible from other rights or laws, no authority was invoked for their establishment; Man himself was their source as well as their ultimate goal. [...] Man appeared as the only sovereign in matters of law as the people was proclaimed the only sovereign in matters of government. The people's sovereignty (different from that of the prince) was not proclaimed by the grace of God but in the name of Man, so that it seemed only natural that the 'inalienable' rights of man would find their guarantee and become an inalienable part of the right of the people to sovereign self-government.[1]

3.1 FROM CIVIL RIGHTS TO SOCIAL RIGHTS: THE STATUTORISATION OF SUBJECTIVE RIGHTS

3.1.1 The political people and the nation

From Rousseau to Hegel – from the man whom posterity made the father of modern democracy to the one whom it stigmatised as the sycophant of state power – political philosophy has never ceased to reflect, through the analysis of the concept of freedom and the determination of the political institutions that render it possible, on the consequences of the abolition of the status differences of the Ancien Régime. The transformation of the *subjectus* into a free subject responsible for himself and for the world in which he lives was the great achievement of the political philosophy of the eighteenth and the first half of the nineteenth century. If we except Rousseau, this was the main contribution of German idealist philosophy to the understanding of political

---

[1]   Arendt, 1979, p. 291.

modernity. This transformation does not mean that the free subject ceased to be subjected, in the sense that his freedom is not something that he discovered or recovered after having emancipated himself from domination, but the correlate of a novel type of domination, one without historical precedent. If the term 'subject' is ambiguous today – an ambiguity that has prompted a flurry of philosophical commentaries – it is because the modern sense of the term has not eliminated the former sense, and this for good reason. The free subject, the subject of right, cannot eliminate the *subjectus* within himself, because his freedom is tied to the power to which he is subjected.

It is likely that in this critique of the illusions attached to the notion of self-legislation, many will see reason to despair of the meaning of democracy and, beyond it, of political action in general. What is the point of engaging in politics, provided one does so not merely to satisfy a taste for power, if the only effect of politics is to change the forms of domination without ever hoping to reduce it? There is, however, a positive aspect to this critique, which is not immediately obvious but can already be indicated in a few words. This critique does appear as a necessary step to radically free us from all communitarian interpretations of the identity of the democratic people. The people – the body politic constituted through the domination that the state exercises by means of equal law – is not the nation. It is true that the history of the modern state and that of nationalism are closely intertwined. But the tragedies of the twentieth century have taught us to be wary of the dangerous confusions produced by these joint histories. The notion of 'constitutional patriotism,' put forward by Dolf Sternberger in 1982 and taken up by Habermas during the quarrel of the German historians of the 1980s,[2] was aimed at freeing political legitimacy from all references to real or imaginary pre-political identities. As long as we perpetuate the myth of self-legislation of the people, however, we will be only halfway there. For the idea of self-legislation compellingly suggests the fantasy of a unified people imagined as a collective that is able to decide its own fate – a unity that the people must possess independently of the state, insofar as the state is power. To affirm the power of the people *against* domination requires a closure of the people that is of its own making, and not the product of domination.

The political people is not the nation. No trace of a nationalistic *ethos* can be found in the works of the three authors (Rousseau, Kant, Hegel) in which I have sought the matrix, or matrices, of the modern conception of the body politic.[3] Hegel even proposed, with the notion of *politische Gesinnung*

---

[2]   See Sternberger, 1990, pp. 17–31.
[3]   One must of course distinguish between nationalism and patriotism. For Rousseau, the people must necessarily feel united, but this feeling is the result of laws and customs deliberately created for this purpose. The admiration he expresses for Moses stems from the fact that the laws Moses imposed on the Jews gave this people a unity that withstood centuries and dispersion. See, in particular, the fragment about the Jews in *Political Fragments* (1994, pp. 33–35).

(political disposition), something very similar to Habermas's constitutional patriotism.[4] What is the nation? Contemporary sociologists and political theorists generally agree that it is an 'imagined' community,[5] based on a sense of belonging that can be fostered by extremely diverse identity factors: a community of language, common customs or faith, a shared political memory, etc. There have been and there are states that gather together several nations, as well as nations that are scattered across several states. Weber noted that 'in ordinary language, "nation," is, first of all, not identical with the "people of a state," that is, with the membership of a given polity.'[6] However, Weber also observed that the centre of gravity of modern nationalism lies in 'sentiments of prestige,' a pride the individual takes in being the citizen of a state that has managed to carve out an honourable place within power relations between states. This attachment to political prestige 'may fuse with a specific belief in responsibility towards succeeding generations. The great power structures *per se* are then held to have a responsibility of their own for the way in which power and prestige are distributed between their own and foreign polities'[7] The stimulation of a sense of national belonging, and even its creation from nothing, is therefore of strategic interest to 'all those groups who hold the power to steer common conduct within a polity.'[8] Ruling elites are not the only architects of what political scientist Roger M. Smith calls 'people-making,' but they are the most important ones. Smith distinguishes between three types of 'stories of peoplehood,' aimed at forging the identity of a people: economic stories that essentially rely on prosperity and well-being, political stories that promise power to both the individual and the collective, and 'ethically constitutive' stories, which are what one is usually referring to when speaking of nationalism. Indeed, the latter designate 'a wide variety of accounts that present membership in a particular people as somehow intrinsic to who its members really are, because of traits that are imbued with ethical significance. Such stories proclaim that members' culture, religion, language, race, ancestry, history, or other such factors are constitutive of their very identity as persons, in ways that both affirm their worth and delineate their obligations. These stories are almost always intergenerational, implying that the ethically constitutive identity espoused not only defines who a person is, but who her ancestors have been and who her children can be.'[9] For political leaders, these ethical stories are interesting in that they offset internal divi-

---

4   See *PhR*, §268 (Hegel, 1991, p. 288). On the notion of *politische Gesinnung* in Hegel, see Kervégan, 2007, pp. 343–59.
5   According to the expression made famous by the work of Benedict Anderson (2006).
6   Weber, 1978, p. 922.
7   *Ibid.*, pp. 921–22.
8   *Ibid.*, p. 922.
9   Smith, 2003, pp. 64–65.

sions and help to mobilise, when necessary, the citizens of a state against an external enemy.

It might be objected that modern republican thought produced a significantly different concept of the nation, one from which all identity references mobilised by nationalism were absent. This concept is found for instance in Title III. 1 of the French Constitution of September 3, 1791: 'Sovereignty is one, indivisible, inalienable, and imprescriptible: it belongs to the nation: no section of the people nor any individual can attribute to himself the exercise thereof.' Yet here the nation is nothing other than the people – as the entire title makes clear. To say that sovereignty belongs to the nation is to say that it belongs to the people *considered as a whole* (the 'body politic'), and that, by virtue of this, it is indivisible, inalienable and imprescriptible, and therefore cannot be appropriated by any fraction or individual.[10] Power, whether of the monarch or of any ruling elite, will always be regarded as delegated. Thus understood, the nation is the sovereign people, which must exercise its sovereignty in the context of an organisation of political powers inherited from past centuries: that of territorial states. To be sure, the territorial character of power implies the need to set criteria for distinguishing between the resident, whose lasting presence on the territory of a particular state makes him a subject of the specific state administration exercised over that territory, and the simple passing visitor. Domination, as the term is understood here, is only ever exerted over persons, and state domination is no exception. However, what distinguishes the latter from previous forms of domination, which relied above all on bonds of personal allegiance, is the fact that territory is the middle term between power and those over whom it is exercised. This is why the control of access to territory is a crucial question for this type of domination, as highlighted, for example, by Christoph Schönberger: 'Territorial domination became possible only when a categorical distinction was achieved between those who had free access to the territory and those who did not. For this reason, the territorial community (*Verband*) needed to be a community of people. It circumscribed the circle of persons who were granted an unconditional right to stay in a particular territory, thus allowing for the latter's legal closure. The institution of nationality (*Angehörigkeit*) made possible inclusion and exclusion at once.'[11]

In the history of the formation of modern states, internal legal-political unification (the monopolisation of legitimate violence, to use the language of Weber) and the delimitation of the territory over which these states claim

---

[10] Moreover, Art. 25 and 26 of the 1793 Declaration of the Rights of Man and of the Citizen attributed to the 'entire people' a sovereignty that was 'one and indivisible, imprescriptible and inalienable.'

[11] Schönberger, 2005, p. 132.

this monopoly (and hence relations with other states) are two integrated and inextricable processes. For this reason, nationalism cannot be regarded as a contingent accident of their history. Because the modern state is a territorial power, it had to define and control its borders, determine an inside and an outside, and identify its nationals and, by contrast, the 'foreigner.' It also needed to secure the allegiance of the populations over which it exercised its domination, for which purpose stories of peoplehood – in particular 'ethical' stories – proved a unique instrument. The 'nationalisation' of the political people is the no doubt inevitable product of state domination *qua* territorial power. Should we conclude from this that the body politic of citizens could only be conceived as a national community? Should we make the logic of democratic citizenship responsible for the closure of the democratic community? It may be that two aspects of state domination are being confused here – ones that, while historically related, are nevertheless conceptually distinguishable. We shall have the occasion to return to this point. But for now, suffice it to note that while the individual subject of right is the product of the modern state, in that the latter imposed equal law by abolishing the status differences of the Ancien Régime, it is in its capacity as territorial domination that this state nationalised the citizen. These two aspects are sufficiently different that, during the French Revolution, some considered adopting as citizens 'those who in the various countries of the world have ripened human reason and prepared the paths of liberty.'[12] This generous conception of citizenship was possible because the civic community was conceived first of all as a community of legally equal individuals, and not as a people that secures control of its destiny by closing its borders. The danger of an interpretation of democratic citizenship centred on the notion of self-legislation is that the people that makes its own laws proceeds to its own delimitation. This danger, or at least this difficulty, is at the heart of current debates on the status of the foreigner.[13] The whole question is whether this status makes sense from the standpoint of democracy, or whether the foreigner is nothing but the outcast of territorial domination.

The moment it appeared on the historical scene, the political people had no choice but to insert itself into the territorial structure of state power. Put differently, the nation of the revolutionary constitutions is the existence of the political people as a state. If we limit ourselves to the French example, we

---

[12] This citation is taken from a text presented to the National Assembly by Marie-Joseph Chénier on August 24, 1792. In concrete terms, this proposal merely resulted in the granting of honorary citizenship to a few famous individuals (among them Thomas Paine, Jeremy Bentham, Anacharsis Cloots, and George Washington). See Weil, 2008, p. 14.

[13] Exemplary from this perspective is the work of Benhabib, *The Rights of Others* (2004), whose arguments I sum up and discuss below. See also Smith's discussion of the positions of Rawls and Habermas on migration policies (2003, p. 135*ff*).

see that the goal of the revolutionary movement was not to upset this structure, but to establish a new relationship between the people and power. In the
revolutionary constitutions, the determination of how public powers should
be organised is always preceded by a text that defines the rights granted to
individuals. From the standpoint of the usual categories of contemporary
political thought, the term 'citizen' seems to be used in an ambiguous manner. While it is poorly distinguished from 'man' in the Declarations of the
Rights of Man and of the Citizen of 1789 and 1793 as well as in the 'Fundamental Provisions Guaranteed' by the Constitution of 1791, it is identified
with national citizenship in the strictly constitutional section of these texts:
Title II. 2 of the Constitution of 1791 and Title 4 of the Constitution of 1793,
which set the criteria for 'French citizenship.' However, this ambiguity stems
entirely from the retrospective interpretation we now make of those texts. The
revolutionary constitutions did not distinguish the citizen from man because
they considered that every man had the 'natural' right to be a citizen of a
free nation. If the revolutionary era did not experience the need to produce a
Universal Declaration of Human Rights, it is because the Declaration of the
Rights of Man and of the Citizen was already a universal declaration. The
rights of the citizen were not reserved for nationals.[14]

3.1.2 The extension of political rights

What was reserved for nationals was the guarantee of the rights of the citizen, granted to all men by a particular state – in short, *French* citizenship.
The latter was defined by a set of criteria, the main one (in addition to age,
see below) being a lasting presence on the territory of that state. The other
criteria merely confirmed the individual's desire to settle on that territory. In
emphasising birth (being born to a French father), the Constitution of 1791
could perhaps lend itself to an ethnic interpretation of nationality. But the
Constitution of 1793, which became the fundamental reference for the subse-
quent democratic tradition, was freed from such ambiguity. Living by one's
labour, acquiring property, marrying a French woman, adopting a child, supporting an elderly person (where the child and the elderly person are tacitly
assumed to be French) – these criteria indicated that the individual's stay on
the territory could not be temporary. The guarantee by a specific state (in this

---

[14] This is what Balibar says, in different words, when he remarks in a note in his book on equaliberty
(with which I fully agree) that 'the statements of the Declaration [he is referring to the *Declaration*
of 1789] are neither nationalist nor cosmopolitan, and, more profoundly, the concept of the citizen
which they embody is not a concept of belonging. It is not the concept of a citizen of a particular
state, city, or community, but, as it were, the concept of a citizen taken absolutely' (2014, p.
307, modified translation). We shall have the occasion to return in greater detail to the theme of
belonging.

case the French state) of rights deemed 'natural'– and hence universal – of the individual was extended to all those who chose to live on its territory. Only passing visitors were excluded, not because they were to be treated as enemies, but because it was admitted that another state provided them with this guarantee.

The Jacobin Constitution includes among the rights of the citizen the 'equal right to take part in the formation of the law and in the nomination of its mandatories or of its agents' (Art. 29). If we consider that this equal participation in the formation of the law is the necessary institutional translation of the principle whereby 'the people, being subject to the laws, ought to be their author,' then the Jacobins appear to have been more Rousseauian than Rousseau himself.[15] Indeed, political rights were for them immediately tied to nationality. While the Constitution of 1791 devotes one article to the requisites of nationality (II. 2, with no age requirement) and another to those of the active citizen (III. II. 2), the Constitution of 1793 conflates the two in a single article: Title 4 of the Constitutional Act, entitled 'On the right of Citizenship,' which specifies on the contrary the age required to exercise the rights of French citizenship. The conditions for obtaining political rights – the right to vote and to stand for election – constituted a major focal point for the political struggles of the nineteenth and first half of the twentieth century. For many historians and political scientists, the greater or lesser extension of the circle of the beneficiaries of those rights is the main criterion by which to measure the progress of democracy during those two centuries.[16] Considering the history of this period as a whole, we find that, despite temporary setbacks, this circle has never ceased to expand: through the reduction and then elimination of property qualifications, the lowering of the voting age, the attribution of political rights to women, but also, in the United States, the abolition of racial discriminations.[17] The distinction between active and passive citizens seems incompatible with the notion of citizenship today. That it did not appear to be so to those who wrote the constitutions of the revolutionary era (if we except the Jacobins) cannot, however, be simply attributed to the bourgeoisie's desire to monopolise power.[18] Rather, it is the symptom of

---

[15] The absence of the notion of universal suffrage in Rousseau is highlighted by Rosanvallon (1992, pp. 56–57, p. 215 and pp. 217–18): 'While Rousseau posited that "the legislative power belongs to the people, and can belong to it alone," by no means did he envision a political system based on voting, in the sense that we understand it today.'

[16] See, for instance, Manin, 1997, p. 132. After showing that representative government was conceived by most of its proponents as an antidote to democracy, he notes that the extension of the right to vote, the elimination of wealth requirements for representatives and, in particular, the advent of universal suffrage 'gave rise to the belief that representation was progressing toward popular government.'

[17] See Shklar, 1991.

[18] See Rosanvallon's analyses on this topic, 1992, pp. 88–118.

the fact that the rights we now qualify as 'political' were not essential to the understanding of citizenship at the time. The citizen was above all man, who had been freed from the shackles of differential statuses and whose 'natural' rights were guaranteed by the rule of equal law. The right to vote became, no doubt very rapidly, the symbol of that equality.[19] And the continuous battle, with its advances and setbacks, for the extension of this right throughout the nineteenth century and the first decades of the twentieth ultimately made it more than a symbol. Political rights have become the very substance of citizenship. At the same time, this politicised citizenship has been untied from the rights of man. In the dominant representations of our time, the rights of man are universal, and the rights of the citizen remain conditioned by national membership.

It is true that the possibility of this shift was already inscribed in the Rousseauian interpretation of popular sovereignty. This is especially apparent in the hesitations of Kant – who, as I mentioned earlier, was a faithful reader of Rousseau – regarding the definition of the citizen (*Bürger, Staatsbürger*). In the opuscule published in 1793, *Theory and Practice*,[20] Kant distinguished between three aspects of the civil state: the freedom of every member of society as a human being, the equality of each with all the others as a subject (*Untertan, subjectus*), and, lastly, the independence of each member of a commonwealth as a citizen. Freedom and equality are granted to all by virtue of a right based on reason, and independence is a *prerequisite* social condition for being accorded the right to vote. By subjecting access to voting rights – presented here as the distinctive character of the citizen – to the condition of independence, Kant justified in principle the non-coincidence between the body of individuals subject to the law and the circle of those who concretely participate in the determination of 'a public will, from which all right proceeds.' 'In the question of actual legislation, all who are free and equal under existing public laws may be considered equal, but not as regards the right to makes these laws.'[21] He therefore distinguished, in the commonwealth, between citizens *stricto sensu* and those who are merely protected by the laws (*Schutzgenossen*). To be sure, Kant set voting qualifications that were infinitely less restrictive than those of the censitary regimes of the next decades. In this text, however, citizenship was already defined in political terms (by the right to vote), and the difference between the rights of man and the rights of the citizen was beginning to rear its head. Two years later,

---

[19]   On the right of suffrage as a symbol of belonging, see Rosanvallon, 1992 and Shklar, 1991.

[20]   *Theory and Practice* is the title under which the 1793 opuscule is generally cited. The exact title is: 'On the Common Saying: "This May be True in Theory, but it does not Apply in Practice."' References here are to the English translation of this text (1991a).

[21]   Kant, 1991a, p. 77.

in paragraph 46 of the *Doctrine of Right*, Kant took up the tripartite distinction he had deployed in *Theory and Practice* between freedom, equality, and civil independence, but with an interesting difference in terminology. Freedom, equality, and independence were now presented, first of all, as the three legal attributes of the 'citizen, inseparable from his essence.'[22] Yet the strictly political definition of the citizen reappeared in the Remark to that same paragraph, in which Kant stated that 'the only qualification for being a citizen is being fit to vote.' The tension between the two definitions of the citizen rendered necessary the distinction *expressis verbis* between active and passive citizens, about which Kant was nevertheless compelled to observe that it 'seems to contradict the concept of a citizen as such.' It is to overcome this contradiction that he proposed to leave the door of citizenship open to all, freedom and equality being expected to allow anyone to 'work his way up from this passive condition to an active one.'

Thus, contrary to a now well-established opinion, the distinction between the rights of man and those of the citizen does not date from the constitutions of the revolutionary period. On the contrary, this distinction resulted from the shift in the centre of gravity of citizenship towards political rights that are themselves tied to nationality – a shift that democratisation, namely the extension of the right to vote, completed by erasing the difference between active and passive citizens, and by allowing, through this erasure, for the final identification of citizens with voters. This identification has fostered confusion, in the democratic imagination, between two aspects of the notion of sovereignty that are distinguished by jurists and also have distinct historical origins. The first is the sovereignty of the nation-state, which determines its relations with other states, and the second is internal sovereignty, which concerns the relations between the people and state power.[23] The political people merged with the sovereign state, accepted the implications of the territoriality of power, and took on responsibility for the distinction between the condition of citizen and that of foreigner. Gerald Stourzh once observed that 'stranger' is a status distinction (of inferior rank), the only one to have resisted until now the process of equalisation of rights that was initiated in the late eighteenth century.[24] But the *status* of foreigner is only ever the projected shadow of the *status* of citizen. Indeed, the rights of the citizen, which the revolutionary constitutions granted to all men, became a statutory qualification precisely when the categories of citizen and national became interchangeable. The sta-

---

[22] *DR* §46 (Kant, 1996, p. 91). All following citations are taken from the same paragraph, pp. 91–92.
[23] See Schönberger, 2005. Hegel, for his part, clearly distinguished between the two notions; see *PhD* §278 and 321(Hegel, 1991, pp. 315–16 and p. 359).
[24] Stourzh, 1996, p. 320. In the original French version of this text, Stourzh uses the term 'étranger,' which should have been translated as 'foreigner' instead of 'stranger.'

tus of the foreigner is not a relic of a bygone era, which would have escaped
the process of equalisation of rights. It is, on the contrary, the outcome of the
identification of the citizen with the national. Consequently, it is linked to the
territorial structure of political power, which, as I indicated above, was not
called into question by the revolutions of the eighteenth century.

A certain – journalistic – reading of the Universal Declaration of Human
Rights suggests it definitively confirms the sharp separation between the
rights of man and the rights of the citizen. It is said that the determination
of the second, which are reserved for nationals, is left in the Declaration to
the discretion of states, whereas the first are fundamental rights which states
are enjoined to respect, for foreigners as much as for their own nationals.
However, the universality expressed in the title does not make it possible to
distinguish between conditional and unconditional rights. Among the rights
recognised to all human beings, the Declaration indeed mentions nationality,[25]
along with the political rights that are tied to it – the right to take part, directly
or indirectly, in public affairs, the right of equal access to public service, and,
finally, the right to vote in regular elections.[26] What is 'universal' is the body
that proclaims all of these rights: the international community represented
by the General Assembly of the United Nations. But by no means does this
Declaration limit the rights of man to what is ordinarily meant by fundamental rights – the right to life, liberty and security of the person (along with the
proscriptions that are their correlate: prohibition against torture, cruel, inhu-
man or degrading treatment and punishment), but also the right to justice,
freedom of expression and worship, and the right to circulate freely.

Thus, the Universal Declaration of Human Rights appears to join together
what was separated by the history of democratisation of the nineteenth and
twentieth centuries – the rights of man and those of the citizen – by subsum-
ing the second under the first. Does it recover, for all that, the 'spirit' of the
declarations of the revolutionary period? The fact that it mentions the right
of every individual to a nationality, thereby establishing the latter as the condition for the enjoyment of political rights, paradoxically leads us to doubt
this possibility. Indeed, the rights declarations of the late eighteenth century
did not evoke nationality, the determination of which was reserved for the
organisational section of the constitutions. This difference may seem minor,
but it is nonetheless important. For it signals a more profound difference: that
of the addressees of these different declarations. The Universal Declaration
of Human Rights addresses states, on behalf of the international political
community, by defining a 'common standard of achievements for all peoples

---

[25] Art. 15: 'Everyone has the right to a nationality.'
[26] Art. 21, Paragraphs 1, 2 and 3.

and all nations'[27] which these states are invited to use as a guide for their legislation, judicial practice, and government policies. True, this declaration includes nationality among the rights of man. But by making nationality the middle term that gives access to some of the rights of man – namely political rights – it leaves the responsibility of granting or denying them to states, thereby reintroducing, in a different guise, the difference between the rights of political citizenship and the fundamental rights of man. On the contrary, the implicit addressees of the revolutionary declarations were not states, but men in general, to whom these declarations were stating their 'natural' rights. In so doing, they assigned these men the responsibility, and even the duty,[28] of upholding these rights. To be sure, the eighteenth century revolutionaries did not call into question the territorial organisation of political power, and it was clear to them that the citizen was to demand the respect and guarantee of his rights from a necessarily specific state. Yet the key point was not this territorial structure, but the fact that these declarations, far from relying on the goodwill of magistrates and government officials, encouraged men, *omnes et singulatim*, to take responsibility for the defence of their rights. It was primarily up to citizens – to all men – to 'compare unceasingly the acts of the government with the aim of every social institution' and to never allow themselves to be 'oppressed and debased by tyranny.'[29] The eighteenth century declarations contained an emancipatory dynamic that is not found in the Universal Declaration of 1948. Their logic implied the recognition of the right to resist. Surely, it is only in the radical Constitution of 1793 that this right is explicitly designated.[30] But the idea of it is also present in Section 3 of the Virginia Declaration of Rights, which states that when any government appears to betray the purposes for which it was established (the common good, the protection and security of the people, the nation and the community), 'a majority of the community has an indubitable, inalienable and indefeasible right to reform, alter, or abolish it, in such manner as shall be judged most conducive to the public weal.' This idea is also present in the United States Declaration of Independence, which, despite precautions, stipulates that every time a form of government fails to guarantee the rights of men, 'it is Right of the People to alter or to abolish it, and to institute new

---

[27] Universal Declaration of Human Rights, Preamble.

[28] Declaration of the Rights of Man and of the Citizen, 1793, Art. 35 (see *infra*, note...)

[29] Declaration of the Rights of Man and of the Citizen, 1793, Preamble.

[30] Art. 33: 'Resistance to oppression is the consequence of the other rights of man.' This is specified in Art. 35: 'When the government violates the rights of the people, insurrection is for the people and for each portion of the people the most sacred of rights and the most indispensable of duties.' Here, I agree with Balibar (*Equaliberty: Political Essays*, 2014 p. 38) who notes that 'the equation that is typical of the revolutionary statements of 1789,' 'that of man and citizen,' has as its consequence, 'among other things, the idea that *the emancipation of the oppressed can be no one's work but their own*' (my emphasis).

Government'. As for the Universal Declaration of Human Rights, from which the notion of a 'right to resist' is absent, it sees in 'rebellion' only a last resort to which men may be compelled when states fail to respect the regime of right that it has determined.[31] While the difference may seem small, it clearly indicates the heterogeneity of the addressees.

3.1.3 The invention of social rights: Citizenship as status

The politicisation of citizenship was the first step in a process that I will venture to call here (while being aware of the unsightliness of the term) the 'statutorisation' of subjective rights. The second step in this process was the development of social rights, which began at the tail end of the nineteenth century and unfolded at different rates depending on the country, culminating towards the middle of the twentieth century in what is known as the welfare state. It is to Thomas H. Marshall that we owe the systematic elaboration of a sociology of the welfare state, which he presented in a series of writings published between 1949 and the mid-1960s. The most famous among these, and one still regarded as a classic of sociology today, is his first book: *Citizenship and Social Class*.[32] It is also to Marshall that we owe the coining of the ideal type of citizenship status. The invention of social rights, whose different phases and aspects he described based on the example of England, represented in his eyes the completion of a three-centuries-long history, which saw the gradual *addition* 'of new rights to a status that already existed and was held to appertain to all adult members of the community' – for all its male members at least. Schematically (as Marshall recognised that the three stages partially overlapped), the 18th century was the century of civil rights, the nineteenth that of political rights, and the twentieth that of social rights. Taken together and apart, these three types of rights constitute citizenship status today (or in 1949, the year of publication of *Citizenship and Social Class*). If we go back to earlier times, we can certainly find equivalents to each of those rights; yet only rarely do we encounter them all together, and, most importantly, at no point do we find them clearly distinguished from each other. The indifferentiation of the rights of the past was the correlate of what appears, from a retrospective standpoint, as an indifferentiation of institutions. Marshall cites in this regard a passage from the *Constitutional History of England*, in which F. W. Maitland remarks: 'The further back we trace our history the more impossible it is for us to draw strict lines of demarcation

---

[31]   See the third 'Whereas': 'Whereas it is essential, if man is not to be compelled to have recourse, as a last resort, to rebellion against tyranny and oppression, that human rights should be protected by the rule of law'.

[32]   Marshall, 1992.

between the various functions of the State: the same institution is a legislative assembly, a governmental council and a court of law. [...] Everywhere, as we pass from the ancient to the modern, we see what the fashionable philosophy calls differentiation.'[33] Regardless of which authors Maitland had in mind when he wrote these lines (in 1908), this 'fashionable philosophy' did anticipate current theories of functional differentiation.

Marshall's works largely contributed to determining the interpretation of the nature of social rights and of citizenship in general that has become canonical among historians, sociologists, and political scientists. In his view, civil rights as understood in the eighteenth and nineteenth centuries were the expression of a power granted to the individual to protect himself against his fellow citizens and against the state. These rights were limited to individual freedom[34] and property, both of which had to be guaranteed against any intrusion or encroachment by a third party – whether by one or several other private individuals, or by public power itself, which was paradoxically responsible for providing that guarantee. Civil rights followed a logic of separation: the right of the individual to freedom and property expressed his desire to 'isolate himself by converting his home into his castle.'[35] Concerning political rights, namely the rights to participate in political power either as an elected official (as a member of a body endowed with political authority) or as an elector, Marshall remarked that they did not appear in the form of new rights, but as an extension, to new categories of the population, of rights that already existed yet had long been reserved for particular groups. In this regard, he considered that the 1918 Representation of the People Act, which had established universal suffrage for the male population in England, was the decisive turning point that made these rights a component of citizenship status.

Most of Marshall's attention went to social rights, as the few pages he devoted to civil and political rights were merely intended to highlight the novelty of the third generation of subjective rights. He distinguished various categories among these, stressing in particular the difference between the rights to education and health, on the one hand, and the right to welfare, on the other. For the individual who possesses them, the first are duties as much as they are rights. Education is the very process of citizen production, a process in which health also participates somehow, since the body of the citizen can be considered part of the national capital.[36] These rights are social

---

33   Maitland, quoted in Marshall, 1992, p. 8.
34   For Marshall, individual freedom includes: liberty of the person, freedom of speech, thought and faith, freedom of contract, and the right to justice.
35   Marshall, 'The Right to Welfare' (first published in *The Sociological Review*, 13 [3], 1965). See Marshall, 1981, p. 91.
36   Marshall, 1981, pp. 90–91.

in the sense that, unlike civil rights, they do not reflect the individual's reluctance towards the demands of society, but, on the contrary, his membership in it. Also social is the right to welfare, under which Marshall classified the benefits individuals can claim when the contingencies of life, old age, lack of training, sickness, and handicaps of all kinds prevent them from accessing through work the resources they need to enjoy the minimum living conditions that are customary in their society. However, welfare is based on an entirely different logic: here rights and duties are not conflated in the individual, but are distributed instead on either side of an asymmetrical relationship. These 'rights claims,' as they are sometimes called, are presented, by individuals who are somehow disadvantaged, to administrative bodies (generally state bodies) that act on behalf of all of society. Society has duties to those of its members who, from the standpoint of its own historically variable norms, cannot adequately meet their own needs. The rights of the individuals concerned are the correlate of the duties of the collective to which *they belong*.

This type of rights is difficult to establish within a strictly liberal conception of subjective rights, which, on this point, is in line with Kant's thinking.[37] This is why, in the middle of the twentieth century, Friedrich Hayek had no difficulty mobilising this liberal logic to launch his critique of 'social justice.'[38] One of the great merits of Marshall's work was to illustrate, through outlining the history of the 'right of the poor' in England between the eighteenth and twentieth centuries, the difficulty that modern capitalist and liberal societies had in conceiving assistance in terms of rights. At first, assistance was precisely only assistance: a form of relief given on humanitarian or charitable grounds to individuals who were excluded from the community of citizens because they were poor. The benefits granted to the destitute with the Poor Law of 1818 in England were actually conditioned on the renunciation of the status of citizen.[39] In the words of Marshall: 'The stigma which clung to poor relief expressed the deep feelings of a people who understood that those who accepted relief must cross the road that separated the community of citizens from the outcast company of the destitute.'[40] The progressive development of the welfare state broke with this miserabilist conception, by including public assistance among the set of rights that constitute citizenship status. This transformation was accompanied by changes in the economic policies of states, including the development of mechanisms of wealth redistribution, as well as by associated changes in the mode of provision of mate-

---

[37] See Kant's critique of paternal government, which can be read as an anticipated critique of the welfare state (1991a, p. 74).

[38] Hayek, 1978.

[39] This entailed confinement in poorhouses in some cases, and denial of political rights in general.

[40] Marshall, 1981, p. 15.

rial security itself. The beneficiary of social rights tied to employment via social insurance systems was no longer construed as a beneficiary of charity, but as a full-fledged member of the community of citizens, who, at some point in his life (unemployment, old age, etc.), receives benefits from a fund to which he has contributed and will potentially contribute again (in the case of the unemployed).[41]

However, the historical perspective from which Marshall analysed the different components of modern citizenship is not limited to the period that runs from the constitutionalisation of civil rights to the invention of social rights. It goes back to 'ancient times'[42] – roughly the feudal era – during which the individual often enjoyed protections analogous to those afforded by social rights today, though on completely different bases. Indeed, given the indifferentiation of institutions, these protections were inextricably confused, in a blend where the civil, the political and the social were indistinguishable. The history of solidarity begins well before the eighteenth century, not only because it can claim the legacies of Roman law's *obligation in solidum*, Republican *concordia*, or Christian *fraternitas*,[43] but also because the particular statuses of the Middle Ages linked together duties and rights, obligations and protections – even though, as one should always keep in mind, status was a 'class marker and an indicator of inequality'[44] in the medieval period. Marshall did not dwell on the exclusive solidarities of orders and of other corporations, but he did consider that, on the local scale of medieval urban communities, equal law was the original source of social rights.[45] However, the lineage from this origin to the social rights of the twentieth century is not direct. This is because the development of the market economy, combined with the political revolution of the eighteenth century, broke these ancient solidarities. Between the two (Marshall was referring to the Elizabethan period in England), the right of the poor served as a transition, with all the ambiguity that this role entailed. This right was the last refuge of social solidarity, which was about to disappear under the blows of capitalism.[46] Between the old and the new, civil rights were located on the side of the new, whereas social rights – or its equivalent at the time, the right of the poor – were on the side of the old.[47] It is this ambiguous, intermediate situation that was brought to an end in England

---

[41] See the analysis of this transformation in France in Robert Castel's essential work, *From Manual Workers to Wage Laborers: Transformation of the Social Question* (2002).

[42] Marshall, 1992, p. 8.

[43] See Brunkhorst, 2005, p. 2.

[44] Marshall, 1992, p. 8.

[45] *Ibid.*, p. 14.

[46] See Karl Polanyi's analysis, in *The Great Transformation*, of the Speenhamland system, to which Marshall also refers (Polanyi, 1944, pp. 81–89).

[47] Marshall, 1981, p. 14.

with the abovementioned law of 1818, which replaced community solidarity with assistance to the excluded.

The history of the right of the poor in the nineteenth and twentieth centuries is a remarkable indicator of the problems encountered, from the perspective of a conception of right based on the autonomy of the subject, in providing a justification for the duties of the state (as the representative of society) to the individual that goes beyond the guarantee of his freedom. We find echoes of this difficulty in certain legal theories of the early twentieth century, such as the *Freirechte* school in Germany, or Duguit's solidaristic doctrine in France. Duguit launched a critique of 'German theory' – from Hegel to Ihering, but also Jellinek – on the twofold ground of its subjectivism (its use of the notion of subjective rights) and its statism.[48] However, it is not this critique that deserves our attention here, but the motivation that lay behind it. The individualistic doctrine, which according to Duguit shares common ground with the hypostasis of the state, cannot conceive the legal rule other than as a limitation of individual rights, such that this rule 'cannot impose active duties, but only abstentions.'[49] Consequently, this doctrine is incapable of justifying the provision of social benefits by the state. By contrast, Duguit (along with Durkheim, Bourgeois and a few others in the same period in France) sought ways to justify those benefits via a concept of solidarity that expresses an awareness of the social interdependence in light of which the opposition between the collective and the individual, between socialism and individualism, loses its *raison d'être*. Individualisation develops in parallel with the complexity of the differentiation between functions and between men. The legal rule is a social product: it is 'society itself, in the sense that the existence of society implies the existence of a rule of conduct.'[50] And the state can only register that rule, which, contrary to what the rights declarations of the revolutionary era postulated, is not immutable but changes with the evolution of societies.[51]

'Solidarity' was the key concept of the legal and sociological theories that strove to integrate social rights in the concept of democracy in the early twentieth century.[52] As I mentioned earlier, this integration reinforced the statutorisation of subjective rights, and thereby revived the old assumption that there can be no democracy without a democratic community. To be sure,

---

[48]   See Duguit, 2003, p. 106*ff.*

[49]   *Ibid.*, p. 141.

[50]   *Ibid.*, p. 92.

[51]   Though Duguit took up Durkheim's thesis that individualisation and the social bond, far from being contradictory, developed and intensified in parallel with each other, he differed from Durkheim in refusing all collective categories. His uncompromising 'methodological individualism' led him to reject in the same breath the 'social consciousness of the sociologist' and the 'national consciousness of the German Historical School' (2003, p. 93).

[52]   I shall return later to the fortune of this word in contemporary sociology and political philosophy. See infra V.1. : 'Citizenship and Solidarity.'

the fact that the protections guaranteeing the security of each member of that community were conceived in terms of the rights of the subject suggests a fundamental difference from the solidarities of the past. However, the justification of these new rights profoundly altered the interpretation of subjective rights in general. From the perspective of the state – whether construed as an autonomous body or as the simple transmission belt of society – the subject is now the object of its social programs. The individual is regarded less as a subject whose freedom ought to be recognised than as an instrument that facilitates the work of social services: he is responsible for asserting his rights, and thereby for helping the administrative bureaucracy implement its program. This subjective right, whose function is purely instrumental,[53] is evidently far removed from subjective rights as understood in particular by Kant. As I recalled above, the Kantian construction of the *Doctrine of Right*, which expounds 'natural right' – i.e., private right – before addressing public right, rests on the axiom that 'a civil constitution is just the rightful condition, by which what belongs to each is only secured, but not actually settled and determined. Any guarantee, then, already presupposes what belongs to someone (to whom it secures it).'[54] When subjective right functions like an operative fiction in the context of government programs, the precedence of private right over public right no longer holds. Here, I follow Luhmann, who notes that attributions cannot be seriously construed as emanations of the individual person, to the point that, far from reflecting an ever broader understanding of the 'freedoms' granted to individuals, the proliferation of subjective rights threatens on the contrary the freedom of the person – at least if we understand it in the sense that Kant did.[55]

Like Marshall, Luhmann took an interest in the history of the right of the poor and in the formation of the welfare state. However, the interpretation he made of them both was quite different, and contained, *in nuce*, a critique of Marshall's general understanding of subjective rights. The divergence begins with the interpretation of civil rights. To say, as Marshall did, that the purpose of these rights was to have the individual convert 'his home into his castle' is to retain from the individualisation of right only one aspect: the self-closure of the individual, which implies that the other is, in general, a foreigner – and a potentially hostile one at that – against whom the individual must above all protect himself. By the same token, the reinterpretation of civil rights in statutory terms, which was made possible by the development of political rights

---

[53] See Dabin, 1964.
[54] *DR* I, 1, §9 (Kant, 1996, p. 45), cited supra, p. 8. Luhmann also refers to this passage (1982, p. 91 and note) to emphasise the extent to which the contemporary usage of the form of subjective rights contravenes the basic presuppositions of its original meaning.
[55] Luhmann, 1982, pp. 91–92.

and above all by the invention of social rights, appears to *re-socialise* civil rights. It is no longer as an individual that the subject enjoys those rights, but as a citizen, and as a citizen of a specific community: the nation. By contrast, Luhmann considered that subjective rights did constitute a vector of inclusion (and this from their earliest occurrences, when they comprised only civil rights), but a paradoxical form of inclusion. Insofar as their establishment went hand in hand with the abolition of all forms of closed corporations, these rights deferred to the individual the task of forging, through private contracts and through the choice of his profession and different (religious, political, etc.) commitments, the bonds that integrate him into society. Consequently, Luhmann refrained from interpreting the emergence of social rights as a re-socialisation of the rights of the subject. The welfare state was innovative in that it made inclusion the *explicit* goal of its political program. From this perspective, no doubt, it seemed to revive the logics of solidarity that in the old forms of socialisation were the corollary of compulsory and particular forms of membership. Yet because the modern state presupposed the functional differentiation of society, it could not rely on the traditional solidarities of statutory bonds, which had long been dissolved. Far from relinquishing the legal form of the rights of the subject, the welfare state was, on the contrary, able to accomplish its program only through creating a large number of new subjective rights.[56]

The difference between modern solidarity and the solidarities of old reveals itself in the unprecedented link that was established by the welfare state between rights and duties. Social rights may seem to restore an original bond between individuals which subjective rights, so long as they were understood primarily as civil rights, had led us to forget. Indeed, the logic of subjective rights makes it difficult to understand duty other than in the language of prohibition, that is, of a limitation of right. Luhmann recognised this when he noted that duties cannot be built on the basis of self-reference, and that the welfare state cannot be justified through a classical, Kantian conception of the subject of right. But do social rights really break with this logic? And is the link between rights and duties 'restored' in the form in which it was formerly understood? Traditional communal solidarities were always tied to specific relationships between individuals playing distinct roles: the tutor and his pupil, the prince and his advisers, the lord and his vassals, the master and his apprentice, etc. Duties were concrete and asymmetrical (for instance, the duties of the tutor to his pupil were not the same as those of the pupil to his tutor); however, they were also reciprocal, in the sense that the specific other to which an individual had duties was himself duty-bound to

---

[56]   See Luhmann, 1982, p. 87*ff*.

that first individual (even though their respective duties were of a different nature). Modern right replaced these concrete reciprocities with a far more abstract bond, which Luhmann refers to as *complementarity*. The difference relates to the basic condition of the subject of right: his freedom, that is to say, his independence from all forms of specific, pre-given social relations – a condition that the invention of social rights did not alter. For this subject, the other he encounters in society is but an *alter ego*, namely an individual endowed with a freedom identical to his own that is realised in property and in the possibility of contracting. Subjective rights have replaced the old symbiosis between rights and duties with a simple authorisation to act, on condition that one does not encroach on the freedom of action of others. Of course, the social bond has not disappeared, but it is now realised only through multiple actions, the initiative of which supposedly rests in each case with the individual. This abstract mode of relating to others, freed from all pre-given sociality, allows for a flexibility and a mobility that are adapted to the conditions of functional differentiation in societies. In the words of Luhmann: in the context of highly differentiated societies, the concept of subjective right 'has imposed itself through its abstraction and adaptation to complexity. This complexity rests on the untying of the bundles of rights and duties in favour of an asymmetrical expectation of complementarity. Asymmetry increases combinatorial possibilities, while freeing them from the dependency that comes with intertwined, concrete social reciprocities. [...] These conquests, however, were not formulated as such; nor were they legally systematised in this form. They were semantically appropriated by the concept of the subject along with its derivatives – freedom, power, capacity or authorisation to act, will, interest, competence, beneficiary.'[57]

Thus, the fact that legal practitioners did not abandon the semantics of subjective rights, despite the critiques of certain legal theorists, does not merely stem from the weight of traditions and linguistic uses. This semantics was preserved because it was impossible to turn back the wheel of history through resuscitating the concrete solidarities of the past. Assigning to the individual the task of asserting his rights remained an extraordinarily economical and, apparently, the only imaginable means of implementing the social policies of governments in the context of societies wherein functional differentiation had reached a point of no return. Thus the concept of subjective right continued to be used by jurists, but as a simple technique in a legal practice for which the transcendental foundation of rights in the autonomy of the subject had not only ceased to be necessary, but also ceased to make sense.[58] Rather than interpreting social rights from the statutory perspective of the different

---

[57] Luhmann, 1982, p. 101.
[58] See Dabin, 1964.

forms of citizenship, as Marshall had, Luhmann saw them as a symptom of the completion of the positivisation of law.[59]

A brief detour through Kelsen would seem to confirm this interpretation. Legal positivism, in the rigorous form that Kelsen gave to it, indeed provided this theoryless practice with the theory that, as it happens, it was doing very well without. It is true that Kelsen's attention did not focus on social rights, and, in this context, it may seem incongruous to invoke him. But while the impossibility of justifying duties from the perspective of a classical conception of subjective rights indicates the limits of that conception, it can be argued that Kelsenian positivism constitutes, on the level of legal theory, the double of Marshall's sociology of rights. This is a highly demystifying double, however, insofar as it helps to justify the welfare state as much as it does an authoritarian state that would deny its citizens, not only social and political rights, but also what constitutes the kernel of modern freedoms: civil rights. As I recalled earlier, the *Pure Theory of Law* begins with duty, understood as the correlate of prohibition. The criterion of right is the sanction determined by the law for certain behaviours, which means that the legal order is essentially a coercive system. Of course, Kant had already linked right and constraint in order to distinguish between the legal and moral levels. But if he was so keen on determining the content of private right before addressing political right – the second being the condition of effectiveness of the first – it is because he wished to avoid what he described as the 'terrifying' consequences of a full positivisation of the law, which he believed he had detected in Hobbes. Indeed, while state constraint was for Kant the indispensable condition for the existence of a legal order – to the extent that he refused to grant subjects a right to resist power, whatever the abuses it may have committed – he nevertheless refused to leave to the discretion of power the content of the rights of the subject. The meaning of the link established by Kelsen between right and sanction is entirely different. This link entails that subjective rights, so long as we choose to retain the term, are nothing other than reflex rights – which is to say, the consequence for individual *A* of the prohibitions limiting the behaviour of individual *B*, provided that the behaviour of *B* can affect *A*. According to Kelsen, the true subject of right is the subject of legal obligations.[60]

What is lost with the statutory interpretation of subjective rights is their normative foundation in the autonomy of the subject, as well as the emancipatory

---

59   See Luhmann, 1982, pp. 88–93. See, in particular, p. 90: The subject has become 'a necessary operative fiction in the political process. As a result, one completely loses sight of the fact that subjective right was originally a particular source of right and a figure opposed to positive law. It is now an instrument of positive law itself.'
60   See Kelsen, 2005, pp. 128–130 and p. 169.

dynamic that was contained in the affirmation of this autonomy. The position defended by Kelsen – his reluctance towards the notion as well as the fact that he accepted to use it in the end – reflects on the level of legal dogma the shift that occurred in the understanding of this notion following the emergence of social rights. Kelsen clearly conceived of rights as something that is granted, a conception that expresses the logic of administrative population management as well as the understanding of politics that goes with it. This is, if you will, politics from above, from the standpoint of rulers. This conception is at the heart of what is referred to today as 'democratic governance,' concerning which one may ask whether it is not a *contradictio in adjecto*. In recent years, the misadventures of the European Constitution – its repeated rejection by 'peoples' who were consulted for form's sake without having a say over the course of its elaboration – show the limits of this administrative concept of democracy. These misadventures might remind those who will listen that the rights declarations that inaugurated democratic modernity created a political subject whose relation to power cannot be reduced to trust. In the complaints of politicians, which are often relayed by journalists, one clearly hears echoes of the old refrains about the ignorance of the multitude. Yet it is vain to expect of political leaders – whether elected officials or experts – that they will sing a different tune. The positions they occupy are positions of power, and, from this standpoint, populations can only be regarded as an object. One might counter that the modern state was also built from above, and specifically by the centralised monarchy. However, it is not from above that the state was democratised, but through the mobilisation of populations which had found, in the form of the autonomous subject implied in the declarations of the rights of man and of the citizen, the wellspring of a mode of intervention in politics that helped them escape minority status. Legal theory may have forgotten what the autonomy of the subject originally meant, but the latter is still alive and continues to sustain the necessarily contentious relationship between democratic peoples and all forms of power.

3.2 THE RIGHTS OF FOREIGNERS

3.2.1 The citizen and the foreigner: The right of world citizenship in Kant

The communitisation of citizenship goes hand in hand with its statutorisation; the former constitutes, as it were, the latter's external face. For while democratisation has translated, on the inside, into the creation of new rights and into a rise in the number of beneficiaries of rights formerly reserved for a few, it has had as its counterpart the growing precarisation of the rights of non-citizens. The more the community is defined with precision, the more it is concerned with fixing its borders. It is true that the territorial framework in which citizenship came to be exercised – i.e., the sovereign state – was inherited from the pre-revolutionary era. But it is the movement of democratisation of the nineteenth and first decades of the twentieth century that turned this originally contingent framework into a constituent element of democracy. The revolutionary concept of citizenship was contaminated by the territorial form of political power, and the merging of the two provided the terrain for the emergence and development of modern nationalism. Thus, the emancipatory dynamic triggered by the rights declarations of the revolutionary period, which assigned each individual the task of asserting and defending his rights, was bypassed by the nationalisation of citizenship. Although this contamination, and the insidious transformation it brought about in the interpretation of the foundation of subjective rights, could remain hidden as long as the internally excluded (whether workers or humble people in general, and later women) were struggling to obtain the right to vote that had become the symbol of full inclusion in the community of citizens, they appeared in broad daylight once the nationalisation of citizenship was complete. At that point, the foreigner became the figure *par excellence* of the outcast. In the light of a citizenship understood in terms of membership, the 'foreignness' of the foreigner could only be conceived as non-membership. As Danièle Lochak observes: 'What ultimately characterises the figure of the foreigner of the nation-state is his "politicisation": The national is defined as a citizen of the state [...] whereas the foreigner is defined as a non-national and (inseparably) as a non-citizen – one who does not belong in the political community constituted as a state.'[61]

While the right of foreigners has a long and complex history, it was entirely reconfigured by the emergence of national identity. It is generally admitted today that, for want of enjoying the rights of the citizen, the foreigner in democratic societies is granted the rights of man, which international law forces states to uphold. The distinction between the rights of man and those of the citizen – which, as we saw earlier, was absent from the declarations of the revolutionary period – has thus imposed itself as a convenient tool for giving a semblance of universalism to legal-political logics that inevitably generate exclusion. This distinction has nevertheless proven extremely difficult to translate into effectively guaranteed rights, not only in countries far removed from the democratic ideal, but also in those that are considered to form the core of modern democracies, whether in Europe or in North America. In the case of the former (China, for instance, but also many African countries),

---

[61]   Lochak, 1985, p. 36.

the failure to respect 'fundamental rights' concerns not only foreigners, but also nationals, such that the ineffectiveness of those rights reflects the ambiguous legal character of norms formulated by international bodies that lack executive power. The case of democratic states is different, and leads to addressing the question of 'the rights of man' other than through the difference between rights merely proclaimed and rights guaranteed by a coercive body. For international law also allows sovereign states to control access to their territories, and thus implicitly supports the measures taken by each of those states to regulate the entry and residence of foreigners. This control is exercised through laws and, especially, through administrative procedures that clearly infringe on rights, even those recognised as human rights, such as the freedom to circulate (think, for instance, of constant identity checks and detention centres) or the right to a private and family life.[62] It is not the fact that the international bodies responsible for human rights lack means of implementation or mechanisms of 'genuine judicial review'[63] that weaken those rights, but the logic of national sovereignty. And if this logic implies that foreigners have no rights other than those that the state affords them, and that it can deny them in practice via the effects of its migration policy, it is because all rights, including the rights of the citizen, are from the perspective of the state granted rights. These aporias, over which anyone who seeks to offer a 'democratic' solution to the question of foreigners inevitably stumbles today, stem from the fact that in thinking democracy as a community, one endorses, wittingly or not, the statutory conception of right generated by the overlap between citizenship and nationality – a conception in which the emancipatory character of the notion of a subject of right has given way to the imperative of belonging.

Here again, the modern conception of citizenship is far removed from the Kantian model of the rule of law, as is attested by common misinterpretations of the 'Third Definitive Article' in Kant's essay on *Perpetual Peace* (1795), which is one of the classic references for contemporary reflections on the status of the foreigner. This text defines 'cosmopolitan' right, which the *Doctrine of Right* had presented as the third level of public right – the first level being constituted of political right, namely the right that governs, within a state, relations between individuals and between individuals and that state, and the second consisting of the law of nations (the traditional name

---

[62] See Lochak, 2007, pp. 62–63: 'When police laws become increasingly coercive, they hinder such basic rights as the freedom to come and go, the right to family life, the right to health, etc. The affirmation of full equal rights becomes completely meaningless.' And, concerning recent developments in migration policy in France, *ibid.*, p. 64: 'We have the appearance of a well-functioning rule of law, but with a legislation that is increasingly detrimental to fundamental rights and with a judge who systematically rules in favour of the legislator and the administration.'

[63] Delmas-Marty, 2009, p. 123.

for international law) which regulates relations between states. Thus, cosmopolitan right is for Kant a right in the strict sense, which means that it does not pertain to philanthropy, but is a necessary complement to political right and the law of nations, so long as one is willing to deploy the public right in its entirety.

'Cosmopolitan right shall be limited to the conditions of universal *hospitality.'*[64] Thus is formulated the only article to determine the content of cosmopolitan right, which, as Kant specifies, is the right of the foreigner who asks to be received in a state of which he is not a citizen. The hospitality requested from the state in question consists in not treating the foreigner as an enemy, and hence in welcoming him. The state is legally obliged to grant this request, on the one condition that the presence of the foreigner poses no threat to its own existence. Kant called this right *Besuchsrecht* ('the right to visit') and distinguished it from *Gastrecht* ('the right to be a permanent visitor'). The latter distinction deserves some attention. The first French translation of this text[65] concealed its significance by construing *Gastrecht* as the right of an individual to be received by another individual, and by opposing to it 'the right of all men to invite foreigners into their society' (*'le droit qu'ont tous les hommes de demander aux étrangers d'entrer dans leur société'*).[66] The reader of this translation is naturally led to think that *Gastrecht* is a sort of right of tourism, and that *Besuchsrecht* involves the possibility of longer settlement. Yet if the distinction between *Gastrecht* and *Besuchsrecht* lies in their respective durations, the temporal difference must probably be reversed. Indeed, with the term *Gastrecht*, Kant was referring to the particular status granted by sovereign princes in the Ancien Régime to specific communities of foreigners, who had been expelled from their countries of origin, often because of their faith (Spanish Jews, French Huguenots), and who were received by another state that saw advantages in their specific professional and economic aptitudes. This hospitality was therefore given to a particular population, and it was based on a convention that determined the rights granted *en bloc* to this population, together with the specific obligations to which it was subject. This institution rested on the pluralist legal logic that underlay the 'special laws' of the Middle Ages[67] – a logic that was still alive in the seventeenth century, as is illustrated by the welcome edicts promulgated for the Huguenots by the

---

[64] Kant, 1983, p. 118.
[65] Kant, 1986, vol. 3, pp. 333–383. This anonymous translation was published in 1796 by Nicolovius in Königsberg (see Heinz Wismann' explanatory note in this volume, pp. 329–331). In the 1974 edition (transl. by Jean Darbellay), '*Gastrecht*' is translated in French as '*droit d'hospitalité.*' The English translation by Ted Humphrey (to which note 66*** refers) does not lend itself to the same confusion.
[66] *Ibid.*, p. 350.
[67] See supra, chap. I.3.

Landgrave of Hesse-Cassel and by the Great Elector of Brandenburg. It is to this kind of edict that Kant was referring when he spoke of a 'charitable agreement' (*wohltätiger Vertrag*) authorising the stay of foreigners.[68]

As a right/privilege granted to a particular community, *Gastrecht* was often limited to one generation, with no guarantee of renewal for the next, and it could generally be revoked. It would be an anachronism to interpret it as a first step towards the integration of the individuals concerned into the community of ordinary citizens – so long as the latter notion makes sense in the context of a society based on a plurality of particular law communities. Kant added that this right was intended to last 'for a certain period.' Does this mean that the right to visit (*Besuchsrecht*), which is what cosmopolitan right consists of, was better guaranteed over the long term? In truth, Kant did not feel the need to specify the duration of that right, because the individuals who claimed it did not aim to settle for long in the foreign country they entered. What Kant had in mind, as is suggested by his discussion of ships and camels (that '*ship* of the desert'),[69] was the conditions for the development of international trade. The latter was necessary for the expansion of civilisation, which Kant, as a good Enlightenment thinker, was certain had originated in Europe and was destined to spread from there to the entire globe. The function of the right to visit was to guarantee by law the possibility of developing international trade, while also condemning the abuses that accompanied it. Kant rejected the argument of *terra nullius* by virtue of which Europeans, in the Americas and in Africa, considered the rights of indigenous peoples to be non-existent. From this perspective, he also justified, *a contrario*, the restrictions that China and Japan imposed on the relations between European traders and their own populations. The provision that the right to visit can be granted only when the foreigner poses no threat to the existence of the society that welcomes him was not aimed at the immigrant – as the term is understood today – or at any other related figure, but at the coloniser. This provision notwithstanding, the right to visit nonetheless had to be recognised in order to provide a legal foundation for the development of peaceful exchanges between nations – namely, commercial and cultural exchanges which offered hope that the logic of peace would someday prevail over the logic of war. If he was to fulfil his own civilising mission, which depended on his mobility, the foreigner could not settle in the country where his commercial interests took him. He could only request a right to visit, and though that visit could last a while, it was not destined to become permanent.

---

[68] The Doctrine of Right speaks of a 'right to *make a settlement* on the land of another nation (*ius incolatus*); for this, a specific contract is required' (Kant, 1996, p. 87).

[69] Kant, 1983, pp. 118–119.

The right to visit is a cosmopolitan right in the sense that it is the means for the construction of a unified political world, which for Kant did not mean a global state, but a federation of states that together aim for peace. But it is also a right of citizenship and, more specifically, a right of world citizenship (*Weltbürgerrecht*). This literal translation draws attention to the fact that the now taken-for-granted equation between citizenship and nationality was by no means evident in the eyes of Kant. If, on occasion, he deemed it necessary to distinguish between the citizen of a state (*Staatsbürger*) and the citizen of a town (*Stadtbürger*),[70] by making the latter equivalent to the French term 'bourgeois,' it is not because he anticipated the difference that Hegel (and Marx after him) would establish a few decades later between the political and social dimensions of collective belonging. The bourgeois construed as the citizen of a town (*Stadtbürger*) is not the individual of Hegelian civil society, concerned primarily with his particular interests. Here, too, we must guard against flattening historical periods. The distinction Hegel made between civil society and the state, to which corresponded his specific understanding of the opposition between the bourgeois and the citizen, registered the emergence of a relatively autonomous sphere of purely social activities with industry and exchange at its core (what he called the 'system of needs'). If the political domain is to be conceptually distinguished from that sphere, and if its primacy is to be affirmed, this is because social integration through work and exchange occurs spontaneously, without actors needing to make collective unity the conscious goal of their action. The quasi-natural character of a social unity whose vector is primarily economic threatens to render meaningless the traditional notion of citizenship, insofar as this notion has always implied – for the Ancients as much as for the humanist writers of the Renaissance – that the individual should put the common good before his particular interests. The Kantian distinction between the bourgeois and the citizen of the state refers to an earlier stage in Western political history: that of the nationalisation of citizenship, which suppressed an older form of citizenship whose territorial framework was the city. True, the *Stadtbürger* – the urban citizen, if you will – foreshadowed the bourgeois of Hegelian civil society by the nature of his activities. It is in the cities of the Middle Ages that trade, crafts and the first forms of industrialisation developed, leading to the constitution of entirely new logics of production and distribution (a new 'mode of production,' to use Marxist terminology) and to the disappearance of the rural economy based on peasant serfdom. Nevertheless, the bourgeois was also a citizen, that is to say, a form of political subjectivity. This is what Weber meant to emphasise when he used the term 'non-legitimate

---

[70] Kant, 1991a, p. 78.

domination' to describe the European medieval city[71]: not that the forms of domination which undeniably existed in the latter were intrinsically illegitimate, but that the European medieval city was the site of formation of a new type of political organisation which broke with the socio-political logic of orders and princely sovereignty. 'The urban citizenry [the bourgeoisie] therefore usurped the right to dissolve the bonds of seigneurial domination; this was the great – in fact, the revolutionary – innovation which differentiated the medieval Occidental cities from all others.'[72] The form of this usurpation was not always revolutionary since the freedoms these cities enjoyed were often granted by princes as privileges. Yet, under the protection of those freedoms, modes of collective organisation of the urban community were established that presupposed some form of equality and political participation for all the individuals engaged in economic activities, and this even where power was monopolised by a stratum of notables.

The bourgeois of medieval cities was an authentic citizen, concerned with the administration of public affairs as much as with his private interests. It is to this figure of political subjectivity that Kant was obliquely referring when he distinguished between the citizen of the state and the bourgeois (*Stadtbürger*, or citizen of a town). One ought to understand that it is precisely because it was possible to think forms of sub-state citizenship such as urban citizenship that supra-state citizenship, namely world citizenship, was conceivable. Citizenship in general did not yet involve the set of civil, political and social rights that developed out of the restatutorisation of subjective rights described in the first part of this chapter. Despite the limitations I noted earlier (i.e., the exclusion of some political rights and, of course, the absence of social rights, the idea of which arose much later), state citizenship as Kant defined it in the *Doctrine of law* and in *Theory and Practice* already constituted the form that was to enable the transformation of subjective rights into statutory rights. Yet, for Kant, the rights of the citizen *of the state* were not the general norm of citizenship in relation to which all other forms of citizenship could merely be construed as an exception or in restrictive terms.[73] Most uses of the Kantian concept of world citizenship today rest on a double misunderstanding. On the one hand, the forgetting of the plurality of forms of citizenship has led to equating this right with fundamental rights, namely the 'rights of man,' which

---

71 'The City: Non-Legitimate Domination' is the title Weber gave to his sociology of the city, which appears as a section of *Economy and Society*. This title has given rise to several questions and divergent interpretations. See, in particular, Breuer (2000) and Colliot-Thélène (2001, pp. 305–24).

72 Weber, 1978, p. 239.

73 The right of world citizenship is *limited* (by the conditions of universal hospitality), not in contrast to the rights of the citizen of the state, but to *Gastrecht*. It is not, as I have pointed out, a right of residence, but a right to visit.

all states have the duty to respect both for foreigners passing through their territory and for their own citizens. On the other hand, the misreading of the distinction between *Gastrecht* and *Besuchsrecht* – the right to be a permanent visitor and the right to visit – has prompted some commentators to lament the fact that Kant limited the length of stay of foreigners, thereby denying them the possibility of enjoying all the rights of the citizen, and hence of integrating without restriction the democratic community. This misreading is manifest in authors who attempt to think the rights of migrant workers and asylum seekers along with Kant. In either of these interpretations, the right to visit – which is the only content Kant gave to the right of world citizenship – proves inadequate to the task.

3.2.2 The 'right to have rights'

Arendt recognised the impossibility of separating the rights of man from those of the citizen in a famous passage of *The Origins of Totalitarianism*. Against the backdrop of the experiences of stateless persons during the inter-war period and World War II, she observed that, without membership in a community of citizens, the rights of man were nothing more than a *flatus vocis*. Reflections on the rights of man in general, and on the rights of for-eigners in particular, are nowadays obliged to refer to this text, as well as to comment on the formula – as beautiful as it is enigmatic – of a 'right to have rights.' The enigma, wherein lies the interest of her text, is that she refused the simplest and most obvious means of justifying this right, which is to make it a moral right founded in the nature of man. As she was too 'political' to invoke this idea that came from what she viewed as a bygone era, she could only take cognisance of the circle in which the right to membership presup-poses membership. The rights of man are only for those who enjoy the rights of the citizen – i.e., those who belong to an organised community, which is the condition for the right of expression and action. Franck Michelman, and Benhabib after him, interpret this 'right to have rights' as a 'right of political inclusion.'[74] Yet this right itself relates to another, more fundamental mem-bership, that is, membership in humanity:

> Humanity, which for the eighteenth century, in Kantian terminology, was no more than a regulative idea, has today become an inescapable fact. This new situation, in which 'humanity' has in effect assumed the role formerly ascribed to nature or history, would mean in this context that the right to have rights, or

---

[74] Frank I. Michelman, 1996, p. 205. Balibar speaks of a 'right to politics' (2014, p. 52), which my interpretation of the centrality of the figure of the subject of right for modern democracy also implies. However, the right to politics is something other than the 'right of political inclusion,' at least if one interprets the latter in terms of membership in a *demos*.

the right of every individual to belong to humanity, should be guaranteed by humanity itself. It is by no means certain whether this is possible.[75]

This passage registers an aporia, and the pessimism of its last sentence reflects Arendt's doubts about the possibility of ever overcoming it. Many contemporary commentators of her reflections on the 'right to have rights' refuse to share this pessimism. 'It remains one of the most puzzling aspects of Hannah Arendt's political thought,' Benhabib remarks, 'that although she criticised the weakness of the nation-state system, she was equally sceptical about all ideals of a world government.'[76] To overcome this scepticism, readers of Arendt have implemented two strategies that are substantially different but can have very similar practical consequences. The first consists in opening up the national *demos* through perpetually renewing discussions of its identity in the public sphere. The second relies on the existence of a global civil society that strongly favours democratic culture, as well as on the constraints exerted on states by the institutionalisation of human rights in various supranational legal and judicial bodies. Benhabib proposes, in the aforementioned work (*The Rights of Others*), an original version of the first strategy that is centred on 'iteration,' a concept she borrows from Derrida while also significantly inflecting it. By this term, Derrida meant that a repetition is never the reproduction of an original, but a variation that always alters what it repeats – the original itself having no real existence.[77] Benhabib draws on this idea to construe democratic practice as a perpetually renewed appropriation of the principles and values upon which a democratic community is built. In this iterative appropriation, the people appears as the author of the law by the very fact that it alters those principles and values through reinterpreting them. This 'fluid' conception of the identity of the *demos* helps open it to foreigners without conditioning their possible integration on an imperative of assimilation. The difference Benhabib introduces in the use of Derrida's concept is that while she recognises that the notion of an 'original meaning' is meaningless in the case of language, the same does not apply to the normative foundation of a political community. The recurring reference, throughout her text, to the opening words of the preamble to the Philadelphia Constitution (1787) – 'We, the people' – indicates that for her all democracies are founded on an original act that constitutes a people through fixing its borders. And while, among what she construes as the three characteristics of the traditional conception of democracy – the self-legislation of the people, the ideal of a

---

75 Hannah Arendt, 1979, p. 298.
76 Benhabib, 2004, p. 61.
77 At least this is what Seyla Benhabib retained, for her argument, from Derrida's analyses in 'Signature, Event, Context' (1988, pp. 1–24).

homogeneous *demos*, and the delineation of a territory – she rejects the latter two in favour of the idea of an always open process of self-constitution of the people, she nonetheless maintains that there exists a 'crucial' link between 'democratic self-governance' and territorial representation.[78] According to Benhabib, democratic autonomy requires closure because democratic representation must be answerable to a specific people. The notion of democracy, understood as the principle whereby the subjects of the law must be its author, always involves an inclusion along with its correlate: exclusion.

The analyses of Brunkhorst illustrate the alternative strategy.[79] Arendt's pessimism regarding the possibility that humanity might one day acquire the consistency of a community of belonging that is able to guarantee the 'right to have rights' can be explained, according to Brunkhorst, by the form that globalisation took in the first half of the twentieth century. Imperialism and totalitarianism: the determining factors of globalisation at the time were the destructive forces of capital and power, and its engine was war. In Brunkhorst's view, the second half of the twentieth century allowed for more optimism, not because capital and power had ceased to exert a decisive and harmful influence, but because a 'denationalised' legal system was gradually established during that period. At present, human rights are guaranteed by a certain number of international legal and judicial institutions, in ways sufficiently efficient to ensure that they do not exclusively depend on the arbitrariness of nation-states. 'For a long time now,' writes Brunkhorst, 'being a citizen of a state has not been a prerequisite to enjoy human rights.'[80] The stateless person today is not necessarily without rights. For Brunkhorst, this extension of legal status indicates a widening of the 'democratic community.' As he sees it, the gap between the circle of citizens endowed with political rights, and the populations subject to the laws of the state who are nevertheless denied the right to vote and to participate via the latter in the elaboration of those laws – a gap that contravenes the principle whereby 'the people, being subject to the laws, ought to be their author' – is filled by human rights. The distinction between the active and passive conditions, which used to cut across nationals and now separates them from foreign residents, is reduced because the latter are guaranteed to be treated 'as if' they were members of the sovereign.[81] Human rights, which Brunkhorst identifies with fundamental rights by including social rights among them, offer a semblance of democratic autonomy to individuals who do not, or do not yet, enjoy political

---

[78]   Benhabib, 2004, p. 219.
[79]   See Brunkhorst, 1999 and 2005.
[80]   Brunkhorst, 1999, p. 174.
[81]   Brunkhorst, 2005, p. 76. One may note in passing the similarity between this argument and that with which Kant solved the problem of the non-coincidence between the body politic and the real people, see *supra*, p. 47.

rights: 'Through human rights, the conceptions of republicanism and democracy that restricted citizenship were transformed into the idea of an expanding community, permanently widening through self-revision, and gradually including all others and strangers.'[82]

The practical conclusions of the two approaches I have just contrasted are not fundamentally different. Both are based on the idea that the dynamism of a *demos* constituted in a never-ending process can solve the contradiction between, on the one hand, the principle that 'all those who are affected by the consequences of the adoption of a norm have a say in its articulation,'[83] and, on the other, the resistance of the gap between the body of citizens with full rights and the body of individuals subject to the law. This similarity stems from the fact that, in either case, the notion of democracy remains attached to that of community: a particular and hence national community for Benhabib, and a global community for Brunkhorst. Along with many others today, Brunkhorst wagers on the development of supranational law to dare what Arendt had not dared herself – as this seemed implausible to her in the post-war context – which is to think humanity as a community of belonging, if not as a constituted community, at least as a community to come. The world republic should and is poised to take over from nation-states, through increasingly reducing the gap that the politicisation of citizenship created between the rights of man and those of the citizen.

I see several reasons to consider as problematic these solutions to the aporia pointed out by Arendt. Regarding the first solution, the difficulty, which I specified in the pages above, lies in what Benhabib calls the 'democratic paradox' – i.e., the fact that the people elaborating the rules of inclusion must also decide upon exclusion. Benhabib's text consists in a long meditation on this paradox, which, *in fine*, she confesses is impossible to resolve. Indeed, the substitution of a dynamic conception of the *demos* for the static conception (illustrated in its extreme form by Schmitt's positions) does not help break the 'crucial link' between democratic autonomy and territorial representation. It is the principle of legitimation of laws itself that requires closure, 'because democratic representation must be accountable to a specific people.' 'I see no way,' she notes in the very last pages of her book, 'to cut this Gordian knot linking territoriality, representation and democratic voice.'[84]

At first glance, the difficulties presented by the 'globalist' solution are of a different nature. They initially result from what Brunkhorst recognises is the dark side of globalisation, namely the development of economic logics

---

[82] *Ibid.*
[83] Benhabib, 2004, p. 218. See also Brunkhorst, 1999, p. 172: 'No person who is affected by the laws should be excluded from participation, and hence from the possibility of changing these laws.'
[84] All these citations are from Benhabib, 2004, p. 219.

– especially financial capitalism – that escape state control, and, thereby, all democratic control. Under the effect of those powers, which resolutely determine the character of global society, there is a good chance that the hopes placed in the international constitutionalisation of human rights will prove to be wishful thinking. Rather than the rights of man being able to overcome the limits of the national figure of democracy, it may be that the tendential denationalisation of law, of which the universalisation of human rights constitutes only a very partial aspect, will have the exact opposite effect. Brunkhorst remarks that the price to pay for the integrated development of global and denationalised economic, political and legal systems may well be democracy itself.[85] While it is difficult to contest that global society is now a reality – in the sense that the life of every individual on the planet is determined by processes that have long been released from national frameworks – it is also clear that this global society produces its own phenomena of exclusion. Nationality is no longer the only criterion, nor even the discriminating criterion between the included and the excluded. No doubt in many countries the lack of proper documentation is equivalent to a 'form of civil death'.[86] But in the various ghettoes that are being produced by global society, nationals do coexist with 'foreigners'. The status of foreigners, on which migration policies essentially inspired by demagoguery focalise public attention, is but the most visible aspect of an exclusion whose decisive factor is not nationality.

The second weakness of the globalist solution to the aporia raised by Arendt resides in the use of the 'as if' argument. As can already be seen in Kant, the latter merely covers over the gap between the body politic and the real people, without ever eliminating it. Indeed, this argument relies on the benevolence of rulers and legislators – a benevolence that can be constrained by the pressure of supranational legal or political bodies, but that does not release the subject from the status of *protégé*. Brunkhorst once quoted a highly pertinent remark by J. H. H. Weiler that vividly expresses the fundamental inadequacy of this status, which is not to be confused with that of citizen: 'You could create rights and afford judicial remedies to slaves. The ability to go to court to enjoy a right bestowed on you by the pleasure of others does not emancipate you, does not make you a citizen. Long before women and Jews were made citizens they enjoyed direct effect'.[87] This ultimately highly restrictive conception of democracy, in which the real autonomy of action of the political subject is erased – as if it mattered little – is the paradoxical outcome of the

---

[85]   See Brunkhorst, 'Ist die Solidarität der Bürgergesellschaft globalisierbar?', in Brunkhorst, 2000, p. 284, and also 2005.
[86]   Benhabib, 2004, p. 215.
[87]   Brunkhorst, 2005, p. 172. This quote is from a text by J. H. H. Weiler, 'To be a European citizen – Eros and civilization' (*Journal of European Public Policy*, 1997, 4, pp. 495–519), p. 503.

literal interpretation of self-legislation. It follows from the continuous thread that some have attempted to weave between the notion of popular sovereignty and the legal arrangements that organised, in the democratic states of the twentieth century, the participation of citizens in the regular functioning of institutions. Democracy presents itself as membership in a community – the nation, or humanity understood as a collective – and this membership is posited as the condition for access to individual rights. In other words: the individual possesses rights only insofar as they are granted to him, whether by a national body or a supranational one.

Chapter 4

Democracy Without *Demos*

What remains or still resists in the deconstructed (or deconstructible) concept of democracy which guides us endlessly? Which orders us not only to engage a deconstruction but to keep the old name? And to deconstruct further in the name of a *democracy* to come? [...] Would it still make sense to speak of democracy when it would no longer be a question (no longer in question as to what is essential or constitutive) of country, nation, even of State or citizen – in other words, *if at least one still keeps to the accepted use of this word*, when it would no longer be a political question?[1]

4.1 DEMOCRACY WITHOUT *DEMOS*: FROM SCHMITT TO KANT

The strictly individualistic logic of subjective rights opens up an entirely different perspective. This is the logic of the declarations of human rights of the revolutionary period, which entrusted, not states or any other instance of power, but men individually or in groups with the task and duty of defending those rights without postulating any form of community membership. Equal freedom – the only *innate* right (to use Kantian terminology) from which derived all the other rights specified in those declarations – could not be founded on community membership, because its affirmation was correlated to the abolition of status differences, namely the elimination of the subordination of rights (the indissoluble rights of man and of the citizen) to a condition of membership.

---

[1]   Derrida, 2005, p. 104.

Human rights activists will naturally object that membership in humanity cannot be put on the same level as particular membership. Yet, the question is precisely whether humanity can be construed as a community in a way that is politically relevant. Formulating this question places us in the compromising company of Carl Schmitt, who not only explicitly asked that question, but also provided a decidedly negative answer to it. Humanity, Schmitt writes in *The Concept of the Political*, 'is not a political concept'.[2] This peremptory statement is an immediate consequence of his agonistic conception of the political whereby the distinction between friend and enemy constitutes the 'specific political distinction', the criterion by which the realm of political action can be identified, in contrast to other realms of action or judgment such as morality, aesthetics, economics, etc. There is politics only where differences are likely to sharpen into antagonisms in which the very existence of opposing parties is at stake.[3] The political world is necessarily a 'pluriverse'.[4] Humanity cannot be a political concept because it has no enemies, at least not on this planet. A world without hostilities, or at the very least without the type of hostilities that can always result in war, is certainly thinkable under the rule of economic and cultural exchange, but the social unity of this world would be comparable to that of 'tenants in a tenement house, customers purchasing gas from the same utility company, or passengers traveling on the same bus'.[5]

The historical background of Schmitt's thesis is well known. The point for him was to denounce the recourse to moral arguments in the political sphere – a denunciation aimed primarily at the provisions of the Treaty of Versailles, which not only enshrined Germany's defeat in World War I, but also attributed to the vanquished nation a 'responsibility' for which it had to pay 'reparations'. While Schmitt's anti-humanism was a reaction to very particular historical circumstances, his critique of the political uses made of the notion of humanity still resonates today with readers who do not necessarily share his agonistic conception of politics, and who are fully aware of his political and ideological trajectory. There is no need to recall the relatively recent events that saw the cynicism of a certain political rhetoric being deployed in the arena of international politics. The latter prevents us from taking at face value the recourse to moral justifications in this domain, and especially the invocation of humanity. Indeed, despite the existence of international institutions, humanity lacks the consistency of a politically organised group, such that anyone can claim to speak and act in its name.

---

2   Schmitt, 1996, p. 55.
3   *Ibid.*, p. 26.
4   *Ibid.*, part 6 (pp. 53–58).
5   *Ibid.*, p. 57.

The fact that Schmitt linked his critique of 'humanist' justifications for war to an agonistic conception of the political – which he did not develop in any way, but simply established as dogma – does not diminish its relevance to the analysis whereby '[w]hen a state fights its political enemy in the name of humanity, it is not a war for the sake of humanity, but a war wherein a particular state seeks to usurp a universal concept against its military opponent'.[6]

The thesis that led Schmitt to reject the political significance of the notion of humanity rests on an equally communitarian conception of the body politic, a conception that is given an extreme form by the criterion of the distinction between friend and enemy. The closure of the Schmittian political community does not tolerate any breach: its borders cannot be 'porous'.[7] This is the reason why the authors who today strive to think democracy in communitarian terms often feel obligated to mention Schmitt's analyses so as to distance themselves from them. One of the ways in which this distance can be established is by giving back to the notion of humanity the political import that Schmitt denied it, thereby making humanity a regulative idea that justifies the opening up of the *demos* to a foreigner viewed not as 'the enemy', but as an other whose otherness is merely provisional. The approach I propose here is radically opposed to this. It seems to me we must concede to Schmitt that humanity 'is not a political concept'; however, the reasons to do so are not his own, but are inspired rather by Kantian positions. This may seem a shocking proposal at first: to suggest that the philosopher of the human Universal could have denied political significance to the concept of humanity is surely at odds with the general use made today of his moral and political work. I must therefore solidly defend this thesis, by imposing on the reader a new detour via an exercise in exegesis.

But first, a brief terminological clarification is in order. One finds in Kant's texts the terms *Humanität*, *Menschheit* and *Menschengattung*. None of these terms appear to correspond to what is called today 'humanity', when it is understood as the superior collective to which all men belong, a membership from which they derive their fundamental rights. The meaning of *Humanität* is easy to establish, and the definition Kant gives to the word is broadly in line with common usage in the German language, while also being more precise. This term,[8] which Kant parallels with the *Humaniora* (Fine Arts), designates for him both the feeling of universal sympathy and the capacity to

---

6   *Ibid.*, p. 54. The passage continues: 'The concept of humanity is an especially useful ideological instrument of imperialist expansion, and in its ethical-humanitarian form it is a specific vehicle of economic imperialism'.
7   Seyla Benhabib, on the contrary, would like borders to be porous.
8   Here I gloss the *Critique of Judgment* §60 (Kant, 1987, pp. 231–32).

communicate universally. This feeling and this capacity together constitute the specifically human sociability. However, sociability (*Geselligkeit*) does not immediately form a political society. It does so only when it takes on a legal character, which presupposes the constitution of a collective body in which constraint enforces compliance with the law. Kant does not consider the possibility that such legalised sociability might extend beyond the confines of a particular people, but he does believe that the art of communication favours the institution of a society – i.e., a state – that combines freedom and constraint, insofar it allows for the circulation of ideas between the most educated classes and the least educated ones. *Menschheit* leads to more confusion, in that while the first confirmed occurrence of the term in the sense of a collective dates back to the second half of the eighteenth century,[9] Kant rarely seems to use the term in this way.[10] In general, *Menschheit* exclusively refers in Kant to a character unique to man, which confers on him the dignity that he alone enjoys among sentient creatures. This character is the moral disposition that attests to man's participation in the realm of the supersensuous, and that justifies that he is the only being 'in the whole of creation' who can be considered an end in itself.[11] Lastly, Kant uses the compound term *Menschengattung*, which I translate as human species rather than humankind, because it concerns what distinguishes man from animals on the level of natural capabilities.[12] Only one of Kant's expressions might correspond to the concept of humanity understood as a collective, namely '*das ganze menschliche Geschlecht*' (totality of human beings), which is found notably in a passage of the *Religion Within the Boundaries of Mere Reason*, on which I shall now dwell briefly.

This passage is located at the beginning of the first section of the third part of *Religion*. Here, Kant determines the concept of an '*ethico-civil state*' (*ethisches gemeines Wesen*), which relates to the '*ethical state of nature*' in a way similar to how the body politic – i.e., the '*juridico-civil* (political) state*' – relates to the '*juridical state of nature*'.[13] The juridico-civil state and

---

9   See *Geschichtliche Grundbegriffe*, vol. 3 (Brunner *et al.*, 1982, p. 1087*ff*).

10   Note, however, the one occurrence towards the end of the third part of 'Theory and Practice', in which Kant evokes the end of man as an entire species ([*der*] *Zweck der Menschheit im Ganzen ihrer Gattung* (Kant, 1991a, p. 91; 1973, p. 112). Yet here Kant merely uses Mendelssohn's terminology, whose thesis he is discussing. He himself prefers speaking of the 'whole of mankind' (*das menschliche Geschlecht im ganzen*) in the rest of the text. The core of his critique consists in saying that it is only from the point of view of providence that human *nature* can be considered as a moral totality, whereas, on the contrary, 'the schemes of men, on the other hand, begin with the parts, and frequently get no further than them. For the whole is too great for men to encompass; while they can reach it with their ideas, they cannot actively influence it' (1991a, pp. 87 and 90).

11   See *The Conflict of the Faculties*, I.1, General Remark (Kant, 1979, p. 85*ff*); and Critique of Practical Reason, I.3 (Kant, 1997, p. 74).

12   See occurrences of the expression in 'Idea for a Universal History from a Cosmopolitan Point of View' (Kant, 1963).

13   The '*juridical state of nature*' is a condition marked by the absence of laws. It is therefore a non-juridical state.

the ethico-civil state are opposed to each other as are public laws and laws of virtue, legality and morality, or even external laws – which rely on coercion – and internal laws – which entail self-constraint. It is worth noting that it is concerning the ethico-civil state that Kant evokes 'the totality of human beings'. Indeed, only this state has as its vocation to embrace all people beyond national differences: unlike legal duties, duties of virtue 'concern the totality of human beings', and, for this reason, 'the concept of an ethical community [ethico-civil state] always refers to the ideal of a totality of human beings, and in this it distinguishes itself from the concept of a political community'.[14] On the scale of what men can achieve, the ethical community takes the form of multiple institutions (*Anstalt*) – i.e., particular churches that organise communities of believers under the direction of leaders. But these are only imperfect representations, commensurate with human imperfection, of the invisible church. In contrast to a body politic, the ethico-civil state 'strives after the consensus of all human beings (indeed, of all finite rational beings)'. The parallelism between the body politic and the ethico-civil state – which founds the second on an injunction similar to that which justifies the first, namely that one ought to leave the ethical state of nature, just as one ought to leave the juridical state of nature (*exeundum esse e statu naturali*) – spans a sizeable difference. The body politic falls under the laws of men, whereas the ethico-civil state falls under divine commands. Only the latter is destined to embrace humanity, understood as the totality of human beings.

But what meaning should one give to Kantian cosmopolitanism under these conditions? In the previous chapter, I mentioned the texts upon which the many authors who invoke Kant's authority so as to give a normative foundation to globalised politics generally draw, and I discussed what Kant meant by the 'right of world citizenship'. Here, I shall focus on a hitherto neglected aspect of Kant's justification of this right: the argument of the sphericity of the earth. The right to visit, he wrote, is the right of all men to 'associate [...] by virtue of their common ownership of the earth's surface; for since the earth is a globe, they cannot scatter themselves infinitely, but must, finally, tolerate living in close proximity, because originally no one had a greater right to any region of the earth than anyone else'.[15]

Seyla Benhabib believes that Kant based the right of sojourn on two different premises: the capacity of all human beings to associate on the one hand, and common possession of the earth on the other.[16] The second premise seems to her unnecessary, and even difficult to understand when it is supplemented by the factual argument of the sphericity of the earth, which she suspects is

14   Kant, 1998, p. 107.
15   Kant, 1983, p. 118.
16   Benhabib, 2004, pp. 29–30.

a 'naturalistic fallacy'.[17] This argument, which puzzled many commentators of Kant's political work, is in fact central to the thesis he defended here. It becomes intelligible, however, when one takes into consideration the radical revision to which Kant subjected the classical theme – inherited from Christianity and developed in various ways by the majority of social contract theorists – of the 'original common possession' of the earth, which was to be reconciled with the justification of private appropriation.[18] Far from seeing in the latter, as did most of his predecessors, a contradiction that had to be resolved one way or another, Kant achieved the tour de force of making the 'original community of land' the very foundation of the right of possession.[19] The key to this tour de force consisted in interpreting the original community of land as an idea of reason 'that has objective (rightfully practical) reality' (DR, § 6) – i.e., as a rational practical postulate that lets every individual appropriate what is not already the possession of another. The main function of the idea of the original community of land, thus understood, was to establish the legal impossibility of a *res nullius*, and hence to open the possibility of appropriation – a possibility that is given to all, not collectively, but distributively. The common in the original community of land was reduced to the license given to all, i.e., to every individual, to declare as his own a portion of the land that no one else had appropriated before.[20]

This being admitted, what role does the reference to the sphericity of the earth play in the order of reasons of Kant's legal and political thought? Of course, it is not this form that matters, but what it implies: the finitude of appropriable land, from which derives men's need to associate together. 'If its surface [of the earth] were an unbounded plane', Kant remarks in paragraph §13 of the *Doctrine of Right*, 'people could be so dispersed on it that they would not come into any community with one another, and community would not then be a necessary result of their existence on the earth'.[21] Let us properly heed these words, which are echoed in the aforementioned passage of the essay on *Perpetual Peace* where Kant defines the right to visit

---

[17]   *Ibid.*, p. 33; 'The claim to the "common possession of the earth" does disappointingly little to explicate the basisof cosmopolitan right', p. 31. For a discussion of the argument of the sphericity of the earth, see *ibid.*, p. 32*ff*, where Benhabib cites and examines the interpretation of Katrin Flikschuh (*Kant and Modern Political Philosophy*, Cambridge University Press, Cambridge, UK, 2000), who, contrary to Benhabib, assigns fundamental importance to this aspect of Kant's argumentation, as I myself propose to do.

[18]   On the interpretations of the Thomist theme of natural common property, see Tully, 1982.

[19]   See paragraphs 6, 11, 13 and 16 of *Doctrine of Right*, cited as *DR* in the text when mention of the page is not necessary.

[20]   See Durkheim, whose interpretation of the Kantian theory of property is one of the most pertinent I have had the chance to read (Durkheim, 1992, p. 133): 'The right that mankind has to the earth implies the right of individuals to occupy limited parts of the earth's surface'. To be more specific, the first right does not imply the second; it is confused with it.

[21]   *DR* §13 (Kant, 1996, p. 50).

as the only concrete expression of world citizenship. If men must come into community with one another, it is only because they are forced to coexist in limited habitable spaces. The sociability of men is not a moral disposition that might be built upon in the hope of escaping the national confines of politics towards a global horizon. It is merely the product – one devoid of signification from the perspective of legal and political rationality – of an empirical fact.[22] It is for a purely factual reason that men must live together, which is to say, that they must *tolerate* one another. Here we find, at the heart of Kantian cosmopolitanism, the fundamental individualism of his conception of rights. In the *Doctrine of Right*, this conception entails the precedence of private law over public law, and justifies seeing in this *Doctrine* the most coherent formulation of a theory of subjective rights, understood as rights pertaining to the individual *as such*.

Again, there is only one fundamental right: the freedom of the individual, namely the individual's independence from being constrained by another's choice. And this freedom is actualised in the possibility of declaring something external to be yours or mine, that is, in possession. As regards the land, the right of possession is a right to settle *where there is space left*. The right of possession is in Kant a right of the first occupant (*DR*, § 9). As I noted earlier, it is by virtue of this principle – which is implied in the restricted interpretation of the right of world citizenship as a simple right to visit – that Kant condemned the predatory practices of European colonisation. And it is this same principle that led him to consider it wise politics on the part of China and Japan to impose drastic restrictions on the access of European merchants to their territories in the eighteenth century. However, Kant did not condemn international exchange – a condemnation that was, after all, a potential corollary of this same principle, though it would have been extreme and out of step with the general evolution of the societies of his time. The reason for this is that he saw civilising virtues in global trade, which he believed favoured peace among nations.[23] Peace is also the central objective of Kant's project of a league of nations (*Völkerbund, foedus Amphictyonum*), which is evoked in particular in the Seventh Thesis of the 'Idea for a Universal History from a Cosmopolitan Point of View'. The task of this league of nations would be to provide a legal framework for relations between states, in order to facilitate the peaceful resolution of conflicts that would inevitably arise between them. Kant's text makes sufficiently clear that this is not a temporary structure that would anticipate a global federal state, but a condition that would allow for

---

[22] Things are different from the perspective of moral rationality: sociability figures among the duties of virtue. The few lines Kant devotes to sociability (Doctrine of Virtue, §48) make clear that it implies the building of 'social' relations, and not the organisation of a common world.

[23] See supra, p. 81.

the full resolution of *the greatest problem* the human race has to solve at the political level, namely that of building a universal civic society that would administer the law within a national framework.[24] Peace between nations is but the condition for fulfilling this ultimate political task, which means that the universal civic constitution is only a means to an end. To be sure, it produces something analogous to a 'civic commonwealth',[25] but something analogous only. The right of world citizenship can be interpreted as the right pertaining to men (and states) as 'citizens of a universal nation of men',[26] but this universal nation exists only in the supersensuous world.[27]

Humanity understood as a collective – as a totality of human beings – definitely has no reality other than a supersensuous one. Kantian cosmopolitanism combines two elements: the requirement for a league of nations favouring peace, and the individual's right to visit all countries. These two elements are related because they derive from the same principle, namely the right to possess. This right entails the protection of original occupants, and hence the closure of national territories, and, at the same time, the right of every individual to settle down anywhere on earth. No doubt the generalisation of the republican form of political power is a factor conducive to the juridification of relations between states. But the *foedum Amphictyonis* is not a first step towards the abolition of national sovereignties, and Kant did not expect this league to force states to respect the fundamental rights of their citizens. Though Kant rejected the right to resist (it being in reality the right to sedition, since Kant otherwise defended the legitimacy of public criticism, which can be seen as a 'soft' form of the right to resist), he was true to the spirit of the rights declarations of the French and American revolutions in that he did not subject human rights to any membership condition, and that he did not conceive those rights as deriving from a granted status. Whereas Carl Schmitt denied the political significance of humanity in the name of a conception of the political that was radically communitarian, Kant developed an individualistic conception of the subject of right that prevented him from holding such a view. In what sense can humanity be invoked to justify equal rights for all?

---

[24] See 'Idea for a Universal History from a Cosmopolitan Point of View', beginning of the Fifth Thesis (Kant, 1963, p. 16). Kant does not specify whether this universal civic society that administers the law is limited to a national framework. But the Seventh Thesis clearly shows that the juridification of relations between states is only a means for the resolution of the 'greatest problem' the human race has to solve, which cannot therefore be this international juridification itself.

[25] See Seventh Thesis (Kant, 1963, p. 19), end of the second paragraph: '*ein Zustand [...], der, einem bürgerlichen gemeinen Wesen ähnlich*'. It seems to me that one should avoid translating 'gemeines Wesen' by community.

[26] In German, 'als Bürger eines allgemeinen Menschenstaats' (*On Perpetual Peace*, Second Section, note 1: Kant, 1983, p.112).

[27] In German, 'als Staatsbürger einer übersinnlichen Welt' (*On Perpetual Peace,* First Definitive Article, note 1: Kant, 1983, p. 112).

Humanity is what men have in common, but this 'common' should not be interpreted in terms of membership in a community. The human individual does not belong to humanity as he belongs to a family, a tribe, a caste, or a nation-state. Humanity is something that he shares with all beings of his species, which is something altogether different.

4.2 LIBERAL INDIVIDUALISM AND DEMOCRACY

And yet, Kant was not a democrat. Making use of his work to reinterpret the meaning of modern democracy by detaching it from all conditions of community membership might be construed as a mark of indifference to the democratic experience of the last two centuries, in which collective identities played a far more important role than did the theoretical presuppositions of subjective rights. Denying the essential contribution of collective subjects, such as nation and class, to the modern understanding of democracy might seem to show a lack of historical sense. As I noted earlier, struggles for political rights – such as those waged by men who were excluded via property qualifications, by blacks in the United States, or by women in Western nations throughout the nineteenth and twentieth centuries and in many countries still today – have been primarily motivated by a demand for the recognition of full membership in the nation of citizens. There is little doubt that the link so naturally established today between democracy and the existence of a democratic community owes far more to the memory and the repetition of those struggles than to the theorem of self-legislation. However, the question remains as to whether these group solidarities, which are generally forged in critical circumstances, can preserve against the test of time and institutionalisation (whether in the form of a nation-state, a trade union, a political party, or any other structure designed to last) the emotional pathos that characterises them, and that might be consubstantial with genuine solidarity. I shall return to this point shortly.[28]

But first, I must say a few words concerning the apparent paradox presented by a conception of democracy that invokes, at least in part, the authority of Kant. Recognising the irreducible difference of power, insisting on freedom understood as autonomy, relating rights to individual subjectivity: such *topoi* traditionally belong to liberalism's panoply of arguments. They also pertain to the Kantian reference. And yet, there is liberalism and liberalism. On the one hand, there is economic liberalism, which strives, above all else, to establish a justification for private property. In its pure form, this liberalism

---

[28] See infra, IV.3. Solidarities in Struggle: The Impossible 'Routinisation'.

accepts without scruple all that ensues from the latter: the pursuit of profit, the unequal distribution of wealth, and the control by a handful of people over what constitutes (whether we like it or not) the core of social life in capitalist societies, namely the means of commodity production, at the cost of a radical dispossession of large segments of the world's populations. More frequently, however, it grants a few fringe benefits aimed at maintaining social cohesion, the disruption of which affects its operation and can even jeopardise its own continuation. On the other hand, there is political liberalism, which, while clearly linked to economic liberalism, it is ludicrous to reduce to the latter, for instance, by claiming that it merely functions as its ideological cover. Here, too, one ought to distinguish variants, which range from safeguarding the independence of the *individual* against interference from the state or any instance presumed to represent the collective, to valuing the autonomy of the *subject*, which entails his adherence to rational law. The first often finds theoretical justification in eighteenth century Scottish philosophy, whereas the second more readily privileges the Kantian reference. Given that the positions I defend here are closer to the Kantian ones, I must specify exactly how I differ from them.

The justification of private property is a central aspect in the first part of Kant's *Doctrine of Right*. It is symptomatic, however, that economic liberalism is unsure of what to do with Kant. Its supporters likely suspect that the autonomy of the subject involves far more than the freedom of enterprise and trade, and that thinking this autonomy in its very foundation might reveal it to profoundly contradict the utilitarian anthropology that constitutes, more or less, the common core of all variants of economic liberalism. As for political liberalism, there prevails among its proponents a conventional and bland reading of Kantian philosophy, one that essentially retains the obligation to obey the law, together with its correlate: the condemnation of the right to resist.[29] That Kant does not endorse all forms of positive law is obvious. The rational subject cannot question the legitimacy of power, but he can contest its mode of exercise, so long as he does so through public criticism in newspapers and scholarly publications. Kantian reformism gambles on the wisdom of enlightened princes who can heed critiques formulated in the public sphere. However, this gamble is nothing other than a gamble. Least of all is it an expression of confidence in the integrity and the enlightenment of political leaders in general. The gap between what ought to be and reality remains the

---

[29]   The work of Lucien Jaume, *La liberté et la loi* (2000), is a perfect example of this reading, though this does not detract from the interest of his analyses, in particular that of the crisis of the universal in the post-Kantian period. However, the importance that Jaume assigns to Kant's trust in the functioning of liberal societies (see p. 257*ff*) prevents him from grasping what I emphasise later: the crucial role played by disobedience in the constitution of the Kantian legal-political subject.

stumbling block of all Kant-inspired liberalism, which must simultaneously condemn disobedience to positive law and recognise there is no guarantee that the latter is rational. Ultimately, what this liberalism refuses to think is the logic of power. The shortcomings of legal and institutional positivity with respect to the rational norm are attributed to the imperfection of men – in this case of leaders – rather than to what is a constitutive dimension of politics, namely domination. In the ideal world of the law, those who govern, legislate and take decisions just as the governed would if they were driven by reason.

This reading of Kant centred on obedience to rational law obfuscates another dimension of his concept of freedom, prompting me to define the scope of his legalism. No doubt it is impossible to legally justify the resistance of subjects to power. This is the reason why the ethical and political significance of the French Revolution can be established only from the outside: via the enthusiastic interest it aroused among the people of Europe, and not the motivations of its actors.[30] But this leads to justifying the revolution *post facto* on the level of mankind's history of moral progress, which is the history of freedom. When browsing through Kant's texts on the Enlightenment, culture, or history, one can only be struck by the recurrence of the theme of man's release from tutelage: the tutelage of nature, but also that of masters of all kinds (priests or political leaders, whether well- or ill-intentioned) who dictate to men the rules by which they shall live. Kant advocates release from instinct – from the 'voice of God' clearly, which is nothing other than the 'call of nature'[31] – as well as emancipation from spiritual advisors, doctors (experts!), and rulers, not just those who oppress, but also the benevolent governments that treat their subjects like children.[32] The definition Kant gives of the Enlightenment in the opuscule commented several times by Foucault – 'man's emergence from his self-incurred immaturity'[33] – is probably the most explicit formulation of his idea of freedom. The free subject is a subject who frees himself by rejecting tutelage, which can only occur in the movement of a history wherein disobedience, to God's prohibitions but also to the laws of despotic powers, plays a decisive role. It may be, as some interpreters argue, that there is in Kant no 'philosophy of history' of the type that Hegel explicitly placed at the heart of the system of objective spirit – namely, a scheme which makes it possible to interpret the chronological succession of different societies and states as different stages in the development of the institutions of freedom. And yet, there is in Kant a tense effort to think the

---

[30] See *The Conflict of the Faculties* (Kant, 1979, p. 141*ff*).
[31] See 'Conjectures on the Beginning of Human History' (Kant, 1991b, p. 223).
[32] See What is Enlightenment? (Kant, 2009, pp. 1–2).
[33] *Ibid.*, p. 1.

possibility of human historicity, which, in his view, can only be that of the becoming-subject.

'Immature' are the men who, whether out of laziness or cowardice, accommodate themselves to tutelage – a state in which the dominant have a vested interest in keeping them. If man were merely a being of needs, he would be perfectly content with the Eden of the beginnings of creation, or, failing that, with life under a paternal government sufficiently concerned about his wellbeing. But man is not merely that: he is neither the uncultured animal of the early (conjectural) history of the human species, nor the 'domestic animal'[34] that his guardians turn him into under the pretext of ensuring his wellbeing. However, if he is more than that, it is because he decides to be so – because he uses his 'ability to choose his own way of life without being tied to any single one like the other animals'.[35] This inaugural act of human history, which initially tore man away from the realm of nature, must be continually renewed against the subjection imposed by some men on others. Only this act and its repetitions make history, because they constitute points of no return. Beyond the vagaries of event history – its ups and downs, its advances and regressions – such an act leaves its mark on the memory of men, who can henceforth recall and repeat it in other circumstances. As Kant observed in 1798, no matter how chaotic its course and uncertain its results, a phenomenon like the French Revolution '*is not to be forgotten*, because it has revealed a tendency and faculty in human nature for improvement such that no politician, affecting wisdom, might have conjured out of the course of things hitherto existing'.[36] For eighteenth century humanity, the French Revolution had the same signification as Adam's transgressive gesture at the time of creation. Indeed, Kant said of this act: 'Now that he had tasted this state of freedom, it was impossible for him to return to a state of servitude under the rule of instinct'.[37]

Freedom cannot be granted to men, not even by an enlightened government (was not the government of God enlightened?). Obedience to the law of the state is certainly necessary for men to live together in peace; yet this obedience, which is the cornerstone of the legal conception of the state (that presented in the *Doctrine of Right*), is not the last word of Kant's theory of political freedom. Neither does it suffice to acknowledge the place Kant gives to public criticism – of the laws, beliefs and dispositions of all kinds that are imposed by instances of tutelage (church, army, state) – to exhaust the ultimate implications of his conception of freedom in society. It is not from the goodwill of rulers that men can expect such freedom. If that were

---

[34]   *Ibid.*, p. 2.
[35]   'Conjectures on the Beginning of Human History' (Kant, 1991b, p. 224).
[36]   *The Conflict of the Faculties* (Kant, 1979, p. 159).
[37]   'Conjectures on the Beginning of Human History' (Kant, 1991b, p. 224).

the case, men's situation would not be very different from that of those who expect these same governments to ensure their wellbeing. Though it is legally unjustifiable, the challenge to established powers, and even the transgression of instituted orders, is a moment as essential for the formation of the free subject as is the recognition of law's virtues, in the same way that disorder is necessary for the development of culture. 'Man wishes concord; but Nature knows better what is good for the race: She wills discord'.[38] What Kant calls here nature and elsewhere providence is the vanishing point of a theory of freedom, which cannot be fully determined within the framework of a political theory whose primary concern is to ensure public order.

The Kantianism of political liberalism sticks to the letter of Kant's texts that bear on politics – the rule of law, the obligation to obey power, freedom of criticism exercised in carefully circumscribed places, the choice of reformism against revolutionary subversion, Utopia converted into a regulative idea, or the league of nations guaranteeing world peace. Of Kant's contribution to the understanding of modern political subjectivity, only the mastery of passions and the subordination of desire to reason are emphasised, because they allow for a critique of utilitarian liberalism. And yet, a more careful reading of the texts on history and culture suffices to trouble this overly proper Kantianism. Kant recognised before Hegel the positivity of the negative in many of his figures, for instance, the figure of disobedience to instituted orders (as I have just mentioned), but also those of ambition, of the instinct of domination and greed, and even of war – which he presented as the equivalent, at the level of relations between nations, of the 'unsocial sociability' of men in the formation of each particular civil society.[39] According to Kant, it is not culture that should be viewed as the final aim of the world's existence, but morality. Yet morality presupposes culture, which progresses only through frictions and antagonisms between men, forcing them to develop their talents. Unless one considers that modern democratic states have reached the end of the history of culture, it is legitimate to also embrace this aspect of the Kantian legacy, rather than to settle for the bland representation of a society pacified by law – one that would have been realised essentially in the civilised world, such that all there would be left to do is convince its citizens of the virtues of the political system in which they are lucky enough to live, while working to spread its benefits to other parts of the world.

Taking into account the place Kant reserves for the negative in human history allows us to see his individualism in a very different light from how it is normally interpreted, and it is doubtful whether liberals are prepared to accept the consequences of this move. It is worth noting that all the figures

---

[38] 'Idea for a Universal History from a Cosmopolitan Point of View' (Kant, 1963, p. 16).
[39] *Ibid.*, p. 15.

of the negative, from radical evil to war through rivalries for domination and wealth, are linked to the becoming-subject. This observation takes us back, via a detour, to the starting point of the *Doctrine of Right*, which is to say, to freedom understood as 'independence from being constrained by another's choice'.[40] In the introduction to the *Doctrine of Right*, Kant says of this freedom that it is an innate right – in truth, the one and only right. In what sense is this right innate? The term cannot refer to one of the natural traits of the human species, i.e., to something that can be observed. That every human individual is independent from constraint by another's choice is obviously not an experiential truth. But is it a rational norm that positive law would be tasked with rendering effective by guaranteeing it? Curiously, Kant does not include this right in the 'rights of men', which are presented in the first part of the *Doctrine of Right* under the title 'Private right', namely those rights whose content is certainly independent from validation by positive law, but that nevertheless require such validation in order to be guaranteed. The latter are 'acquired' rights, and the innateness of freedom is understood in opposition to them. The special fate reserved for this right, which does not fall under the *Doctrine of Right* but is 'put in the prolegomena',[41] seems to me significant: the point is not that innate right does not need to be guaranteed by positive law, but that it *cannot be* guaranteed by it. The right from which derive all the rights that a well-constituted state must guarantee cannot be guaranteed by that state. Freedom, the capacity to have rights that are something other than protections granted by the grace of those in power, has no other guarantee than the individual's desire to release himself from all tutelage.

Thus, the *Doctrine of Right* is constituted on the basis of a repressed negative, which returns to haunt the coherence of its legalism when it addresses the question of citizenship. This negative is the refusal to obey, the rejection of tutelage, including potentially the authority of constituted political powers – a refusal that is necessary for the constitution of the subject, whose duty to obey is then justified by the theory of law. It is this repressed negative which returns in the precariousness of the definition of the citizen I analysed in the previous chapter. 'The only qualification for being a citizen is being fit to vote'[42]; however, being fit to vote is subject to a condition of independence that cannot be granted by an external instance, but must be achieved by the individual himself. The latter must *want* 'to be not just a part of the commonwealth but also a member of it, that is, a part of the commonwealth acting from his own choice in community with others'.[43] Domestics and women

---

[40]   *DR* Introduction, B (Kant, 1996, pp. 30).
[41]   *Ibid.*, p. 31.
[42]   *Ibid.*, p. 91.
[43]   *Ibid.* pp. 91–92.

are deemed immature because they have not expressed that will, which is why their existence 'is, as it were, only inherence': 'They have to be under the direction or protection of other individuals, and so do not possess civil independence'.[44] This is also the reason why the legal freedom and civil equality that are nonetheless granted to them can only be conceded rights. While 'passive' citizens enjoy the *protection* of laws, they are not, strictly speaking, citizens. I leave aside here the case of domestics, which could be examined in a historical light to explain the difference between the relationship that binds the domestic to his employer and that of this same employer to the artisan who accomplishes his task in exchange for a wage.[45] From the perspective of today, the case of women is more interesting. This is because the logic of Kant's argument, if not the letter of his text, leaves open the possibility that women might become subjects of right, provided that they also rise up against the tutelage that men exercise over them. In truth, Kant finds nothing to object to the emancipatory gesture of a human being, whoever he (or she) may be. The 'natural' feminine, about which he merely repeats the conventional ideas of his time and milieu,[46] certainly predisposes women to wallow in the condition of wards – but then the same applies in his view to most men.[47] For women as for men, political capacity or incapacity cannot be founded on natural dispositions, but on the desire for autonomy that is manifested in the rejection of tutelage. If access to full citizenship must remain open to the domestic (through choosing an occupation that allows him to escape his condition), there is no reason of principle that prevents it being open to women as well, so long as these express the will to choose their 'own way of life'.

It is not just what Kant says of women, or the way he takes cognisance of the legal incapacity of domestics without objecting to it, that ought to be viewed as limitations of his political thought attributable to prevailing conditions in the Germany of his time. It is also his cautious reformism, as well as the centrality he assigns, among the rights inferred from human freedom, to private property (which he conceives primarily as possession of the land, though it cannot be reduced to this). The continuing interest of Kant's legal and political theory does not stem from this, but from the fact that he expressed the spirit of the Enlightenment and the revolutionary period, which would continue to resonate in the emancipatory movements of the next two centuries by making the subject's desire for autonomy the ultimate foundation of his

---

[44] *Ibid.*, p. 92.
[45] After discussing the difference between domestics and paid artisans in a note from 'Theory and Practice', Kant ends up admitting that 'it is somewhat difficult to define the qualifications which entitle anyone to claim the status of being his own master' (Kant, 1991a, p. 78).
[46] See *Anthropology* (Kant, 2006, p. 204*ff*).
[47] See *What is Enlightenment?* (Kant, 2009, p. 1).

rights. Therein lies the core of Kant's individualism, which, let us recall, was not conflated with egoism. A passage in *Anthropology* defines as egoistic the man who 'limits all ends to himself', whether to his utility or his happiness. It is significant that Kant opposed to egoism, not altruism or some form of collective solidarity, but *pluralism*, 'that is, the way of thinking in which one is not concerned with oneself as the whole world, but rather regards and conducts oneself as a mere citizen of the world'.[48] In this context, the world does seem to consist of the plurality of human individuals who are obligated to share the earth. Being a citizen of the world means accepting the idea of this necessary sharing, along with the legal regulations that ensue from it. It means accepting the inevitable coexistence of individuals who, because they are all ends in themselves, can claim the same rights. Just that, and nothing more.

4.3 SOLIDARITIES IN STRUGGLE: THE IMPOSSIBLE 'ROUTINISATION'

Rosanvallon once evoked the mobilisations of the people in the street by speaking of the 'revolutionary celebration of the mere emergence of constituent power',[49] as part of a reflection on the plural temporalities of the political. In so doing, he pointed to one of the defining characteristics of the only real phenomenon that can be construed as the presence of the people 'in person'. The highlights of the people's protests create a sense of solidarity, like the outline of a novel community freed of the limitations of known institutional communities. Attempts at organising this community are then regularly made, but they are also rapidly defeated. The community, as it is tested in the 'emergence of constituent power', resists all institutionalisation; it cannot be made to last, lest it be caught in, and hence distorted by, the logics of power and bureaucratisation. Therein lies the irreducibly utopian character of projects of political organisation inspired by inchoate organisations that are conceived in the brotherly enthusiasm of general strikes and insurrectionary movements.

This is not the place to analyse the anthropological dimension of these moments of collective effervescence, which scholars since Durkheim agree have something to do with the sense of the sacred. The social as it is experienced during these episodes marked by the suspension of ordinary time neutralises the problem of domination, as well as the question of rights. Such episodes constantly re-engender the fantasies of a radically new sociability,

---

[48]   *Anthropology* (Kant, 2006, p. 18).
[49]   Rosanvallon, 2000, p. 413.

of unprecedented forms of being together removed from the burdens of daily life, labour discipline, competition and hierarchies, bureaucracy, etc. This is the fantasy of a society founded on a mutual generosity that would not be of the order of assistance or compassion, but would spontaneously follow from the sense of strength that each and everyone derives from immediate participation in a symbiotic collective. May 68 in France symbolised for a generation that breach in the social and political order of daily life, which the explanations of sociologists and political scientists are unable to account for. More than all the 'scientific' analyses of its significance (or insignificance), Maurice Blanchot captured the essence of the event. What was affirmed in May 68, he wrote in *The Unavowable Community*, was an 'explosive communication', 'the opening that gave permission to everyone, without distinction of class, age, sex or culture, to mix with the first comer as if with an already loved being, precisely because he was the unknown-familiar'.[50] This singular communication, without project, was 'an incomparable form of society that remained elusive, that was not meant to survive, to set itself up, not even via the multiple "committees" simulating a disordered-order, an imprecise specialisation'.[51] Blanchot revealed in those few words the secret of this exceptional sociability – the reason why it cannot allow for thinking politics. The people is present in person only when it presents itself as a group of individuals who refuse to take power. It is present only when it presents itself as powerless, not because it lacks force, but because it is willingly powerless since it refuses to take a form which would confer on it a certain duration. To remain amorphous, to be ephemeral, to affirm oneself as powerless (*to do nothing*): These are three aspects of a single reality, the paradoxical reality of the unrealisable community, of the utopian community. Blanchot sees in the Charonne protest the expression of the limitless power of the multitude, and, in the smooth dissolution of that protest, the illustration of the unwritten rules of the only community to escape the perversions of power:

> It must not last, it must have no part in any kind of duration. That was understood on that exceptional day: Nobody had to give the order to disband. Dispersal happened out of the same necessity that had gathered the innumerable. Separation was instantaneous, without any remainder, without any of those nostalgic sequels that alter the true demonstration by pretending to carry on as combat groups. The people are not like that. They are there, then they are no longer there; they ignore the structure that could stabilise them. Presence and absence, if not merged, at least exchange themselves virtually.[52]

---

[50] Blanchot, 1988, pp. 29–30.
[51] *Ibid.*, p. 30.
[52] *Ibid.*, pp. 32–33.

The Charonne protest as interpreted by Blanchot is, however, a limit case. The revolutionary exception generally lasts a little longer than the time of protest; hence, the insurgent people implements more or less formalised forms of organisation. If the established institutions appear sufficiently fragile to suggest a power vacuum, what is at first merely the organisation of struggles is converted in the revolutionary imagination into elementary structures of a new kind of administration, which is likely to take on the technical tasks previously fulfilled by the now ineffective power. These are the chosen moments of dreams of direct democracy, of an administration without domination, to use Weber's expression. Neither the difficulties that necessarily confront the extension of this organisation beyond the assemblies wherein 'all' can be present *in person*, nor the power games that rapidly emerge in revolutionary collectives as elsewhere, are enough to dispel such dreams. Theory has relayed the lived experiences of actors – from Marx who, in *The Civil War in France*, described the Paris Commune of 1871 as the positive form of a 'government of the people by the people', as a state centralisation without bureaucracy and as a very 'possible Communism', to Lenin who drew on Marx's text to interpret the Soviet movement during the Russian revolutions of 1905 and 1917. The 1871 Commune, the Russian Soviets and the German *Arbeiter und Soldatenräte* of 1918–1919 (and in particular the very brief Bavarian Soviet Republic of autumn 1919) became the classical references of the Councilist tradition. To these were added, in the later part of the twentieth century, the Hungarian Revolution of 1956 as well as a few experiments in workers' autonomy, notably in France and Italy in the 1970s.

In the final chapter of her essay *On Revolution*,[53] Hannah Arendt revisits those great moments of revolutionary creativity by interpreting them in light of Jefferson's late writings, which stressed the importance of local municipalities ('townships') for keeping alive, over the long term, the spirit of freedom of the revolutionary period. Via this reference to Jefferson, Arendt establishes a link between the spirit of freedom (which she sometimes names the revolutionary spirit, while also specifying that it is a spirit of foundation, not of subversion) and the federal system. Her praise of 'revolutionary societies' is thus tied to another central theme of her political thought: the thesis of the superiority of the American political system and of the American revolutionary tradition (which she claims is unrecognised) over those of European states. France fully exemplifies in her view the European political system and the tradition that corresponds to it: a Jacobin centralism that reinstates in a new guise the centralism of absolute monarchy, and that finds its theoretical justification in the Rousseauian concept of a general will which excludes plu-

---

[53] See Arendt, 1990.

rality and the confrontation of opinions. For Arendt, the mistake and even the fault of revolutionary theorists – with the exception of Marx's *Civil War in France* and Lenin's *State and Revolution*, penned in the heat of the moment in reaction to an event that these theorists had not foreseen and could not have foreseen – lay in seeing, in these bodies of popular self-organisation, merely temporary phenomena that could help revolutionary parties seize power, but that were destined to disappear after those parties' victories. That the revolutionary societies of the French Revolution, the Commune of 1871, and the Russian Soviets of 1905 and 1917 outlined a new form of government that was incompatible with the domination of any type of party had to be forgotten. The revolutionary leaders worked on extinguishing that memory, crushing by brute force when necessary the organisations of the people that did not die their own death.

The history of these spontaneous forms of popular government is strange and sad, notes Arendt. It is the history of a memoryless repetition of previous experiments, and of the repetition of failure. To explain this recurrent failure, Arendt needs culprits. Both the Kronstadt episode and the suppression of the 1956 Hungarian Revolution serve her purpose, which is to assign responsibility for these failures to the revolutionary parties themselves. Arendt does not question the intentions of the leaders of those parties. She does not accuse them of having pursued private ends while hypocritically pretending to be working for the good of the people. Her critique is more profound: it is aimed at the conceptions of power and politics that these leaders held and shared, whatever they may have thought, with the leaders of the regimes against which they fought. 'Firmly anchored in the tradition of the nation-state, they conceived of revolution as a means to seize power, and they identified power with the monopoly of the means of violence'.[54] Behind Arendt's critique of the partisan approach to politics (i.e., the idea that politics entails competition for power between parties representing opposing social interests) lies a rejection of Weber's definitions of state and politics, which she elucidates in her essay *On Violence*.[55] This essay cites Weber, alongside Bertrand de Jouvenel, to identify the confusion between power and domination that Arendt seeks to unravel by providing her own definitions of power, force, authority and violence. Weber characterised the state as the monopoly of the legitimate use of physical force, and proposed that politics be understood as the fact of 'striving to share power or striving to influence the distribution of power, either among states or among groups within a state'.[56] Politics for Arendt does consist of participation in power, but in a power that cannot be distributed and

---

[54]   *Ibid.*, 1990, p. 256.
[55]   Arendt, 1970, p. 36*ff*.
[56]   Weber, 2009, p. 78.

must not be influenced in any way. In her view, the new form of government that took shape in the Councilist organisation was such that it allowed, in principle, everyone to participate equally, and individually, in public affairs. Arendt does not deny that this is the ancient ideal of the citizen of the *polis*, he who can command and obey, with all that it presupposes and implies: the exclusion of the social – i.e., of questions of allocation and distribution of economic goods – outside the field of politics, and elitism. Arendt recognises this elitism in the very last pages of *On Revolution*, while also refusing to subscribe to an oligarchic conception of government, which is to say, to the idea that the essence of politics lies in rulership and that the dominant political passion is the passion to rule or to govern.[57] The fact remains that, for Arendt, political freedom is in practice reserved for a few, even though politics concerns all citizens. The political elite as she conceives it is composed of individuals in public roles who were neither nominated from above, nor supported from below. Their claims to these titles rest solely on their passion for public happiness and freedom, and on their competencies to serve these ends. Surprisingly, Arendt fails to notice that these claims correspond exactly to the ones made by most political leaders, and that consequently they do not help to distinguish between the virtuosos of freedom and the lovers of power. Worse still, by establishing an insurmountable barrier between the space of necessity – to which economic issues and, more generally, administrative problems pertain – and that of politics rightly understood, she sidesteps all the difficulties of institutionalising political freedom, to the point of arguing, against all likelihood, that those who are excluded from politics are so by their own fault.[58] Free governments, she claims, should not perform administrative tasks, and it was precisely the great mistake of the revolutionary councils to have felt obligated to do so; because of this, they were partly responsible for the failure of their efforts. Here one might be tempted to believe that, just this once, Arendt has joined Weber, who also distinguished true politics from simple administration. But Weber also considered that there is no politics without administration, whereas Arendt is so anxious to purify the concept of politics of all that might, directly or indirectly, be connected to the sphere of 'simple living' (economics and the social) that we no longer know what might be the object around which opinions confront one another in the sphere of action. What she tells us of the possible institutional forms

---

[57] Arendt, 1990, p. 276. Here, too, Arendt appears to be quoting Weber. Though his name is not mentioned in this passage, it is fairly obvious that the definitions of politics and power found in the first pages of *Politik als Beruf* (*Politics as a Vocation*) are for Arendt the paradigmatic expression of what she calls 'our whole tradition of political thought'.

[58] See *ibid.*, p. 280.

of a politics freed of domination is in the end no more precise, and hence no more convincing, than Marx's indications concerning the Paris Commune.

The question Arendt raises is not that of the community, but that of power – not a power exercised by some men over others, but a power emanating from the joint action of individuals who are able to form and articulate opinions specific to each person, to confront these opinions, and to get on with each other despite their differences. The resistance of differences (which Rousseau wished to eliminate) is essential to the existence of public space as a space of expression of individual freedom. The lessons Arendt draws from the exceptional solidarity of revolutionary episodes are the opposite of the dreams of collective fusion that these same episodes inspired in others. And yet, the crux of the problem is the same: it concerns the possibility or impossibility of building lasting institutions out of this exceptional sociability without stifling the ethos – whether of the community or of freedom – that gives it its specific character. Arendt avoids directly confronting this problem by making the exceptionality of the forms of free government a question of space rather than time. 'Freedom', she writes, 'wherever it existed as a tangible reality, has always been spatially limited'.[59] The elite character of these governments stems, in her view, from the fact that they can only survive as islands of freedom in a surrounding sea of necessity.[60] It is doubtful, however, whether these islands are unaffected by what she calls 'necessity', which is to say, the everyday life of men in society that Weber once characterised as the 'site of economic considerations'. The only thing Arendt retains from Weber is the identification – inadmissible in her eyes – of power with domination. She seems uninterested in his sociology of religion. The latter would have enlightened her as to some fundamental presuppositions of Weberian politics, which precisely concern its temporal structures. Weber did not ignore the breaks in the continuum of everyday administration, though he understood them via the figure of the charismatic leader rather than that of popular revolutions. According to Weber, a key aspect of charisma – whether religious or political (and it is sometimes both at once) – is its anti-economic character, which distinguishes it from the two great powers that determine the historicity of human societies: tradition and rationalisation. In its pure form, charisma is 'specifically foreign to economic considerations'.[61] Connected to this is the fact that it can present itself in such purity only *in statu nascendi*. The charismatic leader or prophet finds himself surrounded by an emotional community of warriors, followers, or disciples, who draw their resources either from gifts, from begging, or from (violent or peaceful) extortion – all unsystematic

---

[59]   *Ibid.*, p. 275.
[60]   *Ibid.*, p. 276.
[61]   Weber, 1976, p. 142 (in English: Weber, 1978, p. 244).

and irregular types of income. Thus charismatic communities can only be exceptional configurations; more specifically, to use Weber's very exact terminology (which matters to my argument), they are extra-ordinary (*ausseralltäglich*). As charisma gradually slips into lasting structures of collective action, it is subject to a process of 'routinisation' (*Veralltäglichung*), which goes hand in hand with a fall in the importance of individual action. In short, charisma, which constitutes for Weber the paradigm of the revolutionary exception, is fundamentally averse to institutionalisation. '[I]n fact, it is the strongest anti-economic force [*Unwirtschaflichkeit*], even when it is after material possessions, as in the case of the charismatic warrior. For charisma is by nature not a continuous institution, but in its pure type the very opposite'.[62]

Of course, charisma presupposes a charismatic figure, an individual who stands out from the mass of ordinary men, and whose disciples or companions are not on an equal footing with him. In so far as it is a type of domination, it seems questionable to assimilate it to revolutionary communities or associations, if we make the absence of domination the characteristic trait of the latter. The difference, however, seems secondary to the crux of the problem, which is that of the revolutionary exception and of the conditions of its sustainability. Weber himself identified the link between charisma and the communist ideal – not the 'scientific' communism of Marxism, which, by proposing to reconstruct sociability on the basis of a rational organisation of production, perpetuated rather than subverted the logic of the capitalist world,[63] but its precedents in the history of the warrior and religious communities of the great civilisations. Next to the household, Weber notes, charisma is the 'second important historical representative of communism'.[64] In its (familial and generally patriarchal) household variant, communism did shape the structure of everyday life. The same cannot be said of that communism based on the 'extraordinary foundation of charismatic belief', which prevailed in the warriors' organisations (Weber cites the pirate states of the Ligurian islands and the Islamic state of the caliph Omar) or the religious orders of Christianity and Japanese Buddhism. Such communism always perceives daily economic concerns as a threat, and it can only last as long as it keeps these concerns at bay, that is, as long (and as briefly) as the exception – the danger shared on the battlefield, or the bond of love between disciples of the prophet indifferent to the world around them – endures. If charisma founds communism, communism must, in turn, preserve the purity of charisma against the interference of worldly concerns. The conditions of charisma seal its inevitable fate: the institutional transposition and torsion that transform it until it is replaced by

---

[62] *Ibid.*, p. 656 (in English: Weber, 1978, p. 1113).
[63] On this point, see among other texts the conference on Socialism, in Weber, 2004, pp. 457–91.
[64] Weber, 1976, p. 660 (in English: Weber, 1978, p. 1119). I gloss this passage.

structures adapted to the requirements of everyday life. The followers of the warrior hero create a state; the community gathered around a prophet, an artist or a philosopher becomes a Church, a sect, an academy or a school; the supporters of a new cultural ideal found a party or a press organ; etc.

Among our contemporaries, it is Jacques Rancière who theorised in the most radical fashion the impossible routinisation of the revolutionary exception. Rancière did not, for all that, defend a position of wry scepticism, one which, as he remarks quite pertinently, is often only an avatar of an earlier dogmatism: once revolutionary hope has been abandoned, all there is left to do is accept the world as it is, without ignoring its flaws, but also without maintaining the illusion that these can be remedied. Rancière invites us instead to rethink the concepts of politics and democracy. While this move does not result in any project of social reorganisation, neither does it lead to the conclusion that all political action is vain. Politics, Rancière claims, should not be confused with the state. The latter, to which he also refers as the police, consists in the administration of an assembled community so as to ensure its conservation with as little disruption as possible. Politics rightly understood is precisely not meant to create order and consensus, but is, on the contrary, the expression of a *dissensus*. It is an action without *telos* (and hence with no imaginable institutional end): the repeated questioning of all organised assemblies of men. According to Rancière, if the term democracy is to retain a meaning, it must be dissociated from any representation of an instituted community. Democracy is 'what muddles community, [...] it is the *unthinkable* aspect of community'.[65] In other words, so long as democracy implies the idea of a 'community of equals',[66] it essentially resists institutionalisation and cannot be an organising concept of social experience. Instead, it must persist as that which disrupts all organised social forms. A social organisation, what Rancière calls society, is the product of processes in which the action of men is certainly implicated, but in a manner too complex for the order it constitutes to be attributed to their will. The social order is 'devoid of any immanent reason, [...] it is merely because it is, without any organising purpose'.[67] The idea of an equal society is nonsense, and the 'community of equals' is and can only be an 'inconsistent' community, not because it is ineffective, but because it can never incarnate itself in the structures of a society. Thus, it has no meaning other than that of a regulative idea, which inspires and drives movements of protest against the institutionalised order. The temporality of politics is uneven. It is an always intermittent and transitory

---

[65] Rancière, 1995, p. 67.
[66] 'The Community of Equals' is the title of a very beautiful text included in *On the Shores of Politics* (Rancière, 1995, pp. 63–92).
[67] *Ibid.*, p. 82.

activity, the discontinuous activity of the egalitarian 'exception'[68] that unsettles time and again the fundamentally inegalitarian order of any society. This singular temporality involves the episodic manifestation of the existence of 'the people in person', which does not coincide with any collective identifiable through the usual categories of political theory or the social sciences. The *demos* is embodied in a necessarily fleeting and unpredictable manner, in sporadic eruptions of the egalitarian ideal, in the street, the factory, the university, or even anywhere, via a forced-entry – violent in the sense that it is generally illegal or at the borders of legality – by which beings excluded from the institutionalised political sphere break into a place whose existence depends on their exclusion.

Rancière's 'community of equals' has little to do with what we ordinarily mean by community. As he himself points out, it is not 'proper': it founds no collective or individual identity, and the processes of subjectivation that correspond to it are processes of disidentification and declassification.[69] In the idea of a necessary repetition of the challenge to instituted orders, one can hear echoes of the Kantian thesis whereby the rejection of tutelage is the founding condition of freedom – a rejection that subsists only in the memory of this act, which implies its always-possible reiteration. Where Rancière differs most from Kant, however, is in his distrust of the law, which he considers to be constitutively implicated with the power of experts, and hence connected to the logic of the police and of domination. We can concede to him that the sporadic manifestations of the people in person do not found any lasting collective, and that it is futile to imagine that the community of equals can turn into a society without domination. But this should not prevent us from recognising that the modern legal expression of the egalitarian demand – the figure of the subject of right – introduced into politics an element that profoundly altered the structures of domination. Better yet: it is that which has made thinkable and possible politics and democracy in the sense that Rancière himself gives to these terms.

4.4. FAREWELL TO COMMUNITARIANISM?

The impossibility to stabilise over time a community in which equality is not rapidly undermined by the reappearance of the opposition between the dominant and the dominated raises questions concerning the consistency of the *demos* of democracy. Is this notion necessary to think the reality of contemporary democratic regimes? Would it not be more convenient to do without it

---

[68]   *Ibid.*, p. 88.
[69]   Rancière, 2015, pp. 27–30.

after all? An interpretation of democracy hinged on the concept of subjective rights has the advantage of freeing us from all communitarian presuppositions. To be sure, rights are generally conquered by collective movements; however, the groups that lead struggles aimed at the preservation of acquired rights, the extension of the circle of their beneficiaries or the acquisition of new ones are very unevenly formalised, and their existence is more or less sustained. They do not always generate – and do so less and less in the current context – a sense of belonging to a community, such as nation or class, and they do not mark individual identity in the same way that the latter did. It may seem surprising that the postulate of the unity of the sovereign people is still so prevalent in contemporary theories of democracy considering that the functioning of liberal democracies has obviously little to do with a government of the people, or even with self-legislation. It seems realistic to agree with Robert A. Dahl that 'probably the most we can say about democracy today is that the political and bureaucratic elites who effectively govern most of the time do so under institutionalised influences of popular opinion that make them more constrained than despots'.[70]

To explain the resistance of the notion of the sovereign people, we must concede that, even if we abandon idealised representations of the people's power, and even if we recognise that modern constitutional regimes have not abolished domination nor tended to do so, these representations and regimes have significantly altered the way in which domination operates by subjecting the dominant – be they legislators, ministers or members of the administration – to institutionalised mechanisms of control. Leaders are expected to be *accountable* to the entire population affected by their decisions, and this through fixed procedures among which election by universal suffrage has gradually imposed itself as the key element. The requirement that political leaders subject their action to the evaluation of those they govern – every time at the risk of being removed, at least temporarily, from positions of power – is precisely what perpetuates the communitarian conception of the people, far more so than the inevitable persistence of identities based on culture, religion, ethnicity or a long, shared history. The debates of the 1990s between communitarians and libertarians – at least in their French translation, wherein it is republicanism that was proposed as an alternative to communitarianism – opposed two antagonistic conceptions of the political people, both of which were nevertheless themselves communitarian. The success of the notion of 'constitutional patriotism' (*Verfassungspatriotismus*), which Habermas borrowed from Dolf Sternberger and which, as I noted in my introduction, is very similar to the Hegelian interpretation of patriotism, reveals

---

[70] Dahl, quoted in Roger M. Smith, 2003.

the persistence of the communitarian postulate in recent reinterpretations of the nature of democracy, no matter how new and sophisticated these may be. The difficulties encountered by the different variants of contemporary political philosophy in conceiving the form that democracy might take beyond national borders follow directly from this. These variants are essentially split between a renewal of the traditional cosmopolitan ideal, which looks to the establishment of international institutions that perform functions similar to those of nation-states, and the reaffirmation of the nation-state as the only possible framework for a genuine democracy.

It is now generally recognised, especially in studies devoted to the crisis of representative democracy, that the principle of self-legislation boils down to the imperative of accountability imposed on rulers.[71] And yet, this imperative seems a sufficient argument to continue thinking democracy as tied to the alleged unity of the sovereign people. To whom must rulers be accountable, if not to a collective whose boundaries are definable? Benhabib, in the work I mentioned earlier, reproduces this logic when she claims that democracy necessarily implies a closure of citizenship, and hence exclusion.[72] One of the great merits of her position is to show that the question of the rights of foreigners will remain an aporia so long as we think of democracy as popular sovereignty. However, this aporia is the result of the confusion that developed between popular sovereignty – once a mere legitimating principle of power opposed to that of dynastic sovereignty – and the territorial sovereignty of the state. And it can be undone only by recognising that the closure of the democratic community is an effect of the second term, that is to say, of the national embodiment of citizenship.

The history of legal conceptuality confirms this thesis, as is made clear by Christoph Schönberger's analyses of the notions of *Staatsangehörigkeit* (nationality) and *Staatsbürgerschaft* (citizenship).[73] As Schönberger remarks, the constitutional law of the French Revolution did not clearly distinguish between these two notions because it was primarily centred on the figure of the citizen, whose civil and political rights it sought to determine.[74] Insofar as the French Revolution remained over the next two centuries a fundamental reference of democratic thought, this indistinction contributed to the overlap, frequent among theorists of the nineteenth and twentieth centuries, between the logic of democracy and that of the territorial state. By contrast, in the German tradition, the difference between the two notions was for a while more easily perceptible, though here also it disappeared in the course of the twentieth cen-

---

71 See, for instance, Rosanvallon, 2008.
72 See supra, p. 87.
73 Schönberger, 2005.
74 *Ibid.*, pp. 23–24.

tury. The *Staatsangehörigkeit* was a status that, on the level of national public law, conferred right on a lasting presence in a determined state territory and conditioned the attribution of a number of rights and duties to the individual. The notion of *Staatsbürgerschaft* is older: it appeared in the language of the *Aufklärung* in connection with egalitarian representations that challenged the order of estates (*Stände*), but without initially involving the demand for the participation of all in the formation of the political will.[75] However, in the legal language of the late nineteenth century, the term was generally employed to designate political rights, foremost among them the right to vote.

Thus, the *Staatsangehörigkeit* was a form of collective membership whose specificity was made clear by contrast with the membership relations (*Zugehörigkeiten*) of societies organised in estates (*Stände*).[76] As Schönberger recalls, in the days of the Ancien Régime, there existed a web of intertwining rights tied to multiple memberships (here we recognise Weber's 'law communities') that determined various inequalities: 'There was not *one* determining membership, but a plurality of co-existing memberships. The individual was a member of an estate (*Stand*), he was subject to a lord or was a citizen of the city, yet there existed no universal and abstract membership status'.[77] The great accomplishment of territorial domination was precisely to abolish this plural membership, and to replace it with single membership in the territorial entity of the state. Thus, the territorialisation of power developed in conjunction with the emergence of an abstract and universal conception of belonging. This correlation not only had decisive consequences for the legal status of the individual, but also produced the foreigner – a category that societies of old did not know. As Schönberger further notes, in the estate societies, 'there was no [...] generalised status of the foreigner (*Ausländer*). The stranger (*der Fremde*), too, was involved in multiple relations of status privileges. These relations determined his legal status in an estate society far more strongly than the fact of being born in this or that country'.[78] Because lasting residence on the territory of a state came to condition both access to the rights guaranteed by that state and the duties imposed by it, control of the right of residence became a critical stake in the affirmation of political power. The territorial foundation of power demanded the abolition of differences of estate, but it also entailed the legal closure of the territory, which served as the ground for the reconstitution of the ultimate status opposition of political relevance: that between the national and the foreigner.

---

[75] *Ibid.*, p. 29.
[76] Here, I sum up and gloss the argument developed by C. Schönberger, *Ibid.*, pp. 128–32.
[77] *Ibid.*, p. 128.
[78] *Ibid.*, p. 129.

Let us not, then, blame the democratic people for its own closure. The juridification of the difference between the citizen and the foreigner is not the product of a necessity immanent to democracy, whereby the *demos* must define its borders in order to acquire and maintain control over its destiny. Reading anew the history of modern democracy – both in theoretical terms and in terms of its development throughout the political and social struggles of the nineteenth and twentieth centuries – leads to the conclusion that its essence lies not in citizenship as defined in a national framework or in any other similar but wider framework. States (or the EU) exclude because they are territorial communities, not for reasons inherent to the *modern* concept of democracy. Territorial powers continue to exist, on various scales, and they naturally constitute strong factors of community identification for sedentary populations. Popular passion for sports teams associated with a city or a country attests to the persistence of territorial communities, even though the composition of those teams, driven by the market logic, belies their national character. Still today, the daily life of ordinary individuals unfolds in real spaces that are demarcated by local organisations – for housing, transportation, health services, education, etc. – administered by governments which are also local. A significant portion of political life in states deemed democratic is played out in this context, and it is also in this context that the mechanisms of representative democracy continue to operate, while being modified and occasionally supplemented by elements of participatory democracy. Nevertheless, it is illusory to hope that these specific means of controlling power can extend beyond nation-states without losing their substance. The more power is distant, the more representation is indirect, and the more difficult it becomes to interpret the latter in terms of self-legislation. Moreover, although the current configuration of our world is not erasing the territorial forms of organisation of power, it is bringing to an end the hegemony that these forms enjoyed during the golden age of nation-states. With the loss of this hegemony, the identification that the political history of the nineteenth century and the first decades of the twentieth had established between the sovereign people and the democratic people comes undone.

As a result, one must avoid conflating the people of constitutions, invoked to found the legitimacy of power when traditional modes of legitimation lost their credibility, with the living people, which forced the expansion of the rights of the citizen and democratised states. To consider that democracy constitutively excludes is to consider it in its sovereign modality, which is only one manifestation of the territorial sovereignty of states. The impasses of this sovereign democracy have been known for a long time, and they were already perceptible in Rousseau's conception of the general will. The latter was only the projection of the unity of power from which individuals could expect the guarantee of their rights. However, because the living people has never had the required homogeneity of the 'body politic', the unity of the general will has also at times validated, in spite of Rousseau, the tyranny of the majority. The election of political leaders is a means of controlling power, but so long as it is seen as the expression of the will of a constituent people, it cannot prevent the dominant from claiming the legitimacy – which it supposedly confers on them – to restrict the rights of minority factions (religious, ethnic or otherwise) in the populations over which they exercise power. Against etymology and archaic representations of democracy – which, let us recall, belong to a period when the notions of legitimacy and sovereignty were unknown – one must ultimately recognise that only the demand for equal rights breaks the communitarian logic implied in the postulate of the sovereign people. This demand encapsulates and sums up the whole meaning of democracy as understood by the moderns, namely, a democracy that does not presuppose any *demos*. Echoing the quote from Derrida with which I began this chapter, I would argue that the deconstruction of the concept of democracy has, in a way, already been accomplished. The bond forged between this term and the nation and the state has always been contingent: it was inherited from a structure of power that preceded the revolutions which gave birth to modern political regimes – and therefore also preceded their democratisation – and it is destined to fade away as the sovereignty of nation-states gradually unravels. However, there is no reason to renounce thinking a democratic citizenship, which, even if it is not bound to the national framework, remains political insofar as it always maintains an essential relation to power. The democracy to come is emerging in the forms taken by the demand for equality when it is confronted with the new topology of power with which it is forced to cope.

Chapter 5

The Future of the Political Subject in the Context of Globalisation

In reality, increasingly numerous aspects of the life of the world's constitutive units depend on what other units are or do today, and on what they were or did in the past. Most importantly, an even more concrete aspect of this intensive interdependence is that it reaches individuals more and more directly, and not through the institutions or the communities to which they belong and that have until now formed their horizon or their 'world'.[1]

5.1 CITIZENSHIP AND SOLIDARITY

There now exists an extensive literature on the changes that the practices and understanding of citizenship have undergone as a result of the phenomena gathered under the term 'globalisation'. It is no longer clear that national sovereignty, and with it national citizenship, is 'the "natural" political condition of humankind',[2] as Giddens phrased it in his summary of the history of the 19th and first three quarters of the twentieth century. However, interpretations of post-national citizenship are as diverse as are those of globalisation itself. Before discussing these interpretations and specifying the new perspectives that the concept of 'democracy without demos' might open up, I must say a few words concerning the doubts that have been raised against the notion of post-national democracy – the possibility of which is far from unanimously accepted. The strongest objections have often come from French authors. This, of course, can be explained by the weight of the republican tradition,

---

[1] Balibar, 1997, pp. 422–23.
[2] Giddens, 1987, p. 259.

which makes it difficult to disconnect citizenship from membership in the national community. Characteristic of this is the attitude of Rosanvallon, who in his most recent works interrogates the current transformations and the future of democracy, yet pays only marginal attention to what he calls cosmopolitanism. His understanding of democracy as 'the attempt to institute a community out of a group of individuals'[3] prevents us from seeing, in the reconfiguration of contemporary democratic practices, anything but the desire for a community or a solidarity expanded to the scale of humanity, which are necessarily less strenuous than the community or the solidarity of the nation of citizens.[4]

Much could be said about the uses that have been made in recent years, in France and elsewhere, of the term 'solidarity', or of the more abstract, less affectively charged expression that often serves as its substitute: 'the social bond'. This term and this expression have become key words in contemporary sociological thought as well as in certain currents of political philosophy.[5] The interpretation of the political following the thread of solidarity – which functions, as Slavoj Žižek pertinently remarks, as the 'signifier of the impossible fullness of society if ever there was one'[6] – constitutes a response to the economistic reduction of sociability to market relations, or, to put it in Weberian terms, to that communalisation without community which is fundamentally alien to fraternisation and is thereby opposed to all other forms of communalisation.[7] What is being pursued or formulated with the term 'solidarity' is a fundamental anthropology that might replace the minimalist and simplistic one that liberal economic theory naively takes for granted. The current success of 'solidarity' is, on the level of theory, the answer to the political hegemony of that caricatural form of liberalism that has justified the basic public policy orientations of large Western democracies over the last three decades. Even before the current crisis revealed the illusory character of growth conceived solely in terms of financial profitability, it was sufficiently clear that this economic doctrine, embraced by most political elites in the name of governmental rationality, implied the gradual unravelling of the social security systems that had been established or consolidated in the aftermath of World War II, and that had functioned since then as a sort of social

---

3   Rosanvallon, 2000, p. 402.
4   See Rosanvallon, 2000, pp. 421–22, where he opposes the solidarity of citizenship to the solidarity of humanity, the second being weaker and less strenuous than the first. He refers to this passage at the end of *Counter-Democracy* (2008, pp. 315–16), where he repeats that '[e]ven though there is no officially constituted *demos*, the goal is still to construct a common humanity, though of course the demands on individuals are less strenuous at this level'.
5   On the current success of the notion of solidarity following several decades of oblivion, see Marie-Claude Blais's introduction to her book: *La solidarité, histoire d'une idée*, Blais, 2007, pp. 9–15.
6   Žižek, 1999, p. 178.
7   Weber, 1978, p. 637.

compact upon which the legitimacy of governments rested.[8] The erosion of these protection systems, together with a rise in inequalities whose magnitude cannot be camouflaged with statistical manipulations, has revived the search for another form of sociability, one that does not claim affiliation with communism as was the case in the past. Solidarity – the slogan with which French radical theorists of the early twentieth century anticipated the social state that would be gradually put in place in the next fifty or sixty years – has become, at the beginning of this century, the 'magic term'[9] that retrospectively justifies the institutions of the welfare state, at a time when neo-liberal ideology and the public policies it inspires are working to dismantle it.

It is little wonder that this pursuit has translated in France into a renewed interest in the work of Durkheim. Of course, sociologists never ceased to honour this author, whom Aron and Parsons enshrined in the pantheon of their discipline's founders. In doing so, however, they also decontextualised him. By contrast, recent interpretations of Durkheim proceeded to re-contextualise his work, and rediscovered by the same token its philosophical and political import. This was the occasion for a long series of authors – from Léon Bourgeois to Célestin Bouglé through Léon Duguit or Alfred Fouillé, remembered until then only by specialists of the history of French political thought – to be drawn from obscurity.[10] The work of Durkheim now appears as one of the expressions of a French 'republican moment' whose memory was repressed by the confrontation between liberals and Marxists. Anxious to escape the conventional oppositions that structured this divide – i.e., equality vs. freedom, predominance of the collective vs. that of the individual – the new republicans have sought to determine the forms of a society wherein the intervention of public power, far from undermining individuals' freedom, is, on the contrary, what makes it possible and truly equal for all.[11] This is the problem that the French radicals of the early twentieth century were already tackling, an endeavour for which Durkheim's *Division of Labour in Society* unquestionably provided the most solid theoretical foundation. And this is why it is worth considering the political implications that Durkheim himself drew from his interpretation of modern individualism.

'How does it come about that the individual, whilst becoming more autonomous, depends ever more closely upon society? How can he become at the same time more of an individual and yet more linked to society?'[12] Thus Durkheim summed up, in the preface to the first edition of the *Division*

---

[8]   See Castel, 2002.

[9]   Blais, 2007, p. 325.

[10] See in particular the works of Marie-Claude Blais, 2007, and Jean-Fabien Spitz, 2005.

[11] This is precisely what is at stake in the distinction between freedom understood as non-domination and freedom understood as non-interference. See Pettit, 1997, and Spitz, 2005.

[12] Durkheim, 1997, p. xxx.

of Labour, the question he purported to answer in his book. The title of this work reflects Durkheim's debt to economists, which he made explicit in one passage: economists deserved credit for having first pointed out the spontaneous character of social life.[13] Yet Durkheim seized on the theme of the division of labour only to re-elaborate it, and this, by turning it against economic ideology – that is to say, against utilitarianism, whose sociological expression in the person of Spencer he specifically targeted. According to Durkheim, the core error of 'Utilitarians' lay in 'the manner in which they conceived the genesis of society. They supposed that originally there were isolated and independent individuals who thus could only enter into relationships with one another in order to co-operate'. In other words, they made the mistake of 'deducing society from the individual'. To this, Durkheim opposed the central thesis of his work: 'Collective life did not arise from individual life; on the contrary, it is the latter that emerged from the former'.[14] The purpose of the present book does not justify me in dwelling on the details of Durkheim's demonstration. Nevertheless, the political reinterpretation made today of his work – in particular, of the *Division of Labour* – calls for a few comments. There is no doubt that Durkheim's intentions were at once scientific and political, to the point where it is difficult to distinguish between the two. In the *Division of Labour*, the political intent is concealed behind the ambiguity of the notion of solidarity, which Durkheim presented as an anthropological thesis, while also making it a moral imperative. The thesis that human individuality is not a given of nature, but is imbued with the social, is, indeed, anthropological. That the individual in modern societies affirms his personal difference changes nothing to the fact that society 'lives and acts in him' through beliefs and rules.[15] The development of individual personality, which is characteristic of modern societies, is a particular modality of this presence of the social within individuality itself. Durkheim tried to account for this presence – and for its different expressions depending on the type of society – by distinguishing in the consciousness of the individual between individual and collective aspects, the respective importance of which changes in the course of social evolution. The problems inherent to this conceptualisation are well known.[16] Durkheim's aim was to reject the opposition between the individual and the social; however, the distinction between common consciousness and collective consciousness merely internalised this opposition. The difficulties he had in conceptually

---

[13] *Ibid.*, p. 320.
[14] *Ibid.*, pp. 220–21.
[15] 'Rôle des universités dans l'Education sociale du pays' (The role of universities in the social education of the country), quoted in Blais, 2007, p. 287.
[16] On this topic, see Bruno Karsenti's remarkable analyses in *L'homme total* (1997).

articulating the fundamental anthropological thesis that was to help sociology elucidate the spontaneous sociability of market society – without imagining, as economists did, that the individual could be understood by himself and that only the social needed to be explained – do not detract from its relevance. This thesis has fuelled the most fertile thoughts of the twentieth century. Until Luhmann,[17] the correlation between the phenomenon of individualisation (the becoming-individual of the individual) and the emergence of a new way of structuring the collective was a central theme of sociology. And the more general idea according to which the constitution of the social and that of psychic individuality are, in the end, only two faces of a single process was raised to a quasi-ontological level by Gilbert Simondon, with the concept of transindividuality.[18]

And yet, the step is a long one from this thesis to the affirmation that 'every society is a moral society' because it forces the individual to consider himself as part of a whole. To be sure, Durkheim presented this obligation first as a disposition that naturally develops in individuals out of the experience of interdependence. But he also confessed his normative ambition when he proposed to compare the normal type with himself. According to Durkheim, this was a 'strictly scientific operation' that would allow the sociologist to see that the normal type is not 'entirely at harmony within itself'[19] – i.e., that reality comprises, from the perspective of the theory, imperfections which the sociologist can attempt to remedy. An ethical dimension was thus re-inscribed, via the notion of solidarity, in the discourse of empirical sociology. Men are not only *de facto* solidary; they must also want to be so for society to function properly. A similar shift from the analytical to the normative register accounts for the political conclusions Durkheim infers from his thesis in *Professional Ethics and Civic Morals*.[20] Those who today believe that they can find in Durkheim the means to rebuild republican democracy should read this text carefully. Indeed, the rejection of the postulate whereby the rights of the individual are inherent in the individual[21] (which is to be expected from an author who stresses the social genesis of individuality) naturally leads to a paternalistic conception of the state – a conception that was already announced in the *Division of Labour*, in which Durkheim assigned to the state the mission of 'reminding us of the sentiment of our common solidarity'.[22] *Professional Ethics* explains how the state must be constituted if it is to meet this task. The state – which Durkheim identifies with the institutions of government, and more specifically with the

---

[17] See Luhmann, 1989b.
[18] See Simondon, 2007, especially p. 173*ff*.
[19] Durkheim, 1997, p. xxvii.
[20] Durkheim, 1992.
[21] *Ibid.*, p. 57.
[22] Durkheim, 1997, p. 173.

specific group of officials responsible for asserting the authority of the collective over individuals – elaborates the collective representations that exist only in a diffused form (in the guise of myths, religious dogmas, moral traditions, etc.) in the rest of society. The representations that guide the actions of state officials differ from those other collective representations 'by their higher degree of consciousness and reflection'.[23] In more concise terms, the state thinks the social: it is the 'social brain'[24] by virtue of which officials acting on its behalf are entitled to govern. This is, indeed, a matter of governance. For while the opposition between the diffuse character of collective psychic life in all of society and the clarity and precision that this life acquires in state bodies might suggest that the state merely expresses representations latent in society, Durkheim makes clear that this is not the case. Society does not think through the state, but the state thinks for it. 'When the State takes thought and makes a decision, we must not say that it is the society that thinks and decides through the State, but that the State thinks and decides for it. It is not simply an instrument for canalising and concentrating. It is, in a certain sense, the organising centre of the secondary groups themselves'.[25]

What did Durkheim mean by democracy when he stated that it is 'the political system by which the society can achieve a consciousness of itself in its purest form'?[26] Needless to say, this was not the concept of democracy of the traditional division into three types of governments, long considered obsolete by the time of Durkheim. And, of course, neither was it the democracy that Marx had characterised as the 'resolved mystery of all constitutions'.[27] At the end of the nineteenth century, the term democracy could only designate the institutional arrangement that had been gradually put in place, through many twists and turns, since the French Revolution. These institutions were not based on the Rousseauian idea that 'the will and thought of those governing are identical and merge with the will and thought of those governed'[28] – an idea which, according to Durkheim, was radically unsuited to the complexity of modern societies. The administration of these institutions entailed a rationality that was built through deliberations informed by increasingly abundant technical knowledge, including statistical information and administrative data. The 'crowd' did not possess such knowledge, and could not use it even if it did, because 'it has no unity'. The government 'is better placed than the crowd' to know 'what is expedient' for societies.[29] That such a conception

---

23   Durkheim, 1992, p. 50.
24   *Ibid.*, p. 53.
25   *Ibid.*, p. 49.
26   *Ibid.*, p. 89.
27   Marx, 1977, p. 30.
28   Durkheim, 1992, p. 91.
29   *Ibid.*, p. 92.

implies a radical rejection of direct democracy and of its substitutes (e.g., the imperative mandate) is hardly surprising. More startling for a reader of today is Durkheim's distrust of what is generally considered to be the cornerstone of modern democratic institutions: the election of deputies via universal suffrage. Durkheim reproaches this method of leader selection for maintaining a direct link between the governed and their representatives – a link that undermines the latter's independence, which is the condition of enlightened governance. Durkheim shares with Weber (who has rarely been viewed as a democrat) the conviction that, with the exception of a few primitive populations, 'there are no societies where the government is carried out direct by all in common: It is always in the hands of a minority chosen either by birth or by election; its scope may be large or small, according to circumstances, but it never comprises more than a limited circle of individuals. In this respect there are only slight shades of difference between the various political forms'.[30] Democracy consists in the respect of the laws, not because the laws are the expression of the will of the people, but because they are conceived by leaders who, we must assume, are concerned with the public interest which they alone are entitled to define. Ultimately, the confidence that the dominated place in those who dominate them is the key foundation of democracy.[31]

To be sure, this confidence is placed in capable leaders. And leaders' capability presupposes a specific arrangement of the political system, the two characteristics of which are the visibility of deliberations and government action and the transparency of society for power – or, to use Durkheimian terminology, the communication and extension of government consciousness. It would be a mistake, however, to see in this requirement for visibility and transparency an anticipation of the public sphere, understood in the Habermasian sense. For the flows of exchange between the dominant and the dominated, as conceived by Durkheim, are decidedly uneven. The initiative to communicate belongs to the government: the latter publicises its action to help everyone understand the reasons for it, and the feedback it expects can only consist of answers to the questions it poses.[32] That the gaze and action of leaders can reach into every corner of social life is the strength of modern

---

[30] *Ibid.*, p. 85. Compare with Weber, 1994, p. 361: "[...] d'une manière générale, la politique est toujours le fait d'une minorité [...]".

[31] See this characteristic passage: 'It is not because we have made a certain law or because it has been willed by so many votes, that we submit to it; it is because it is a good one—that is, appropriate to the nature of the facts, because it is all it ought to be and because we have confidence in it. And this confidence depends equally on that inspired by the organs that have the task of preparing it. What matters, then, is the way in which the law is made, the competence of those whose function it is to make it and the nature of the particular agency that has to make this particular function work' (Durkheim, 1992, pp. 107–108).

[32] See *ibid.*, pp. 81–82.

democratic governments – a strength that was prepared by the centralising action of the monarchy, itself already a sort of democratic government.[33] The information transmitted from society to power merely contributes to power's reflection because, 'since it is framed to think along special lines, it has to take thought in its own way'.[34] If we add to this picture Durkheim's proposal to restore a system of corporations that rest on occupational differences and that are intended to form the basis of political representation and social organisation as a whole, we see why it is legitimate to describe his political conceptions as paternalistic. Although Durkheim sometimes says that the state should not oppress the individual, his main preoccupation is to free the state from the individual: to free it, ultimately, from the pressures and influences of the 'multitude'. The political elite determine for the people what constitutes its best interests, and must make every effort – from publicising their action to educating the people – to convince it of the correctness of their decisions. The metaphor of the 'social brain' should not be taken lightly coming from an author who saw social progress in women's abstention from participation in political life, and who justified the latter by the greater difference observed between the brain volume of Parisian women and men as compared with the gap between male and female skulls in Ancient Egypt.[35] Here we are far from the position defended by Kant, who, whatever he may have thought of women's character, refrained from justifying by nature the tutelage exercised over any category of human beings.

Transposed on the political level, the sociological critique of utilitarian anthropology results in an extremely restrictive interpretation of the autonomy of ordinary individuals. The duties of citizens appear far more essential to the proper functioning of society than do their rights – at least their political rights. Some might dispute that this theorisation of paternalistic elite government inevitably ensues from the theses put forward in the *Division of Labour*. Nevertheless, it seems to me that, in its general orientation if not in its details, such theorisation is already anticipated in the ambiguity of the term 'solidarity', which straddles between the empirical and the normative. The term's ambivalence ultimately springs from Durkheim's communitarian conception of the 'social bond', which he does not appear to distinguish from social cohesion. And yet, the social bond does not necessarily presuppose the existence of a bounded collective. One can think the social constitution of individuality without postulating the existence of a whole of which

---

[33] *Ibid.*, p. 89.
[34] *Ibid.*, p. 92.
[35] See Durkheim, 1997, p. 19. It is almost embarrassing to find, in the writings of one the great founders of modern sociology, who is celebrated today as an authority on republicanism, a sentence that seems a caricature of anti-feminist thinking: 'Even now there is still a very large number of savage peoples where the woman takes part in political life'.

individuals would be parts. This is the direction Simondon indicates, when he states that if we want to definitively dismiss the representation of the social and the individual as two distinct, substantial realities, we must stop construing them as the terms of a relation. By contrast, the notion of social cohesion implies the identification of the social bond with 'society' conceived as a closed totality. It functions as a barely euphemised equivalent of the social order, and establishes by the same token a direct link between sociological inquiry and the concerns of political officials. All sociologists who claim an affiliation with Durkheim would probably not agree with the political conclusions he draws from the central thesis of the *Division of Labour*. Yet the simple shift from the social to society – together with its harmonics 'social cohesion' and 'social integration' – presupposes that the sociologist has already adopted the perspective of rulers on the social. Zygmunt Bauman is not wrong to say that the agent of this sociology – the one that sets the goals and tries to meet them – 'was the sovereign state', such that the discipline constituted itself as 'the intelligence branch of its practice'.[36] The society of sociologists is the social understood from the point of view of the state: a group of individuals, a population which is to be constituted as an orderly community whose structures must be determined by an enlightened political elite and the experts who advise it. If the works of Durkheim and other theorists of republican solidarism are experiencing renewed popularity today, it is because the communitarian demand appears as a salutary counterforce to the competitive society of *homo economicus*. But many forget that communitarian solidarity can also serve as an alibi for paternalistic power, which is as unconcerned with the autonomy of the political subject as is economic utilitarianism – though for opposite reasons. While it may be true that the institutions of the welfare state should be viewed as a democratic advance in that they consecrated new rights of the subject, the protected citizen is not the truth of the modern political subject. As the orientations of current liberal policies show very well, the power that grants rights can just as easily reduce or revoke them. The only real guarantee of acquired rights is what made their conquest possible, namely the right of everyone, individually, to claim rights: a pre-legal right that is not of nature, but has reality only through the action of individuals, who become subjects only by freeing themselves from tutelage.

---

[36] Bauman, 2002, p. 2. On the 'society of sociologists', see also Dubet, 2009, ch. 1.

5.2 THE DENATIONALISATION OF CITIZENSHIP

Citizenship, understood as a status linked to nationality that covers all the civil, political and social rights gradually acquired by the populations of Western societies between the late eighteenth and mid-twentieth centuries, is now defeated. Nation-states themselves largely contributed to the hollowing out of national citizenship, by granting part of the rights formerly reserved for citizens to ever more categories of foreigners – i.e., aliens residing legally and permanently on their territory, but also sometimes illegal aliens. In a book widely regarded as a landmark in the recent literature on post-national citizenship, Yasemin Soysal compares the rights now accorded to resident aliens in most European countries to the ones they enjoyed in the 1960s.[37] After distinguishing between the integration policies implemented by those different countries – policies which bear the stamp of quite distinct conceptions of civic belonging – she concludes that, overall, national citizenship is no longer a discriminating factor in access to civil rights and social rights (i.e., public education, health care, labour protection, or social insurance). To be or not to be a citizen no longer makes a fundamental difference in this regard. Let us recall the example of the German Foreigners Law promulgated in 1965 by the Federal Republic of Germany, which granted all basic rights to foreigners, '*except* the basic rights of freedom of assembly, freedom of association, freedom of movement and free choice of occupation, place of work and place of education, and protection from extradition abroad'.[38] It would be difficult to imagine today a legal text that would so drastically restrict 'basic rights'.[39] Soysal rightly remarks that the order in which these rights were accorded to foreigners is almost the reverse of that in which they combined to form the status of citizenship as theorised by Marshall. First came social rights, along with some civil rights such as freedom of association and freedom of expression, and then, belatedly and with more difficulty, some elements of political rights. Only political rights in the strict sense – the rights to vote and to stand for election in the host country – are still denied to foreigners today. Even so, the latter restriction fully applies only in the case of national elections. Foreigners from the EU are allowed to participate in local elections in all countries of the EU, and non-EU permanent residents are permitted to do the same in some of those countries. Thus the rights reserved for nationals tend to be reduced to the election of national parliaments and, in some cases, to the election of the head of government. The symbolic significance of this

---

[37] Soysal, 1994.
[38] Quoted in Soysal, 1994, p. 122. My emphasis.
[39] In the case of irregular migrants, however, administrative practices do lead to restrictions that are not far removed from those codified in this law.

right is all the more celebrated now that it is all that remains of the status of national citizen.

Of course, one cannot deplore this widening of the circle of civil and social rights beneficiaries. But should one see in this, as Soysal suggests we do, the sign that a radically new concept of citizenship is emerging, one that would be founded no longer on national belonging but on universal personhood? Soysal tends to interpret changes in the institutional forms of citizenship as the effect of a new mode of legitimation. As she sees it, the logic of nationality gave way to the logic of human rights, and the latter now manifests itself as a new form of membership – specifically, as membership in humanity. This interpretation is determined in part by Soysal's choice of method. Instead of explaining the success or failure of immigrants' integration by their cultural origin, she points to the role of public policies in the host countries after first highlighting, as I mentioned earlier, the differences between them.[40] In her view, that despite those differences roughly the same outcome is produced everywhere in the end stems from the growing influence exerted on national governments by 'transnational discourse and structures celebrating human rights as a world-level organising principle'.[41] The recent tightening of migration policies in European countries, which was already perceptible at the time Soysal wrote her book (published in 1994), does not seem to her to contradict the general trend in the evolution of citizenship rights. Such tightening merely reflects the gap between the legitimating principles of those rights and the modalities of their material realisation, which remains the responsibility of states. Curiously, Soysal does not seem to notice that this gap casts doubt on the consistency of the 'transnational community',[42] which she believes is being formed through the recognised universality of human rights and the various institutions in charge of enforcing them. It is indisputable that the promulgation of normative texts that are universal in scope and approved by most states, as well as the existence of legal and judicial supra-national bodies that are created and recognised by those same states, alter the conditions for the exercise of national sovereignty. Moreover, there is no denying that both these texts and the action of these bodies have contributed to the extension of civil and social rights to foreigners. Still, the transnational community – supposing we choose to retain the expression – is of a very different nature than the national community, and it seems excessive to describe individuals' relation to it as one of membership. The implementation deficit of universal rights

---

[40] Soysal proposes a typology that distinguishes between corporatist, statist, liberal and fragmental models of incorporation.
[41] Soysal, 1994, p. 3.
[42] *Ibid.*, 1994, p. 142.

results from the fact that the transnational community is not a collective held together by the authority of a power with the monopoly of legitimate coercion. Legitimate principles do not amount to a legitimate power – namely, to a power that forces recognition of its authority by breaking resistance, as the monarchical state (the forerunner of the democratic nation-state) used to do when faced with the resistance of particularistic 'law communities'.[43]

Soysal is right to say that the denationalisation of a great portion of citizenship rights was the work of nation-states. But by focusing on public policies, she not only ignores how the subjected – in this case foreigners – have contributed to transforming their own status, but also conflates the principles invoked by those policies with the motivations of their proponents. One ought to recall that, in the case of nationals, both the granting of new rights and the extension of certain categories of rights to new holders (for instance, the right of suffrage to the entire male population and later to women) have always been the outcome of a power struggle. They are the result of circumstances favourable to the dominated, either because the state needed to mobilise them to achieve its own economic or military ends, or because it sought to thwart the menacing threat of revolutionary uprisings. While the history of social rights in Germany begins with Bismarck, the latter saw no contradiction between 'a legislature and an administration willing to accommodate the demands of the working masses' and the suppression of the parties that defended the interests of those same masses, because for him the aim of state-run insurance systems was 'to produce, in the great mass of the needy, that conservative reflex which is born of the sense of having a right to a pension'.[44] Bismarck stated in a brutal fashion the truth that lies behind the motivations of political leaders, for whom rights granted to the dominated, and especially to those who have only their labour to offer, are but a means to gain the adhesion necessary to the proper functioning of a society whose unequal structures must not be fundamentally challenged. Without sharing Bismarck's cynicism, Weber said roughly the same thing, in 1917, when he defended the principle of equal and universal suffrage by arguing that, without it, 'never again would the nation stand against any external threat as it did in August 1914',[45] and that, so long as the existing social order would last, 'the inequality of the outward circumstances of life, particularity of *property*, may be mitigated, as may the relationships of social dependence which it produces, but it can never be eliminated altogether. Thus those who are privileged by it will never even come close to losing all their influence on

---

[43]   See supra...
[44]   See Lothar Gall, pp. 640–41. The quoted passages are by Bismarck himself.
[45]   Weber, 1994, p. 233.

national politics, which they exert to a far greater degree than their numbers warrant'.[46]

A discussion, however brief, of the circumstances that facilitated the expansion of citizenship rights and their extension to new beneficiaries naturally goes beyond the scope of the present book.[47] This reminder is merely intended to offer a prosaic interpretation of the evolution of foreigners' rights, which, we can assume, was also determined by the strategic considerations of governments of the host countries – these being influenced, for instance, by their relations with immigrants' countries of origin. Saskia Sassen cites the example of Salvadorans who migrated to the United States during the civil war that tore their country apart between 1981 and 1992. The post-civil war governments of El Salvador, which did not want these migrants to return because of the high level of unemployment in the country and because of the economic benefits generated by the remittances they sent to their families, supported their fight for residency rights in the United States.[48] Similar examples abound. The proliferation of official texts that recognise, at the international level, the validity of human rights as well as of the courts responsible for enforcing them, has not changed the fact that the greater or lesser effectiveness of these rights is always subordinated to governmental reason. Their effectiveness therefore remains a function of power struggles – whether direct or indirect (including through the mediation of immigrants' states of origin) – between the populations that claim rights and the authorities that grant or refuse them. Contrary to what Soysal implies, the link between human rights and the universality of the human person was not established in recent decades. This innovation dates back to the era of the revolutionary declarations, which, whatever may have been claimed afterwards, did not distinguish between the rights of man and those of the citizen, but called on all men to demand that their respective governments guarantee all of these rights to their own nationals. The tension between the universality of these rights and what Soysal calls the 'material realisation of individual rights' by the nation-state is not new either. It follows from the principle of state sovereignty, which remains to this day one of the pillars of international law. This principle implies, in particular, that each state defines and controls the conditions of access to its territory, which explains

---

46 *Ibid.*, p. 103.
47 On this topic, see Sandra Halperin's stimulating article in *Millenium* (2009). Halperin argues that the determining factor in the democratisation of Western societies was war. It was the need to mobilise the working classes that pushed those in power (who, she admits in a Marxist vein, primarily defend the interests of the propertied classes) to lift all restrictions on the right to vote. She notes that it is only after World War II that universal, equal, direct and secret suffrage became the norm in all Western Europe. Under post-war conditions, a balance of power favourable to the dominated imposed a historic class compromise that forced capital to organise itself in a primarily national framework, thereby rendering possible the extension of social rights.
48 Sassen, 2006, pp. 295–96.

why the status of foreigners is always more precarious than that of nationals, and this even in those states where human rights are most respected. In the case of the European Union, the Schengen Agreement eroded this aspect of national sovereignty by abolishing the internal border controls of the European area. Yet we know that this internal liberalisation was accompanied by a significant tightening of controls at the external borders of Europe. Far from outlining, at the regional level, what a transnational community might look like, the EU reproduces on a larger scale the logic of all real communities, which can only include through excluding. While an institution like the European Court of Human Rights, in charge of ensuring the application of the European Convention, can sometimes assert the universality of human rights against states, the institutions and policy of the EU are nevertheless always ruled by governmental reason.[49]

Nation-states have been agents of the gradual denationalisation of citizenship rights. But the reason for this is not that they consented to the universal values and norms upheld by certain discourses or transnational structures. They did not even want this denationalisation, of which the evolution of foreigners' status is merely one aspect. Just as important, in this regard, is the abandonment by states of some of the prerogatives and competences that allowed them to grant and guarantee the social rights of citizens and hence made possible the social compromise on which the legitimacy of the welfare state rested. Today, one speaks of the dilution of sovereignty,[50] but also of the dilution of loyalty to the state.[51] The one and the other are of course related. The citizen remains attached to the nation-state so long as he sees in it the fundamental structure upon which his rights and living conditions depend. The adhesion of citizens is no longer as necessary for states as it was in the days when on-going or looming wars between European nations called for a general mobilisation. States do not even need to mobilise citizens economically. There is no shortage of workers, and if their demands are too high, large companies can easily move to countries where labour is cheaper. Far more so than the mobility of populations, it is the mobility of capital that undermines the foundations of national citizenship. Of course, the political structures of democratic states, which constrain leaders to regularly expose themselves to voters' sanction, make it impossible to abolish social protections overnight or to attack civil liberties frontally. On-going changes in the justification of social benefits – the shift from the language of 'rights of all' to that of 'assistance to the poor' – are nevertheless symptomatic of a watershed, one that, as we are beginning to sense, is not a mere matter of conjuncture. The disaffili-

---

[49] On the difference in logic between the institutions of the European Convention and those of the EU, see Delmas-Marty, 2009.
[50] Delmas-Marty, 2009, quoting H. Ruiz Fabri, p. 14.
[51] Sassen, 2006, p. 283.

ation of the most disadvantaged is only the most visible aspect of a process that already affects poor workers and a portion of the middle class, who are increasingly asked to provide for their own health care or to build a decent pension through privately-funded schemes.[52]

At the same time, one sees the development of instruments of population control – files and administrative practices of all kinds which only the naïve fail to see are undermining the civil liberties of nationals themselves – based on the assumption that, from the perspective of governmental reason (of the police, as understood by Rancière), virtually every citizen is a suspect. This is another facet of the erasure of the difference between the national citizen and the foreigner, and one that leads to a far less optimistic interpretation than that proposed by Soysal. The control of foreigners is only one element in a generalised politics of population control. Such politics is obviously not without historical precedent, but it now has new technical means at its disposal. The latter combine the advantage of being effective, to a degree that governments could only dream of in the past, with that of displaying supposed 'neutrality', which exempts the state from resorting to the brutal methods used by the dictatorships of yesterday and today. The surveillance of populations is already well under way despite resistance from some citizen groups, but also from a few institutions still attached to principles of freedom in which political leaders essentially see, in the name of security, obstacles to rational governance. The war on terror precipitated this development. The infamous Patriot Act, approved by the US Congress one month after the attacks of September 11, 2001, legalised a series of police intrusions into the privacy of US citizens. It also considerably extended the scope of so-called 'secret' operations by official surveillance bodies – i.e., operations that are exempt from the disclosure requirement generally considered to be one of the cornerstones of democratic regimes. It would be wrong to view this recent episode in American political life as an accident, on the grounds that the new presidency has cancelled or will perhaps cancel its most conspicuous provisions. The Edvige database in France, though less serious than the Patriot Act, suggests that the security imperative naturally leads the governments of democratic countries to reduce the civil rights of citizens in favour of population control. It is significant, and particularly worrying, that the main argument put forward to justify this project was not the terrorist threat, but the need to 'tackle new forms of delinquency, and especially gang delinquency'.[53] This formula clearly tar-

---

[52] On the theme of disaffiliation, see Castel, 2002. On recent trends in the evolution of the welfare state, see Castel, 2009.

[53] Declaration by Frédéric Lefebvre, one of the spokespersons for the UMP (*Union pour un mouvement populaire*), a political party of the classic French right recently renamed *Les Républicains*. One of the most controversial provisions of this project consisted in registering minors as young as 13 in this database.

geted some specific strata of the population, namely those who reside in 'the neighbourhoods' (*les quartiers*) – as the term goes – and have been deprived of a future by the logic of the liberalised economy. The reappearance, under a different name, of nineteenth century 'dangerous classes' shows full well that the regression of social rights is normally accompanied by the challenge to civil rights. While these developments do not, for the time being, warrant the apocalyptic diagnoses that have been made by some, they nevertheless suggest that the formality of democratic institutions, and in particular the regular election of political leaders, does not suffice to found democracy on the confidence that populations are expected to place in their leaders. This confidence can be misplaced, as the episode of the Bush administration makes clear. For this reason, it is dangerous to assign to those leaders the responsibility to look after the rights of citizens. As I noted earlier, conceded rights can always be revoked. Only the vigilance of the subjects of rights ultimately ensures their protection. This means that these subjects must be ready to mobilise to preserve the rights they have already won, just as they did to conquer them in the first place, and as they might have to do again in order to acquire new ones in the future.

5.3 NEW SCENES OF CIVIC CREATIVITY: THE CITY

Why do you think you have rights?
   Well, one part is just what we were saying. I am an honest person, thank God. I don't steal from anyone. I am a worker. I fulfill my obligations at home, with my family. I pay my taxes. But today I think the following: I have right because the *Constituinte* [i.e., Constitution] gives me these rights. But I have to run after my rights. I have to look for them. Because if I don't, they won't fall from the sky. Only rain falls from the sky. You can live here fifty years. But if you don't run after your rights, how are you going to make them happen?[54]

Citizenship cannot be reduced to the enjoyment of codified rights. A whole section of the literature on the contemporary transformations of citizenship focuses on the practices of individuals and groups rather than on their formal rights. There are now studies on: the involvement of citizens in organisations other than traditional political parties and trade unions, which belies their alleged depoliticisation; the formation of cross-border ties of exchange and solidarity between certain groups of immigrants and their parents or friends

---

[54] Response from a resident of a suburban neighbourhood of São Paulo, Jardim das Camélias, quoted in Holston, 2008, p. 253.

back in the home country; the constitution of 'global classes' composed of managers of multinational corporations as well as of international researchers and high-ranking officials, or, at the other end of the social spectrum, of unqualified workers moving from country to country at the whim of the needs of the labour market.[55] However, by lumping together these heterogeneous phenomena under the umbrella of post-national citizenship, one runs the risk of emptying this concept of all specific content. To avoid this confusion, it may be useful to retain the question of rights as a common thread. Some of the ambiguities that haunt the nature of citizenship today stem from the fact that it has been submerged in the broader theme of social identities. One often hears that these identities are plural. Though this has always been the case, this plurality is more visible today than it was at the time when national citizenship could claim to encompass all identities, while simultaneously subordinating them. But not all identities – whether old or new – are civic, and neither are all forms of solidarity. The specificity of modern civic identity is that it developed from the figure of the subject of right, which is to say, from the individual entitled to assert his rights as an individual. As I wrote earlier, the individualisation of the subject of right was the real innovation of the late eighteenth century revolutions. It was formulated in the terms of human nature, and it is on this point that all critiques, from those of Burke to those of Kelsen, converged. What these critiques systematically ignored is the fact that the individualisation of the subject of right was the product of a history: that of the destruction or the subordination of statutory rights by state power, thanks to which this individualisation instigated a new form of historicity of the legal-political subject. Paradoxically, the 'natural' character of those rights did not mean that they were fixed once and for all, but that, unlike and contrary to the rights of old, they were undetermined. Critics were quick to condemn this indeterminacy. Its advantages became apparent only in light of the construction and evolution of citizenship throughout the nineteenth and twentieth centuries, as it opened the possibility for the conquest of new rights – i.e., for the space of modern democratic politics. Today, however, if this politics is to have a future, it must emancipate itself from the framework that presided over the re-statutorisation of citizenship, that is to say, it must release the subject of rights from national identity.

Strictly understood, citizenship still has to do with rights, and specifically with rights that are actualised in practices – in the exercise of recognised rights, in their defence when they are under attack, and in the struggle for new ones. Although governments are generally wary of the excessive politicisation of society, the logic of liberal democratic institutions requires that

---

[55] On this very broad conception of post-national citizenship, see Sassen, 2006, pp. 287–289, as well as her bibliography.

the citizen express his interest in public affairs through voting. In the more demanding republican imagination, the good citizen is not content with voting, but also participates actively in collective life, in the various bodies – be they local or national, professional or associative – that are open to him. When one considers the practices of citizens rather than the government policies of contemporary societies, the denationalisation of citizenship appears in a different light, one that partially offsets the pessimism of the above analyses. The scenes on which the history of modern citizenship continues to unfold are not, or at least not only, those of yesterday. They no longer coincide with the national frame, and this either because they are more local, or because they reach beyond that frame. Marshall's classic model does not allow us to account for that fact, as Soysal pointed out when discussing the rights of foreigners in European countries, and as James Holston also did in the remarkable book he devoted to the development of 'insurgent citizenship' in the outskirts of large Brazilian cities.[56] As Holston admits, the interest of Marshall's ideal type is that it offers a concept of citizenship that does not reduce it to political rights. And yet, the narrative of cumulative progress from civil rights to political rights and then to social rights cannot serve as a universal norm of citizenship development. It no doubt accounts for the specific history of England, perhaps even for that of some other European countries, but it is wholly inadequate in the case of Brazil. The analysis of the history of citizenship in Brazil in the nineteenth and twentieth centuries leads Holston to challenge not only the linear character of this development and the order of the three-stage sequence, but also the postulates that the nation-state is the only possible framework for the constitution of citizenship rights and that class differences are the unique factor in their transformation. Last but not least, Holston accuses Marshall of having treated illegalities as an aberration, as something alien to the construction and effectiveness of rights. He himself invites us to view these, on the contrary, as a central element in the formation and development of those rights.[57]

The role of illegalities in the constitution of citizenship is particularly evident in the case of Brazil, where modern citizenship, though conceived in the nineteenth century in reference to the French and American examples, took a wholly singular form, combining a large extension (including heterogeneous populations) with an extremely unequal internal structuration. Holston's central concern is to show that the struggles that were waged by underprivileged populations massed together in the margins of large Brazilian cities, and that were aimed at the legalisation of their property claims and the development of their neighbourhoods, upset the unequal order of Brazilian citizenship. They

---

[56]   Holston, 2008. See also Holston, 1999, 2001, and Hoston and Appadurai, 1999.
[57]   Holston, 2008, p. 24 and p. 317, notes 9 and 10.

did so by forcing recognition, for the benefit of the individuals concerned, of rights hitherto reserved for privileged minorities and even of new rights in the area of public services, including sanitation and education. Particularly interesting from the standpoint of my argument is Holston's analysis of how the argumentation of favela residents, as well as the strategies they deployed in order to have their claims met, evolved over time. Towards the mid-1980s, he notes, these residents began to construe their needs as rights and to defend them as such. Rather than relying on the good grace of local potentates who exchanged their favours for votes, they broke with the logic of clientelism by taking their claims to the courts. With the help of 'alternative' lawyers, they gradually acquired a legal competence that made them full actors in the public sphere, while simultaneously redefining the contours of that sphere. To use Holston's own formulas, the new line of argument and its accompanying strategies reflected a 'change in citizen subjectivity': 'The rights arguments constituted their proponents as bearers of the *right to rights* and as worthy of that distinction as any other class of citizen. In this performance, they produced a transformation in the understanding of Brazilian citizenship itself of great social consequence, from a distribution of privilege to particular categories of citizens to a *distribution of the right to rights for all citizens*'.[58] Here we see the re-emergence – via a completely different path than the one Arendt had followed in her famous reflections on the right to have rights – of this enigmatic figure of a right that resists all institutionalisation, yet seems to form the basis of all the rights of the modern citizen. Whereas Arendt limited herself to observing an aporia, namely the rightlessness of stateless persons, the rightless citizens of contemporary Brazil imposed new solutions through their practices. They were only able to do so because they did not claim membership in the national community to justify their demands, which would have made little sense in the context of a national citizenship that had institutionalised the unequal distribution of rights. As Holston remarks, it is little wonder that, in these conditions, the language of human rights became the general idiom of citizenship during that period.[59] The reason for this is not only that favela residents made demands that were met with particularly violent police repression, but also that they aimed for equal rights – the right to housing, education, health and sanitation – which they claimed had to be granted and guaranteed to all without discrimination. Favela residents reactivated, no doubt unwittingly, the spirit of the rights declarations of the

---

[58] *Ibid.*, p. 241. My emphasis. See also p. 253*ff*, 'New Foundations of Rights', where Holston lists the mixed justifications put forward by his interlocutors to explain why they think they 'have rights': legitimate privileges of honest workers, fair compensation of stakeholders (contributor rights), or rigorous application of the Constitution's provisions.

[59] *Ibid.*, p. 250.

revolutionary period by invoking equality rather than membership – an equality that can become effective only if individuals 'run after rights' that 'won't
fall from the sky'. 'This demand for equal rights not only grounds specific
demands for access to resources and institutions on behalf of members, but
also aims to produce a universal equality, dignity, and access. In this manner, the insurgent public sphere of citizenship entails a particular project of
social justice and fosters a specific democratic imagination, one focused on
equalisation and not differentiation'.[60]

5.4 NEW SCENES OF CIVIC CREATIVITY: THE WORLD?

The megalopolises of today concentrate many of the problems that are
associated with the new structuring of the world commonly referred to as
globalisation. But the struggles waged by the inhabitants of these megalopolises remain local, even though many of the parameters that determine these
struggles – from economic logics to the existence of universally recognised
principles that individuals can invoke when fighting for their rights – situate
them in the context of the globalised world. The question of the future of
democratic citizenship nevertheless arises on other levels, ones that require
us to take an overview of the topology of the global space of powers. The
pluralisation of heterogeneous and non-hierarchical powers is at the heart of
globalisation. The dilution of national sovereignty is one of the most visible
manifestations of this process, as well as the most easily documented. However, it is more difficult to fix a positive image of the new ordering of powers
that is replacing the order of states and international law. The new powers that
are undermining state sovereignty are of various kinds: economic, of course,
but also political and legal or quasi-legal. Jurists, in particular, confess their
perplexity regarding the dissolution of the normative space of state territory
– what Delmas-Marty calls 'the great legal complexity of the world'.[61] Many
now recognise the need to review in depth the fundamental postulates of the
classical theory of law, whether that of the state's monopoly on the enactment
of legal norms or that of the unity of the law. But the form of the pluralistic
legal theory that might be used instead – including the concept of law that it
would mobilise – remains an object of dispute.

It is in the context of this pluralisation of powers that the opportunities
that are still open today for democratic citizenship – i.e., for the egalitarian
demand – ought to be assessed. A convenient way to approach the problem
is to postulate the formation of a 'global civil society' destined to play,

---

[60]   *Ibid.*, p. 249.
[61]   Delmas-Marty, 2009, p. 13; Kerchove and Ost, 2010.

before the instances of domination of the globalised world, a role similar to that of civil society in liberal democracies: namely, the exercise of functions of control, legitimation and protest in which the force of constituent power manifests itself. The global forums from Porto Alegre to Mumbai, the protests against the G8 or G20 summits, and the information and denunciation activities of various NGOs (including in the areas of human rights and the environment) can be viewed as different manifestations of that global civil society. It is true that the practices of individuals and of groups of individuals mobilised to defend their rights are no longer bounded by state borders, and that the new topology of powers has caused the emergence of new forms of organisation. But does this mean that global citizenship is about to replace national citizenship? The question mark is necessary here, for the notion of globalisation is as ambiguous as the term 'world' to which it refers. To construe globalisation as a sort of substitute for the nationalisation of powers and political practices is to remain attached to a territorial understanding of the structuration of politics: it is to presuppose that all forms of power coincide with the control of a geographic space and of the populations living within it. This is why some prefer to speak today of a fragmented world. And yet, the term 'fragmentation' must also be used with caution. The fragments of our world cannot be compared to the pieces of a puzzle that a gifted analyst might hope to fit together so as to form the image of a coherent totality. The metaphor of networks, which is also often used to describe the structures of contemporary social relations, is more appropriate. The network is a series of links with no fixed boundaries: it is a flexible structure that is always open to new extensions, but that does not seek to encompass all of the world's populations. Networks are specific: there are those of finance, this or that type of industrial production or trade, terrorism, international bureaucracies, environmental activists, etc. The globalised world is made of multiple networks that are juxtaposed and overlapping at once.

This means that the unity of the globalised world is not, and probably never will be, of the same type as the unity of the state. This is true even for regional powers like the European Union. Although it is always mentioned among the phenomena that reflect the erosion of state sovereignty, and although it contributes as such to the political restructuring of the contemporary world, the EU cannot be construed as a realisation, on a small scale, of what the whole world tends to be, and this because it is a systematic (though uneven) construction resulting from a deliberate project. Still, the political category under which it might be classified is indeterminate today. The difficulties encountered in having the draft European Constitution validated by the European peoples reflect the impossibility of applying the classical concepts of public law – the notions of state and federation, but also of people and legitimacy – to this strange entity. Such concepts are even more inadequate when it comes to thinking the structuration of powers on a global scale. Initially, the people understood as constituent power was a fiction necessary to legitimate the sovereign state, when dynastic legitimacy was swept away with the collapse of the Ancien Régime's hierarchical orders. If the people has become more than a mere fiction, it is by virtue of the unity of state power, both because of the government (linguistic, educational, social) policies that were put in place over time, and because the egalitarian demand was naturally asserted within the framework of the nation state – the political leaders of the state being its necessary addressees. The oft-lamented lack of consistency of the European people, let alone that of the global *demos*, is not provisional – at least not if the powers that shape our world remain fragmented, as we now have every reason to suppose.

The concept of law itself is also becoming increasingly indeterminate. A number of contemporary jurists view the norms and regulations that are being spontaneously generated by instances of various kinds – independently of states or interstate conventions – as a form of law. The term quasi-law has been used at times to distinguish the latter from state law. By this, however, is not meant a temporary law that would require, as does Kant's private law, the guarantee of a public power in order to become peremptory law. Gunther Teubner, in particular (he is not alone in defending this thesis, but it is far from unanimous among jurists), insists that the law of the globalised world should not be viewed as an insufficiently developed law that suffers from structural deficits when compared to national law. On the contrary, he invites us to see in this law an already well-established legal order whose character-istics simply differ from those of state law.[62] For Teubner, the *lex mercatoria* exemplifies these characteristics in that it breaks the 'taboo' of the unity of state and law, and this both because it supposes that private contracts, which lack a higher authority to guarantee them, constitute in themselves sources of law, and because by eluding political control it also eludes the process of democratic legitimation. It is true that by privatising in this way the founda-tion of law, one runs the risk of losing all criteria for distinguishing, in the vir-tually infinite multiplicity of social control systems, between what is and what is not law. But Teubner refuses to settle for this indistinction. In the wake of Luhmann, he invites us to think the law as a system defined by the use of a specific code – i.e., the opposition between law and non-law – by means of which it constitutes itself and sets its boundaries in relation to other systems that form its environment (*Umwelt*). There is no point here in exploring the subtleties of systems theory. I only mention Teubner's proposal to show that the advocates of pluralistic legal theory are fully aware of the difficulties this

---

[62]   Teubner, 1996a.

theory raises. By renouncing the exclusively statist concept of law, which was central to the legal dogma of the nineteenth and twentieth centuries, one abandons a solid and well-marked terrain to venture into an unknown where one must find new bearings. And yet the 'great legal complexity' of the contemporary world makes this adventure necessary. If one is to translate into theory the state of the world as it is revealed by empirical studies, the statist definition of law is simply no longer operational. The sociological definition of law proposed by Weber, which had the peculiarity – remarkable at the time – of not being restricted to state law, immediately comes to mind. In a recent article devoted to the role of the state in coordinating the partial legal rationalities of the contemporary world, Martin Herberg evokes in a footnote the question of the criteria that make it possible to recognise a normative structure as law. Without dwelling on it, he refers to the 'minimum criterion' he finds in the Weberian definition, whereby the law is 'what happens factually because the probability exists that men participating in a collective action will interpret determined ordinances as valid and act accordingly in practice – that is to say, they will orient their action in conformity with these ordinances'.[63] What I propose here is a similar return to Weber, by focusing, in light of my overall argument, on his equally non-statist definition of subjective right.[64] By defining subjective right in general as an individual's guaranteed chance 'of invoking in favour of his ideal or material interests the aid of a "coercive apparatus" which is in special readiness for this purpose', while also claiming that this coercive apparatus can belong to a non-political authority and that the means of coercion themselves are not necessarily violent, Weber probably sought to develop first of all a concept applicable to previous historical periods. This is indicated by his reference to the Church practice of excommunication and to 'the prospect of magically conditioned advantages or disadvantages in this world, or of reward and punishment in the next'. However, by also mentioning the retaliatory measures used by private groups – such as blacklists or boycotts by association of creditors or landlords – Weber made this broadened concept of subjective rights also relevant to the analysis of our present and future.[65]

Like the notions of people, law and right, the concept of legitimacy can no longer be used without prior re-examination. The legitimacy deficit of the new economic, political and legal powers is frequently highlighted in studies inspired by the contemporary transformations of political and legal structures. For the most part, however, this question is raised only marginally. Rarely is

---

[63] Herberg, 2008, p. 116.
[64] See supra, ch. 1. I develop this theme in greater detail in two articles, see Colliot-Thélène 2009 a and 2009 b.
[65] All citations are from the 'Sociology of Law', Weber, 1978, pp. 315–317.

it tackled upfront, and when it is, the conclusions drawn leave little room for optimism. In an article published in 2008, Jens Steffek summarised the results of an empirical study he conducted on the topic in collaboration with another author.[66] His point of departure was the observation that while the transfer of decision-making powers from the state to inter- or supra-national bodies did not abolish state power, it nonetheless greatly altered the character of political domination. This transfer largely took place on the initiative of nation-states, specifically of their governments. The state officials, experts and diplomats who form the elite now endowed with these decision-making powers are selected by heads of executive bodies, usually without the intervention of parliaments. The increasing shift of political power's effectiveness in favour of the executive – through the proliferation of multilateral agreements and international organisations that began at the end of World War II and has continued ever since[67] – has thus significantly impacted 'democratic theory's requirement that the addressees of a binding law influence the legislation process. Citizens are now affected by rules laid down beyond the borders of the nation-state, and can no longer view themselves as participating in any meaningful way in their elaboration'.[68] The study Steffek conducted with Patricia Nanz assessed the democratic character of thirty-two international institutions in function of the place they make for civil society organisations (the notion of CSOs being somewhat broader than that of NGOs, as it also includes actors like churches or trade unions). The conclusion Steffek draws from this study is that, while some progress can be seen in terms of the consultation of CSOs and the (very relative) transparency of the operations of some international institutions, there have been virtually no advances as regards the participation of civil society representatives in the decision-making process. The integration of these representatives is most often a trompe l'oeil, as it is limited to forums that are isolated from the sites of decision making and that are rarely attended by the real decision makers. Thus, Steffek concludes that

---

[66] Steffek, 2008. The article refers to a study by Jens Steffek and Patricia Nanz published in 2005: 'Assessing the Democratic Quality of Deliberation in International Governance: Criteria and Research Strategies', in *Acta Politica*, 40 (3), pp. 368–383.

[67] For the record, and without being exhaustive, let us mention, besides the United Nations established in 1945: the IMF, founded in 1944; the World Bank, created in 1945 under the name International Bank for Reconstruction and Development; the WTO (World Trade Organisation), established as such in 1995, but taking over from the GATT (General Agreement on Tariffs and Trade) which dated back to 1947. On the side of legal or judicial institutions, the European Court of Human Rights was founded in 1959, while the International Criminal Court, created in 1998, has had a legal existence since 2002. To these various institutions should be added, on the legal side, the different *ad hoc* tribunals constituted under the auspices of the UN Security Council (International Criminal Tribunal for the former Yugoslavia in 1993, International Criminal Tribunal for Rwanda in 1994, etc.), and, on the political or economic side, the more or less formalised intergovernmental summits of the G8, expanded on occasion to the G20 or G13.

[68] Steffek, 2008, p. 181.

'the institutional presuppositions of democratic self-determination have long been undermined by executive multilateralism'.[69]

This diagnosis would certainly have been even more negative if the study had not been limited to organisations established on the initiative of states, but had also included non-political (industrial or commercial) transnational powers. As I have just noted, these powers also produce quasi-legal rules whose effects can extend to populations that are never consulted. The heterogeneity of transnational powers – the decisions of which escape all control (even indirect control) by the representative bodies of civil society – is one of the main reasons why we cannot raise the question of their legitimacy in the same terms as we did, and still do, concerning the power of the nation-state. Steffek's criterion for assessing the degree of legitimacy or illegitimacy of international political institutions is the traditional principle of self-legislation. According to this principle, the participation of populations affected by the rules and decisions that bind collective destinies founds the legitimacy of established powers, insofar as this participation can be viewed as an activation of constituent power. But does it make sense to evoke constituent power with regards to expressions of civil society that are, of necessity, as fragmented as the powers over which they try to exert influence? On the mere level of the operation of political institutions, the unreality of constituent power came to light in the vicissitudes of the process of ratification of the European constitution. When the people voted against the will of executive authorities, the latter regained control and overrode the popular veto. On this occasion, executive multilateralism – to use the expression Steffek himself borrows from Michael Zürn[70] – showed that it had little regard for the principle of self-legislation. If executive authorities are concerned at all with legitimacy, it is only as a *post facto* confirmation of their own decisions, or of the decisions made by experts to whom they delegate their powers. This delegation is convenient to these authorities, as it allows them to invoke higher powers, often masquerading as anonymous ones (e.g., the 'objective logic' of markets), and hence to deny their responsibility in the workings of the world. Here again, it must be stressed that the denationalisation of politics was largely the work of nation-states themselves, and that the key political conflict of our time is not between states and supranational or global powers. These powers exist only thanks to the tacit consent of states, and are even at times created on their initiative. Globalisation does not mean the end of states, but the transformation of their role. And this transformation, which translates into the increasing and probably irreversible prevalence of the executive over the legislative, suffers from an imbalance that was present from the very beginnings of modern

---

[69]   *Ibid.*, p. 199.
[70]   *Ibid.*, p. 179. The reference goes to Zürn, 2004.

democratic regimes – that is, when these were not yet qualified as such. From Rousseau to Madison, and, much later, to Durkheim, the autonomy of the executive was considered necessary for good governance. But many also saw in it the seeds of a possible degeneration. The illusion was that such degeneration could be contained by constitutional or ordinary laws derived from procedures that helped found their authority on the alleged will of the people. The fragility of this theoretical construction was revealed when the sites of production of collective rules – i.e., law or quasi-law – began to shift. Given that the concept of legitimacy is a central piece of this construction, and that it seems difficult to assign to it a content that does not directly or indirectly refer to the will of a constituent power (regardless of how it is determined), it would be wise to stop assessing the opportunities still open for democracy today in light of this notion. Popular legitimacy only made sense when it was opposed to dynastic legitimacy, or else to legitimacies that relied on divine authority or the cosmological order. Most powers of domination today invoke neither of these. They are neither legitimate nor illegitimate; they simply exist. And they are 'democratisable' only insofar as populations can – through various means – assert before them the equality of rights of all and compel them to more or less respect this equality. True, the possibility of this happening is fairly low, but it is not non-existent. In any event, it is on this possibility that the future of democracy depends.

Conclusion

The subject of right is the figure of the modern political subject. At the end of the two-century-long history of Western political regimes, a faithful interpretation of this figure is the democratic citizen who mobilises to defend his rights or to conquer new ones. This figure of political subjectivity is the product of the modern state, that is to say, of the unicity of the power from which the individual can expect the guarantee of his rights. The citizen has never ceased to be subjected because power is still an external instance to which he turns to make claims, to protest, etc. This subject is now a citizen in that the rights he claims are equal rights. But the premise underlying this relationship is that the instance of power to which he turns has the capacity to respond – that it controls, to a certain extent, the key parameters that determine the conditions of individuals' social existence. To be sure, for the ordinary individual, the privileged interlocutor supposed to recognise and guarantee his rights remains the nation-state. And yet, modern democratic citizenship appears weaker today, because the condition that made it possible – the unicity of the power that determines the conditions of existence of the subject – is undermined as nation-states see their room for manoeuvre being increasingly reduced. The 'realistic' discourse of political leaders, who invoke the constraints of the global economy to justify the gradual withdrawal of rights that had been gained with the welfare state, is a discourse of powerlessness that erodes the conditions of legitimacy of democratic power. Opposed to this are the 'populist' discourses of the right and left, which are certainly unrealistic, but nevertheless pertain to the modern democratic logic since what they demand of the nation-state is that it demonstrates it still has enough power to be the privileged interlocutor of rights-claiming citizens. The nation-state has not disappeared, and nothing suggests that it will do so in the short or medium term. But power is no longer singular. And because the singularisation of power was key to the structuration of the modern political subject, the identity of the latter has now become problematic. To whom should this subject now turn to secure the respect of his acquired rights or the recognition of new ones when his traditional interlocutor confesses and displays its own impotence?

The disaffection of citizens towards political parties, as well as the development of forms of activist commitment around sub-, supra- or trans-national interests, reflect the fact that citizens' field of political action is no longer determined exclusively by their relation to the nation-state. Does democracy gain or lose from this reconfiguration of its sites of expression? Those who dream of cosmopolitan citizenship, and thus seek to revive the ideals that have accompanied, in various forms, the history of the nation-state since its beginnings, find in this new activism the confirmation of their predictions and hopes. It is doubtful, however, whether the cosmopolitan scheme is suited to account for what is not an extension, but an unprecedented structuring of the topology of political action. Moreover, this scheme of analysis does not suffice to prevent the withdrawal into communitarian interpretations of democratic identity. Compared to the ideal of global citizenship, which presupposes a global equivalent of the state, national citizenship certainly appears narrow and even regressive. But if global citizenship proves illusory, it is only understandable that some will see in the national *demos* the import and allure of the 'ethical totality'.

One of the main advantages of interpreting modern democracy in the light of its history – i.e., of the process that turned the constitutional regimes built since the late 18ᵗʰ century into what we now call 'liberal democracies' – is that it allows for a flexible conception of democracy, freed from the utopia of a unitary *demos*. I noted earlier that the conception of citizenship as linked to national membership was the result of the territorial structure of the power with which the individual had to negotiate his rights. But I also highlighted that, even under conditions of state monopoly over the recognition and guarantee of rights, the latter's extension – whether in terms of the circle of beneficiaries or in terms of their content – rarely took place on the initiative of established powers. More specifically, whenever these powers formalised new rights or expanded the circle of beneficiaries of already existing rights by inscribing them in the law, they generally did so under the effective or anticipated pressure of protests from populations without power. It is disadvantaged social classes and 'minorities' of all kinds that imposed, through the various peaceful and violent means that constitute the means of expression of 'those who have no part', the institution of new rights, which transformed, step by step, the definition of citizenship. As Sassen remarks,[1] the formal-

---

[1]   See Sassen, 2006, pp. 292–293.

ising moment – i.e., that of the legal positivisation of rights – is easier to identify than the sometimes invisible struggles that preceded it and rendered it necessary. Without minimising the crucial character of the legislative act, it is important to remember that the protests of the powerless have decisively contributed to giving modern democracy its specific features. Conversely, by deconstructing the interpretations of democracy as self-government or self-legislation, we discover that, far from tending to eradicate power, democratisation has always presupposed it as the addressee of demands. Thus, if we are to do justice to the historical reality of modern democracy, we must guard against opposing institutions to the contestation of institutions, and must, on the contrary, strive to understand the game that binds the two to each other. We ought to recognise that there can be no rights without power, even though – but these are limit cases – there are forms of power that deprive individuals of all rights.

In this sense, the interpretation of contemporary democracy I propose here is not an apology for rebellion or anarchy. Placing subjective rights at the heart of our understanding of democracy implies recognising that power understood as domination – which may take on harder or softer forms – is a constitutive element of what we name politics. In the terminology of today, one would speak instead of governance. One can distinguish between good and bad governance, but the distinguishing criterion, so long as it is set by rulers themselves or by theorists who adopt the point of view of rulers, can only be that of effectiveness, namely the ability to garner the support of the governed to policies elaborated by others than themselves. Good governance is one that prevents potential resistances from the human material over which it is exercised. In this perspective, which necessarily considers the governed from above, the autonomy of the subject is an obstacle that must be dealt with through persuasion rather than coercion. Convincing the subjected that one works in their best interest, so that they will contribute to the realisation of policies that cannot succeed without their active or passive support (i.e., their lack of resistance): such is the goal of good governance. Even participatory democracy – which some propose to develop today to compensate for the now overly obvious formalism of representative democracy, but also to revive a civic sentiment believed to be disappearing – is for rulers only a means among others to secure the consent of the governed to power. Consenting to power, that is to say, to tutelage. When such participatory democracy turns to resistance, it is denounced as an attack on the rule of law and on electoral legitimacy, which is the only legitimacy that ultimately matters for those in power.

One can certainly choose to qualify good governance as democratic. But one should also keep in mind that it has little to do with popular government, and that while it makes domination acceptable to the dominated, it does not tend towards the abolition of domination in any way. The autonomy of the subject is fairly secondary here, as it is reduced to a technical means for administering mass societies. Regardless of whether governance is good or bad (that is, incapable of garnering support and forced to use violence), it remains a domination exercised by some men or groups of men over other men. This point should be emphasised, not only against the utopia of an administration of things that would replace the government of men, but also against the representation whereby societies are organised for the most part spontaneously, with human intention playing hardly any role in the matter. This liberal myth, which was generated by the spectacle of market sociability and theorised in its most radical form by Hayek,[2] is curiously found in an author like Rancière when he affirms that the social order is 'without any organising purpose'.[3] It goes without saying that no actor or group of actors alone controls the multiple processes which combine to determine the unequal distribution of power and wealth among men – whether at the level of national societies or that of the entire world. And yet there do exist sites of power where individuals make decisions that have a direct and often predictable impact on the conditions of existence of subjected populations. The economic crisis we are currently experiencing[4] is not of the same order as a natural disaster; nor is it an accident whose (regrettable) possibility is inscribed in the anonymous logic of market sociability. Rather, it is the result of deliberate, so-called deregulation policies that were decided at the end of the 1980s by international bodies (the IMF and the World Bank, to mention only the most famous), and that were implemented by these same bodies with the cooperation of states. To be sure, no individual state could really choose to comply or not with the directives formulated by these supranational powers.[5] But international bodies – be they political or economic (the border between these being difficult to discern) – are also composed of men, and they usually owe their existence and their power to the will or consent of the political leaders of nation-states, or at least of the most important among them. Nation-states, and more specifically the governments of those states, have cooperated in the 'denationalisation' of economic regulation. And if they have tried to soften the social impact of these policies, it is only to reduce disaffection among their constituents and to prevent wild protest movements that would disrupt the proper functioning of the deregulated economy. Market sociability may well be a process without a

---

[2] See Hayek's well-known opposition (1978, Volume 1, p. 35*ff*) between order as *taxis*, which is a deliberate arrangement, and order as *kosmos*, namely an ordered structure produced by the action of several men with no particular human purpose.

[3] Rancière, 1995, p. 82.

[4] The present book was written in 2010.

[5] Note also that all states are not on an equal footing in terms of the influence they can exert on these supranational powers.

subject, in that it results from the intersecting actions of an indefinite number of actors. But the specific forms it takes in different periods are attributable to the choices of specific men and groups of men.

The presence of domination in all forms of power, including those that pretend to be a simple administration adjusted to 'objective' constraints, is what makes democracy possible. While this may seem a paradoxical affirmation to those who remain attached to the idea of popular government, it is easily understood if we admit that democracy is only one way of organising the relationship between the dominant and the dominated, the core of which resides in the demand for equal rights. Indeed, one must recognise that if sociability were essentially determined by systemic constraints, as is claimed by liberal economic theory, individuals would be hard pressed to find an addressee for their rights claims. Arendt rightly points out that, in a fully developed bureaucracy (by which she means an anonymous power without individuals or classes that might be construed as its source), 'there is nobody left with whom one can argue, to whom one can present grievances, on whom the pressures of power can be exerted'.[6] Far from leading us to despair of the meaning of political action, the observation that democracy is unthinkable without power helps, on the contrary, to locate within the mutating social and political space of our time, the still partly inchoate forms in which democratic practice can be perpetuated or renewed. The processes of denationalisation that I have just mentioned have led to a pluralisation of the powers with which individuals must negotiate the recognition of their rights. What remains unchanged is the correlation between rights and powers. Without instances of power able to enforce the claims raised by individuals or groups of individuals, such claims never acquire the consistency of rights. What is new, at least from the perspective of the nation-state logic that has structured the functioning of politics for more than two centuries, is the plurality of the powers with which rights-claiming individuals and groups of individuals are confronted today.

Should we expect democratic progress from this plurality? It is impossible to tell at this point in time. Some analysts, who focus above all on the promulgation of human rights texts with a universal scope and on the creation of supranational legal bodies that issue decrees on the basis of those texts, believe they are seeing the emergence of a normative order freed from the limits of the state order. This, they argue, can only benefit democracy, insofar as it allows individuals to assert the rights they believe to be theirs against the judicial or political authorities of the states in which they reside. These analysts deplore only the – allegedly provisional – limits of this supranational law, and in particular the fact that the enforcement of judgments

---

6   Arendt, 1970, p. 81.

issued by the courts representing it is still subject to the will of states. They often invoke, and rightly so, the example of the European Court of Human Rights. But the exclusive focus on this type of body wrongly suggests that the emergent global legal-political order is destined to reproduce, on a larger scale, the pyramidal structure of the state order, when in fact one merely needs to widen the analytical lens to demonstrate the improbability of this hypothesis. To consider the laws and legal bodies that give human rights a supranational scope as different manifestations of a cosmopolitan order in the making, or to interpret their limited effectiveness as due to their lagging behind economic globalisation,[7] is to remain dependent on the historical teleology that was once inspired by the formation of nation-states. It is not wrong to say that these texts and supranational bodies have broadened the range of instruments individuals have at their disposal to assert their rights. However, it would be a mistake to view the latter as the expression of a 'new organising principle of the world' that would tend to replace the logic of the powers of domination, and illusory to imagine that we are witnessing the formation of a 'transnational community'. Both the advocates and the opponents of globalisation assume a shift in the key locus of politics from the national to the global level, which would imply the gradual decline of states. And yet, when alter-globalisation activists protested against the WTO in Seattle in 1999 or the G8 summit in Genoa in 2001, they were still dealing with states – that is, with institutions that owe their existence to the will of states and that are populated with state representatives. Conversely, workers who demonstrate against a company closure at the local level are very often confronted with transnational powers. Globalisation has little to do with what the Socialist or Communist Internationals once aspired to (at least initially), insofar as the 'capitalist system' represented for them a unitary principle of organisation of the world whose subversion they called for so as to put an end to all domination. Struggles for rights no longer converge in the utopia of radical transformation; they are now fragmented, and this fragmentation reflects both the fragmentation of powers and the inextricable entanglement of the local, national, regional and global levels on which they operate.

It is the centralised unity of state power – in its monarchical and then democratic form – that freed individuals from community allegiances. The paradox of this form of domination is that it aroused, in the populations it subjected, the psychic dispositions that facilitated its own contestation. A strictly economistic reading of modern history tends to identify individualism with the inward focus on private interests and has sustained, since the first decades of the nineteenth century, discourses on both the right and the

---

[7]   See Soysal, 1994, and Brunkhorst, 1999, for the first interpretation, and Delmas-Marty, 2009, for the second.

left that deplore the erosion of civic sentiment. Such a reading forgets that individualism also contains a legal and political component that crystallised in the notion of subject of right. The new world to which the economic and political transformations of the seventeenth and eighteenth centuries gave rise was not only that of property owners, industrialists and merchants, but also that of individuals who no longer felt the need to invoke membership in an order, a class or a caste to found the rights they were claiming. The importance of the reference to human rights in contemporary political theory and practice indicates that the figure of the subject of right may well survive the conditions that produced it. To be sure, in as much as this figure has served as a support for the struggles of the dominated, it has ceased to be a strictly legal notion. This is all the more true now that the contours of law itself are losing the sharpness they once had, when law was firmly bound to the sovereign power of the state. But what remains vivid in this confused situation, where the boundaries between the political, legal and economic domains are no longer easy to determine, is the notion that everyone has the right to have rights. This is the concept formulated by Arendt, which loses its aporetic character as soon as rights cease to be subordinated to communitarian membership. Inequalities between human beings are today at least as important as they were in the most inegalitarian societies of old, and the disparities in 'opportunity' between individuals – based on where they are born, their social origin, the property they inherit, etc. – are now colossal.[8] And yet, with a few exceptions (which often concern women's rights), no set of beliefs can legitimate these inequalities today. The force of the idea of equal rights is evidenced, in particular, by the discretion required of the dominant and affluent who, because they cannot found their privileges on a cosmological or theological order, are left to choose between somewhat hackneyed 'bourgeois' justifications (work, merit, talent), hypocrisy or cynicism. Kant was probably right in thinking that there are ideas whose formulation marks a point of no return in the historicity of human societies, and this not because they determine once and for all the forms of future societies, but because, once they have appeared, they can be forever used and re-actualised in new circumstances. In this sense, the 'right to have rights' has made history. Of all the elements that give our world its complex form, this right remains the key vector of an always-possible democratisation – even though this democratisation is never complete or safe from regression.

---

[8]　To get an idea of these disparities, one only needs to consult tables of life expectancy across countries and continents (about eighty years in Western countries against about fifty years and often less than forty years in most African countries), or to recall that more than one billion human beings do not have access to the basic resource of drinking water.

By taking as a starting point and bedrock principle the notion of subjective right, my reflection on modern democracy was necessarily bound to also appear as a contribution to the history of subjectivity. That subjectivity has a history is a commonplace of contemporary philosophy. Nevertheless, for the most part, philosophers pay little attention to the legal and political aspects of that history, or else they treat them as marginal concerns. Thus, in an article of about sixty pages allegedly devoted to reviewing late twentieth century literature on the question of subjectivity – an article in which Kant features prominently – the subject of right and the citizen are mentioned only in a brief parenthesis.[9] If the metaphysics of subjectivity is a thing of the past, as various schools of contemporary philosophy insist on repeating, are we then to believe that the subject of right, understood as a mere regional expression of said metaphysics, is also doomed to disappear? Or, on the contrary, might we suggest that the legal notion of person (not as it was represented in Ancient Rome, but as it came to be defined when the modern revolutions put an end to statutory logics) was one of the elements that contributed to forging the modern concept of the subject? I shall leave unresolved this perhaps undecidable question of the order of causes. It can only be regretted that metaphysicians are the only ones to inquire into the future of the subject, while the major political philosophies of today seem to have forgotten the central intuition of modern political philosophy: that the way in which the individual understands himself – in brief, the subject – is closely linked to how he relates to power, and that this self-understanding consequently varies according to the form this relationship takes. The 'psychic life of power' cannot be reduced to internalisation of the law or to consent to obedience or voluntary servitude, even though it is undeniable that the construction of the subject entails a necessary moment of heteronomy. The autonomy of the subject is not the fantasy of a rationalism oblivious to the social conditions of psychic structures, but the theorisation of a historical fact whose institutional dimension (the state's monopoly on the guarantee of rights) came with a psychic dimension (the individualisation of the subject of right). The ongoing transformations of institutions have been widely commented upon in the contemporary literature of political science, law or sociology. Political philosophy, however, has been slow to take cognisance of these changes, as it is split today between those who struggle to redefine the normative foundation of a just order to be

---

9   This is the otherwise remarkable article by Jocelyn Benoist (1995), 'La subjectivité' (Subjectivity), published in one of the three volumes of *Notions de philosophie* (Notions of Philosophy), an edited collection that brings together contributions from the cream of French academic philosophy. Benoist, who starts from the premise that there is a history of subjectivity that must be known in its broad lines if one is to 'give back to the concept its full problematic depth' (p. 504), evokes the legal-political subject in just these few words: '[...] let us not forget the subject of right and that modern figure of political subjectivity: the citizen' (p. 530).

realised by states (or, at least, by supranational powers that would essentially retain the form of states), and those who think that they can give new meaning to the term democracy by turning their back on institutions, and even on institutionalisation in general.[10] Insofar as the position defended in this book makes rights claims the vector of democratisation, while also inviting the reader to doubt the overall goodwill of those in power, it might seem closer to the second of these two strands of political philosophy. Nevertheless, my position also opposes the denial of political reality that pervades all proposals to define the terms 'politics' and 'democracy' in ways that protect them from compromise with domination. Under cover of restoring against ordinary language uses the genuine meaning of those terms, such arbitrary semantics helps to elude reality. There is no need to invoke the authority of the Ancients or of any other philosophical quibble to conclude that politics cannot be reduced to the action of professional politicians. The history of the last two centuries has made this sufficiently clear. Yet we should not ignore the fact that the field of politics is not only structured by power relations – i.e., by asymmetric relations in which domination is always present – but is also essentially constituted by them. No doubt we can dream of other relations between men, and perhaps even recognise that 'the ultimate and most sublime values' of human life 'have retreated from public life either into the transcendental realm of mystic life or into the brotherliness of direct and personal human relations'.[11] But these relationships are precisely not what constitutes politics, and the subjective aspects they produce and maintain are not those of political subjectivity. So long as democracy retains a political meaning, it necessarily remains bound to the specific field of activity constituted by the subject's relations to powers that tend to subject him. All attempts to wrest the concepts of politics and democracy from that field risk making us forget that, whether we like it or not, the fates of contemporary societies and of their populations continue and will continue to be determined by these powers. And while relying on them is certainly dangerous, these powers (at least some of them) nonetheless condition the very existence of the political subject as a subject of rights, which means that anyone who wishes to participate in politics as anything other than an object must negotiate with them. Negotiating entails, first of all, abandoning the illusion that the action of these powers has no impact on our lives, on the structure of our subjectivities, or on the modalities of action through which we sometimes oppose them. Negotiating also involves identifying and recognising these powers in their diversity (for the most visible are not necessarily the most determinant), as well as distinguishing between those with which the only possible relation is one of

---

[10]   See Colliot-Thélène, 2009c.
[11]   Weber, 2009, p. 155.

confrontation, and those that, owing to their conditions of existence (elections) or their stated objectives (certain supranational legal bodies), can offer,
willingly or not, the guarantee without which the rights of individuals have no
reality. It is not by deserting the field of power relations that the democratic
subject can hope to continue the task accomplished in the last two centuries.
On the contrary, it is by intervening in that field with means adequate to its
new structures, and this to assert the egalitarian demand from which he draws
his very substance.

Bibliography

Allard, J. and Antoine G. (2005) *Les Juges dans la mondialisation*, Paris: Le Seuil.

Anderson, B. (2006) *Imagined Communities: Reflections on the origin and spread of nationalism*, New York: Verso.

Anter, A. (2000) 'Max Weber und Georg Jellinek: Wissenschaftliche Beziehung, Affinitäten und Divergenzen' in S. Paulson and M. Schulte (eds.) *Georg Jellinek: Beiträge zu Leben und Werk,* Tübingen: Mohr Siebeck, 67+.

———. (2001) 'Von der politischen Gemeinschaft zum Anstaltsstaat: Das Monopol der legitimen Gewaltsamkeit'. In E. Hanke and W. J. Mommsen (eds.) *Max Webers Hersschaftssoziologie*, Tübingen: Mohr Siebeck 121–38.

Anter, A. (2014) *Max Weber's Theory of the Modern State: Origins, structure and significance*, New York: Palgrave Macmillan.

Arendt, H. (1970) *On Violence*, Boston, MA: Houghton Mifflin Harcourt.

——— (1979) *The Origins of Totalitarianism*, London, UK: HBJ Book.

——— (1990) *On Revolution*, New York: Penguin Books.

Balibar, É. (1997) *La Crainte des masses*, Paris: Galilée.

———. (2014) *Equaliberty: Political essays*, Durham, NC: Duke University Press.

Bauman, Z. (2002) *Society Under Siege*, Cambridge, UK: Polity Press.

Benhabid, S. (2004) *The Rights of Others*, Cambridge, UK: Cambridge University Press.

Benoist, J. (1995) 'La subjectivité', in D. Kambouchner (ed.) *Notions de philosophie II*, Paris: Gallimard, 501–61.

Bernardi, B. (2006) *La Fabrique des concepts*, Paris: Honoré Champion.

The Bible: Authorized King James Version with Apocrypha, Oxford, UK: Oxford University Press (1997).

Binoche, B. (1989) *Critiques des droits de l'homme*, Paris: PUF. Reprinted in the second part of B. Binoche and J-P. Cléro (eds.) *Bentham contre les droits de l'homme*, Paris: PUF (2007).

Blais, M-C. (2007) *La Solidarité : Histoire d'une idée*, Paris: Gallimard.

Blanchot, M. (1988) *The Unavowable Community*, Barrytown, NY: Station Hill Press.

Bobbio, N. (1999) 'Kelsen and Legal Power', in S. L. Paulson and B. Litschewski-Paulson (eds.) *Normativity and Norms*, Oxford, UK: Oxford University Press, 435–50.

Bodin, J. (2009) *On Sovereignty: Six books of the commonwealth*, abridged and translated by M. J. Tooley, Oxford, UK: Seven Treasures Publications.

Breuer, S. (1999) *Georg Jellinek und Max Weber: Von der sozialen zur soziologischen Staatslehre*, Baden-Baden: Nomos.

——— (2000) 'Nichtlegitime Herrschaft', in H. Bruhns and W. Nippel (eds.) *Max Weber und die Stadt*, Göttingen: Vandenhoeck & Ruprecht, 63–76.

Brunkhorst, H. (1999) 'Menschenrecht und Solidarität – ein Dilemma?', in H. Brunkorst *et al*. *Recht auf Menschenrechte*, Frankfurt am Main: Suhrkamp.

——— (2000) 'Ist die Solidarität der Bürgergesellschaft globalisierbar?', in H. Brunkhorst and M. Kettner (eds.) *Globalisierung und Demokratie*, Frankfurt am Main: Suhrkamp, 274–86.

——— (2005) *Solidarity: From civic friendship to a global legal community*, Cambridge, MA: MIT Press.

Brunner, O. Conze, W. and Koselleck R. (1972) *Geschichtliche Grundbegriffe, Bd. 1*, Stuttgart: Klett-Cotta.

——— (1982) *Geschichtliche Grundbegriff, Bd. 3*, Stuttgart: Klett-Cotta.

Burke, E. (1955) *Reflections on the Revolution in France*, New York: Bobbs-Merrill Company.

Castel, R. (2002) *From Manual Workers to Wage Laborers: Transformation of the social question*, Piscataway, NJ: Transaction Publishers.

——— (2009) *La Montée des incertitudes*, Paris: Le Seuil.

Colliot-Thélène, C. (2001) *Etudes wébériennes*, Paris: PUF.

——— (2005) 'La fin de la violence légitime', in M. Coutu and G. Rocher (eds.) *La légitimité de l'État et du droit*, Québec: Presses de l'Université Laval, 23–46.

——— (2009a) 'Après la souveraineté: que reste-t-il des droits subjectifs?' *Jus Politicum 1: Le Droit politique, Dalloz*, Paris: Dalloz, 117–36.

——— (2009b) 'Pour une politique des droits subjectifs: La lutte pour les droits comme lutte politique', *L'Année sociologique* 59, 231–58.

——— (2009c) 'Philosophie politique: Pouvoir et démocratie', in *Histoire de la Philosophie*, Paris: Le Seuil, 643–62.

Crouch, C. (2004) *Post-Democracy*, Cambridge, UK: Polity Press.

Dabin, J. (1964) 'Droit subjectif et subjectivisme juridique', *Archives de philosophie du droit* 9: *Le droit subjectif en question*.

Delmas-Marty, M. (2009) *Ordering Pluralism: A conceptual framework for understanding the transnational legal world*, Portland, OR: Hart Publishing.

Derrida, J. (1988) *Limited inc*, Evanston, IL: Northwestern University Press.

——— (2002) *Acts of Religion*, New York: Routledge.

——— (2005) *Politics of Friendship*, New York: Verso.

Descombes, V. (2004) *Le Complément de sujet*, Paris: Gallimard.

Dubet, F. (2009) *Le Travail des sociétés*, Paris: Le Seuil.

Duguit, L. (2003) *L'État, le Droit objectif et la Loi positive*, Paris: Dalloz.

Durkheim, E. (1992) *Professional Ethics and Civic Morals*, translated by C. Brookfield, New York: Routledge.

———— (1997) *The Division of Labor in Society*, translated by W. D. Halls, New York: Simon and Schuster.

Foucault, M. (2005) *The Hermeneutics of the Subject: Lectures at the collège de France, 1981-82*, edited by F. Gros *et al.*, translated by G. Burchell, New York: Palgrave Macmillan.

Gall, L. (1984) *Bismarck*, Paris: Fayard.

Giddens, A. (1987) *The Nation-State and Violence*, Berkeley, CA and Los Angeles, CA: University of California Press.

Goyard-Fabre, S. (1975) *Kant et le problème du droit*, Paris: Vrin.

Habermas, J. (1998) *L'Intégration républicaine*, Paris: Fayard.

Hahn, A. (2000) *Konstruktionen des Selbsts, der Welt und der Geschichte*, Frankfurt am Main: Suhrkamp.

Halperin, S. (2009) 'Power to the people: nationally embedded development and mass armies in the making of democracy', *Millenium: Journal of International Studies* 37.3: 605–30.

Hamilton, A. *et al.* (1961) *The Federalist Papers*, C. Rossiter (ed.) New York: Penguin Putnam.

Hayek, F. A. (1978) *Law, Legislation and Liberty, Volume 1: Rules and order*, Chicago, IL: University of Chicago Press.

Hegel, G. W. F. (1894) *Philosophy of Mind*, translated by W. Wallace, Oxford, UK: Clarendon Press.

———— (1991) *Elements of the Philosophy of Right*, edited by A. Wood, translated by H. B. Nisbet, Cambridge, UK: Cambridge University Press.

Herberg, M. (2008) 'Globalisierung des Rechts, Öffnung des Staates: Der Staat als Koordinator pluraler Teilrechtsordnungen', in A. Hurrelmann *et al. Zerfasert der Nationalstaat?* Frankfurt am Main: Campus Verlag.

Hobbes, T. (1982) *Leviathan*, London, UK: Penguin Classics.

Holston, J. (1999) *Cities and Citizenship*, Durham, NC: Duke University Press.

———— (2001) 'Urban Citizenship and Globalization', in A. J. Scott (ed.) *Global City Regions*, Oxford, UK: Oxford University Press, 325–48.

———— (2008) *Insurgent Citizenship*, Princeton, NJ: Princeton University Press.

Holston, J. and Appadurai A. (1999) 'Cities and citizenship', in J. Holston (ed.) *Cities and Citizenship*, Durham, NC: Duke University Press, 1–18.

Jaume, L. (2000) *La Liberté et la Loi*, Paris: Fayard.

Jellinek, G. (1976) *Allgemeine Staatslehre*, Frankfurt am Main: Athenäum Verlag.

Jouanjan O. (2005a) '"Le monde subjectif dans lequel se joue la vie du droit…": Une interprétation de Georg Jellinek', in M. Coutu and G. Rocher (eds.) *La Légitimité de l'État et du droit*, Québec: Presses de l'Université Laval, 115–36.

———— (2005b) *Une histoire de la pensée juridique en Allemagne (1880-1018)*, Paris: PUF.

———— (2009) 'Les aventures du sujet dans la narration villeyenne de l'histoire de la pensée juridique', *Droit et Société* 71: 27–45.

Kant, I. (1963) 'Idea for a universal history from a cosmopolitan point of view', in *On History*, edited and translated by L. W. Beck, New York: Macmillan.

—— (1973) *Kleinere Schriften zur Geschichtsphilosophie, Ethik und Politik*, Hamburg: Felix Meiner Verlag.

—— (1979) *The Conflict of the Faculties*, edited and translated by M. Gregor, Lincoln, NE: University of Nebraska Press.

—— (1983) *Perpetual Peace and Other Essays*, translated by T. Humphrey, Indianapolis, IN: Hackett Publishing Company.

—— (1986) *Œuvres philosophiques, t. III*, Paris: Gallimard, 'Bibliothèque de la Pléiade'.

—— (1987) *Critique of Judgment*, translated by W. S. Pluhar, Indianapolis, IN: Hackett Publishing Company.

—— (1991a) 'On the common saying: "this may be true in theory, but it does not apply in practice"', in H. Reiss (ed.) *Kant: Political Writings*, translated by H. B. Nisbet, Cambridge, UK: Cambridge University Press, 61–92.

—— (1991b) 'Conjectures on the beginning of human history', in H. Reiss (ed.) *Kant: Political Writings*, translated by H. B. Nisbet, Cambridge, UK: Cambridge University Press, 221–34.

—— (1994) *Métaphysique des moeurs: Tome 2: Doctrine du droit, Doctrine de la vertu*, translated into French by A. Renaut, Paris: Flammarion.

—— (1996) *The Metaphysics of Morals*, edited and translated by M. Gregor, Cambridge, UK: Cambridge University Press.

—— (1997) *Critique of Practical Reason*, edited and translated by M. Gregor, Cambridge UK: Cambridge University Press.

—— (1998) *Religion Within the Boundaries of Mere Reason and Other Writings*, edited and translated by A. Wood and G. di Giovanni, Cambridge, UK: Cambridge University Press.

—— (2006) *Anthropology from a Pragmatic Point of View*, edited and translated by R. Louden, Cambridge, UK: Cambridge University Press.

—— (2009) *An Answer to the Question: 'What is enlightenment'?* translated by H. B. Nisbett, London, UK: Penguin Books.

Kantorowicz, E. H. (1951) 'Pro Patria Mori in medieval political thought', *The American Historical Review* 56.3: 472–92.

Karsenti, B. (1997) *L'Homme total*, Paris: PUF.

Kelsen, H. (1928) *Der soziologische und der juristische Staatsbegriff*, Aalen: Scientia Verlag.

—— (2005) *Pure Theory of Law*, Clark, NJ: The Lawbook Exchange.

—— (2013) *The Essence and Value of Democracy*, edited by N. Urbinati and C. I. Accetti, translated by B. Graf, Lanham, MD: Rowman & Littlefield Publishers.

Kerchove, M. van de and Ost, F. (2010) *De la pyramide au réseau?* Bruxelles: Facultés universitaires Saint-Louis.

Kersting, W. (2004) *Kant über Recht*, Paderbonn: Mentis Verlag.

Kervégan, J-F. (2007) *L'Effectif et le Rationnel*, Paris: Vrin.

Lefort, C. (1986) *The Political Forms of Modern Society: Bureaucracy, democracy, totalitarianism*, Cambridge, MA: MIT Press.

Lochak, D. (1985) *Étrangers: de quel droit?* Paris: PUF.

—— (2007) *Face aux migrants: État de droit ou état de siège?* Paris: Textuel.

Luhmann, N. (1982) 'Subjektive Rechte. Zum Umbau des Rechtsbewusstseins für die moderne Gesellschaft', in *Gesellschaftsstruktur und Semantik: Studien zur Wissenssoziologie der modernen Gesellschaft, Bd. 2*, Frankfurt am Main: Suhrkamp, 45–104.

—— (1989a) 'Staat undStaatsräson im Übergang von traditionaler Herrschaft zu moderner Politik', in *Gesellschaftsstruktur und Semantik: Studien zur Wissenssoziologie der modernen Gesellschaft, Bd. 3*, Frankfurt am Main: Suhrkamp, 65–148.

—— (1989b) 'Individuum, individualität,individualismus', in *Gesellschaftsstruktur und Semantik: Studien zur Wissenssoziologie der modernen Gesellschaft, Bd. 3*, Frankfurt am Main: Suhrkamp, 149–258.

Maier, H. (1971) 'Zur neueren Geschichte des Demokratiebegriffs', in K. von Beyme (ed.) *Theory and Politics / Theorie und Politik, Festschrift zum 70. Geburtstag für Carl Joachim Friedrich*, The Hague: Martinus Nijhoff, 127–61.

Manin, B. (1997) *The Principles of Representative Government*, New York: Cambridge University Press.

Mann, T. (1994) *Buddenbrooks: The decline of a family*, New York: Vintage Books.

Marshall, T. H. (1981) *The Right to Welfare and other Essays*, London: Heinemann Educational Books.

—— (1992) 'Citizenship and social class', in T. H. Marshall and T. Bottomore, *Citizenship and Social Class*, Concord, MA: Pluto Press.

Marx, K. (1977) *Critique of Hegel's 'Philosophy of Right'*, edited by J. O'Mally, translated by J. O'Mally and A. Jolin, Cambridge, UK: Cambridge University Press.

—— (1983) *Marx-Engels-Werke, Bd 1*, Berlin: Dietz Verlag.

—— (2012) *On the Jewish Question*, Chicago, IL: Aristeus Books.

Michelman, F. I. (1996) 'Parsing "a right to have rights"', *Constellations* 3.2: 200–08.

Negri, A. (2009) *Insurgencies: Constituent power and the modern state*, Minneapolis, MN: University of Minnesota Press.

Palmer, R. R. (1953) 'Notes on the use of the word "democracy" 1789-1799', *Political Science Quarterly* 68.2: 203–06.

—— (1959) *The Age of the Democratic Revolution*, Princeton, NJ: Princeton University Press.

Pettit, P. (1997) *Republicanism: A theory of freedom and government*, Oxford, UK: Oxford Press.

Polanyi, K. (1944) *The Great Transformation: The political and economic origin of our time*, Boston, MA: Beacon Press.

Quaritsch, H. (1986) *Souveränität: Entstehung und Entwicklung des Begriffs in Frankreich und Deutschland vom 13. Jh. bis 1806*, Berlin: Duncker & Humblot.

Rancière, J. (1995) *On the Shores of Politics*, New York: Verso.

—— (1998) *Disagreement*, Minneapolis, MN: University of Minnesota Press.

—— (2005) *Dissensus: On politics and aesthetics*, London, UK: Continuum.

Reinhard, W. (1999) *Geschichte der Staatsgewalt*, Munich: C. H. Beck.

Rosanvallon, P. (1992) *Le Sacre du citoyen*, Paris: Gallimard.

—————— (2000) *La Démocratie inachevée*, Paris: Gallimard.

—————— (2008) *Counter-Democracy: Politics in an age of distrust*, New York: Cambridge University Press.

—————— (2012) *Democracy Past and Future: Selected essays*, New York: Columbia University Press.

Rousseau, J-J. (1994) *Social Contract, Discourse on the Virtue Most Necessary for a Hero, Political Fragments, and Geneva Manuscript*, translated by R. D. Masters, C. Kelly and J. R. Bush, Hanover, NH: Dartmouth College Press.

—————— (2003) *On the Social Contract*, translated by G. D. H. Cole, Mineola, NY: Dover Publications.

—————— (2005) *The Plan for Perpetual Peace, On the Government of Poland, and Other Writings on History and Politics*, translated by C. Kelly and J. R. Bush, Hanover, NH: Dartmouth College Press.

—————— (2013) *Letter to Beaumont, Letters Written from the Mountain, and Related Writings*, translated by C. Kelly and J. R. Bush, Hanover, NH: Dartmouth College Press.

Runciman, D. (1997) *Pluralism and the Personality of the State*, Cambridge, UK: Cambridge University Press.

Sassen, S. (2006) *Territory, Authority, Rights: From medieval to global assemblages*, Princeton, NJ: Princeton University Press.

Schmitt, C. (1996) *The Concept of the Political*, translated by G. Schwab, Chicago, IL: The University of Chicago Press.

—————— (2008) *Constitutional Theory*, translated by J. Seitzer, Durham, NC: Duke University Press.

Schnapper, D. (1998) *Community of Citizens: On the modern idea of nationality*, Piscataway: Transaction.

Schönberger, C. (2005) *Unionsbürger*, Tübingen: Mohr Siebeck.

Shklar, J. (1991) *American Citizenship: The quest for inclusion*, Cambridge, MA: Harvard University Press.

Simondon, G. (2007) *L'Individualité psychique et collective*, Paris: Aubier.

Sintomer, Y. (2007) *Le Pouvoir au people*, Paris: La Découverte.

Smith, R. M. (2003) *Stories of Peoplehood: The politics and morals of political membership*, Cambridge, UK: Cambridge University Press.

Soysal, Y. N. (1994) *Limits of citizenship*, Chicago, IL: The University of Chicago Press.

Spitz, J-F. (2005) *Le Moment républicain en France*, Paris: Gallimard.

Steffek, J. (2008) 'Legitimität jenseits des Nationalstaates: Vom exekutiven zum partizipativen Multilateralismus?' in A. Hurrelman *et al.* (eds.) *Zerfasert der Nationalstaat?* Frankfurt/New York: Campus Verlag.

Sternberger, D. (1990) *Verfassungspatriotismus*, Frankfurt am Main: Insel Verlag.

Stourzh, G. (1996) 'The modern state: equal rights. Equalizing the individual's status and the breakthrough of the modern liberal state', in J. Coleman (ed.) *The Individual in Political Theory and Practice*, Oxford: Clarendon Press, 303–28.

Teubner, G. (1996a) 'Globale Bukowina: Zur Emergenz eines transnationalen Pluralismus', *Rechtshistorisches Journal* 15: 255+.

——— (1996b) 'Des Königs viel Leiber: Die Selbstdekontruction des Rechts', *Soziale Systeme* 3: 229+.

Tuck, R. (1979) *Natural Rights Theories: Their origin and their development*, Cambridge, UK: Cambridge University Press.

Tully, J. (1982) *A Discourse on Property: John Locke and his adversaries*, Cambridge, UK: Cambridge University Press.

Villey, M. (1983) *Le Droit et les Droits de l'homme*, Paris: PUF.

——— (2003) *La Formation de la pensée juridique moderne*, Paris: PUF.

Weber, M. (1976) *Wirtschaft und Gesellschaft*, Tübingen: Mohr Siebeck.

——— (1978) *Economy and Society: An outline of interpretive sociology*, edited by G. Roth and C. Wittich, Berkeley, CA: University of California Press.

——— (1994) *Political Writings*, edited by P. Lassman and translated by R. Speirs, Cambridge, UK: Cambridge University Press.

——— (2009) *From Max Weber: Essays in sociology*, edited and translated by H. H. Gerth and C. Wright Mills, New York: Routledge.

Weil, P. (2008) *How to be French: Nationality in the making since 1789*, Durham, NC: Duke University Press.

Žižek, S. (1999) *The Ticklish Subject: The absent centre of political ontology*, New York: Verso.

Zürn, M. (2004) 'Global Governance and Legitimacy Problems', *Government and Opposition* 39.2: 260–87.

Index